Reforming Law Reform

Reforming Law Reform

Perspectives from Hong Kong and Beyond

Edited by Michael Tilbury, Simon N M Young
and Ludwig Ng

Hong Kong University Press
The University of Hong Kong
Pok Fu Lam Road
Hong Kong
https://hkupress.hku.hk

© 2014 Hong Kong University Press, with the exception of Chapter 3

ISBN 978-988-8208-24-1 *(Hardback)*

All rights reserved. No portion of this publication may be reproduced or transmitted in any form or by any means, electronic or mechanical, including photocopying, recording, or any information storage or retrieval system, without prior permission in writing from the publisher.

British Library Cataloguing-in-Publication Data
A catalogue record for this book is available from the British Library.

Digitally printed

Contents

List of Contributors		vii
Acknowledgements		ix

Part A: The Context of Law Reform

1	Law Reform Today *Michael Tilbury, Simon N M Young and Ludwig Ng*	3
2	Changing Fashions and Enduring Values in Law Reform *Michael Kirby*	23
3	Sources and Channels of Law Reform in Hong Kong *Wong Yan Lung*	43

Part B: Law Reform Commissions

4	Hong Kong's Law Reform Commission *Stuart M I Stoker*	53
5	Law Reform: The UK Experience *Martin Partington*	67
6	Lessons from Law Reform in Ontario and Elsewhere in Canada *Patricia Hughes*	87
7	Lessons from a Small University-based Law Reform Body in Australia *Kate Warner*	113

Part C: Law Reform in Diverse Contexts

8	Tortoise in Coma: Reform of Hong Kong's Insolvency Law *Ludwig Ng*	135
9	The Dynamics of Labour Law Reform in Hong Kong *Rick Glofcheski*	145

| 10 | Equal Opportunities Law Reform in Hong Kong: The Impact of International Norms and Civil Society Advocacy
Carole J Petersen and Kelley Loper | 173 |

Part D: Law Reform and Privacy

11	Reviewing the Personal Data (Privacy) Ordinance through Standstill and Crisis *Allan Chiang*	207
12	Privacy and Law Reform: What Can We Learn from the Hong Kong Process? *John Bacon-Shone*	231
13	Reforming Privacy Law in New South Wales: Lessons for Law Reform Agencies *Michael Tilbury*	239

Part E: Final Word

| 14 | Reforming Law Reform: Concluding Reflections
Michael Kirby | 259 |

| Index | | 277 |

Contributors

John Bacon-Shone, Professor, Faculty of Social Sciences, The University of Hong Kong

Allan Chiang, Privacy Commissioner for Personal Data, Hong Kong

Rick Glofcheski, Professor, Faculty of Law, The University of Hong Kong

Patricia Hughes, Executive Director, Law Commission of Ontario; former Professor and Dean of the Faculty of Law, University of Calgary, Alberta, Canada

Michael Kirby, AC CMG, first Chairman of the Australian Law Reform Commission; former Justice of the High Court of Australia and President of the New South Wales Court of Appeal

Kelley Loper, Assistant Professor, Director of the LLM in Human Rights Programme, Deputy Director of the Centre for Comparative and Public Law, Faculty of Law, The University of Hong Kong

Ludwig Ng, Partner, ONC Lawyers, Hong Kong

Martin Partington, Emeritus Professor, School of Law, University of Bristol; former Law Commissioner (2001–2006) and Special Consultant (to 2008), Law Commission of England and Wales

Carole J Petersen, Professor, William S. Richardson School of Law, University of Hawaii; Director, Spark M Matsunaga Institute for Peace and Conflict Resolution

Stuart M I Stoker, former Secretary, Law Reform Commission of Hong Kong

Michael Tilbury, Chair of Private Law and Kerry Holdings Professor in Law, Faculty of Law, The University of Hong Kong; former Law Commissioner, New South Wales Law Reform Commission

Kate Warner, Professor of Law, University of Tasmania; Director, Tasmanian Law Reform Institute, Australia

Wong Yan Lung, SC, former Secretary for Justice, Government of the Hong Kong Special Administrative Region (2005–2012)

Simon N M Young, Professor, Faculty of Law, The University of Hong Kong; Barrister, Parkside Chambers; former Director, Centre for Comparative and Public Law (2007–2013); former member of the Law Reform Commission of Hong Kong's sub-committees on criminal hearsay and double jeopardy

Acknowledgements

This book originates from the ONC Conference on Law Reform organized by the Centre for Comparative and Public Law in the Faculty of Law, The University of Hong Kong, on 17 September 2011. We thank ONC Lawyers and other donors for their financial support of this project. We also thank the Dean of the Law Faculty (Professor Johannes Chan SC (Hon)) and Head of the Law Department (Professor Douglas Arner), both of whom spoke at the conference, for their support. We thank all the speakers and participants in the conference, including former legislator Margaret Ng and Law Faculty member, Eric Cheung, who previously served on the Law Reform Commission of Hong Kong (HKLRC). We thank the Government of the Hong Kong Special Administrative Region (HKSARG), especially the Secretary for Justice (Mr. Wong Yan Lung), and the HKLRC (including the secretariat) for their support and assistance. In particular, we acknowledge the HKSARG's copyright in Chapter 3. We thank our student researchers, Ian Chau and Afra Li, and, finally, we thank Sharron Fast, Flora Leung, Raymond Lam and Chris Munn for their invaluable assistance.

Acknowledgements

Part A

The Context of Law Reform

Chapter 1
Law Reform Today

Michael Tilbury, Simon N M Young and Ludwig Ng

Law Reform: The International Context

This book is about law reform, specifically the process of law reform. Its principal focus is the question whether the institutions of law reform in Hong Kong are appropriate to deliver effective law reform, by which we mean timely and on-going reform that produces laws that are clear, accessible and just, and that respond to the present-day, often shifting, needs of Hong Kong's society and economy. This is an important question for Hong Kong. Hong Kong's legal system, with its independent judiciary, is often said to be a cornerstone, if not the cornerstone, of Hong Kong's competitive advantage in the region of the world in which it finds itself. That advantage is diminished by the extent to which the legal system consists of laws that do not adequately address contemporary problems.

The necessity for continual law reform is not unique to Hong Kong. It is experienced in all countries whose economies and societies are in a state of constant flux. The need is felt particularly in common law jurisdictions, like Hong Kong, where the legislature and the courts — the institutions that hold sway over the development of the two principal sources of law, legislation and case law respectively — are not always the most suitable vehicles for reform of the law. This is obvious in relation to case law. Judicial reform of the common law is always piecemeal and slow, dependent, as it is, on the chance of the right case presenting itself for decision. Moreover, even when the right case does come along, judges can only reform the common law within the bounds of their constitutional function, and, in particular, within the constraints of the doctrine of precedent. To the extent to which they are perceived to be acting beyond the limits of that doctrine, they will, invariably, expose themselves to a "charge" of judicial activism, implying that they have acted beyond their proper function. In practice, this means that judicial reform of the law is often dependent on further happenstance: that the case in question ends up in a court of final appeal, where the doctrine of precedent does not apply with the same force.[1]

This may be thought to leave reform of the law where it properly belongs: with the legislature. In the Westminster system, however, legislatures are usually under the control of the executive government whose legislative programme may have no space for law reform that is not on the political agenda; or that is not perceived to have community support; or that is opposed by powerful interest groups. Indeed, even where a government is prepared to entertain the possibility of reform of a particular area of law, it may not be apparent which government department should be responsible for the reform; and, even where it is, the department in question may lack the expertise in legal policy that is necessary to undertake the process of reform effectively. In Hong Kong, effective law reform through legislation is further compromised by the existence of a dysfunctional legislature, which is, at least partly, attributable to the fact that it is not yet a fully democratic body.[2] And, in politically sensitive areas, reform can be stalled by public perceptions that the Chinese central authorities are directing the change, in defiance of the high degree of autonomy promised to Hong Kong under the Basic Law.[3]

Responding to the need for professional law reform on a continual basis, the government of the United Kingdom created the Law Commission of England and Wales and the Scottish Law Commission in 1965.[4] Their purpose is to promote law reform,[5] and, to this end, to "take and keep under review all the law with a view to its systematic development and reform, including in particular the codification of such law, the elimination of anomalies, the repeal of obsolete and unnecessary enactments, the reduction of the number of separate enactments and generally the simplification and modernisation of the law".[6]

---

[1] For Hong Kong, see *Solicitor (24/07) v Law Society of Hong Kong* (2008) 11 HKCFAR 117, [18]–[19] (Li CJ).

[2] Consider the Basic Law of the Hong Kong Special Administrative Region of the People's Republic of China, art 68.

[3] For examples, see n 30.

[4] Law Commissions Act 1965 (UK).

[5] Ibid s 1(1).

[6] Ibid s 3(1).

To accomplish these objectives, the Law Commissions are established as permanent bodies, comprising full-time commissioners supported by research and administrative staff, including parliamentary drafters. Following the example of the United Kingdom, law reform commissions were established in many common law jurisdictions, though their functions and structure were, and are, not always the same as those in the United Kingdom.[7]

By the early 1980s, almost two decades after the establishment of the Law Commissions in the United Kingdom, it could be said, as a broad generalization, that law reform was "in full flower" in the Commonwealth.[8] The flower was not, however, to bloom for long. By the late 1980s and the early 1990s, many governments had lost an appreciation of the need for full-time law reform commissions and had begun to reappraise the need for them, one reason being that they were regarded as expensive luxuries.[9] The result, particularly in Australia and in Canada, was that law reform agencies were downsized, abolished or simply allowed to wither away.[10] The downsized agencies represented a retreat to a view that had prevailed in the era before full-time law reform commissions were created: that professional law reform could be accomplished through agencies whose members are part-time, though they may be supported by some full-time research and/or administrative staff. Alternatively, the total abolition of law reform bodies could be justified by assigning their work to government departments, particularly to units devoted to legal policy reform within such departments.[11]

---

[7] For the creation and spread of law reform commissions in select parts of the Commonwealth, consider W Hurlburt, *Law Reform Commissions in the United Kingdom, Australia and Canada* (Juriliber, 1986); G Powles, "The Challenge of Law Reform in Pacific Island States" in B Opeskin and D Weisbrot, *The Promise of Law Reform* (Federation Press, 2005) ch 28; M Kamuwanga, "The Challenge of Law Reform in Southern Africa" in ibid, ch 29.

[8] M Kirby, *Reform the Law: Essays on the Renewal of the Australian Legal System* (OUP, 1983) 30.

[9] For example, Victoria, Legislative Assembly, *Parliamentary Debates (Hansard)*, 6 November 1992, 550–552 (Hon Jan Wade, Attorney-General, justifying the abolition of the Law Reform Commission of Victoria on grounds of expense [among others]).

[10] See P Handford, "The Changing Face of Law Reform" (1999) 73 *Australian Law Journal* 503.

[11] Consider the extensive remit of the Programs Branch of the Department of Justice Canada, aimed at achieving the strategic outcome of developing and maintaining a

Of course, law reform commissions that mirror at least the objectives of the UK Law Commissions continue to exist throughout the Commonwealth, at least on paper. Lack of political independence and lack of funding have, however, meant that many of these agencies have made little progress in achieving their objectives.[12] This exposes them to questions about the need for their existence and to the continual threat of abolition or defunding. These questions and this threat are not confined to such agencies. In 2010, the Law Commission of England and Wales, arguably the most successful law reform commission in the common law world, was faced with the threat not only of a substantial cut in its funding, but also to its independence, if not its very existence.[13] While the Commission weathered the storm, by the end of 2011, its Chairman, Lord Justice Munby, was still concerned that the Commission was under threat.[14]

Unsurprisingly, the turmoil affecting law reform agencies over the last two decades or so has led those concerned with the need for on-going professional law reform to devise other ways in which law reform can be accomplished within their jurisdictions. The most promising development has been the emergence of partnerships between universities, governments and other interested parties. Under this arrangement each party to the agreement contributes to the funding of law reform activity, which takes place either within the law faculty of a university or in close connection with a university faculty or faculties of law. This model, which can be traced back to the Alberta Law Reform Institute (which was established by agreement between the government, the University of Alberta and the Law Society of Alberta as long ago as 1967),[15] may prove particularly suitable for smaller jurisdictions, as it has done in Alberta[16] and

---

"fair, relevant and accessible justice system": see <www.justice.gc.ca/eng/pi/pb-dpg. index.html> accessed 31 January 2013.

[12] See Kamuwanga (n 7) 431–432 (law reform agencies in Eastern and Southern Africa).

[13] See Lord Justice Munby, "Shaping the Law — The Law Commission at the Crossroads" (the Denning Lecture for 2011) 5–6 <www.lawcom.gov.uk/publications/lectures.htm> accessed 31 January 2013.

[14] Ibid 3.

[15] See Hurlburt (n 7) 215–223. The Institute was originally styled "The Institute of Law Research and Reform".

[16] By June 2010, the Institute had issued 97 reports with a good implementation rate: see Alberta Law Reform Institute, *Annual Report July 2009–June 2010*, 35–46, available at <www.law.ualberta.ca/alri> accessed 31 January 2013.

as it appears to be doing in Ontario[17] and Tasmania.[18] Whatever the future of this specific model of law reform, the co-operation arrangements that it promotes between governments and universities are capable of wider application in the achievement of effective law reform. An example of such co-operation occurred in the recent project of the Law Reform Commission of Hong Kong (HKLRC) on reforming offence exceptions to suspended sentences of imprisonment. The Law Society of Hong Kong commissioned the University of Hong Kong's Centre for Comparative and Public Law (CCPL) to prepare a report on the subject, which then served as the main impetus for the HKLRC's project. Agreeing with the recommendations contained in the CCPL report, the HKLRC was able to move swiftly to publishing a consultation paper in June 2013 without the need to form a sub-committee to study the matter.[19]

It is important that the work of professional full-time law reform commissions be put in context in evaluating the overall law reform record of any jurisdiction. Law reform commissions do not have a monopoly on law reform. As Professor David Weisbrot, a former President of the Australian Law Reform Commission, has pointed out, law reform exists in a "crowded field".[20] Successful law reform initiatives may result from the work of other sources, including committees of parliaments; departments of government; specialist tribunals (such as anti-discrimination tribunals); specialist bodies (such as environmental protection agencies); Royal Commissions; and even private consultants and advocates.[21] Moreover, many of these bodies may produce consultation documents, engage in public consultation and, generally, adopt techniques that have been pioneered by law reform commissions.

Law Reform: The Hong Kong Context

A crowded field of law reform also exists in Hong Kong. In addition to the Administration, the Legislative Council (LegCo) and the Courts, the HKLRC possesses a general law reform mandate, which, because it is expressly

---

[17] See Chapter 6 (Hughes).
[18] See Chapter 7 (Warner).
[19] The consultation paper can be accessed on the HKLRC website: <http://www.hkreform.gov.hk/en/docs/exceptedoff_e.pdf> accessed 1 August 2013.
[20] See D Weisbrot, "The Future of Institutional Law Reform" in Opeskin and Weisbrot (n 7) 18, 20–22.
[21] Consider Chapter 10 (Petersen and Loper).

articulated, places the commission at the centre of any evaluation of the state of law reform in Hong Kong. Specialist bodies nevertheless continue to pursue law reform agenda in particular contexts. It is, therefore, necessary to consider the contribution that can be made to law reform through these various sources, and in particular to evaluate how that contribution measures up in comparison to the work of the HKLRC.

Law making and law enforcement, and hence law reform, lie at the very heart of the constitutional functions of the Executive[22] and of LegCo.[23] However, the limited accountability of the Executive to LegCo,[24] combined with the fact that LegCo is not a fully democratic body,[25] mean that neither the Executive nor the Legislature is fully accountable politically to the people of Hong Kong. This generates great difficulty in achieving effective law reform through the Executive and LegCo in the face of the slightest opposition to reform from vested interests. We acknowledge, of course, that it is nevertheless possible for successful law reform to originate in government departments or bureaux.[26] Indeed, government bureaux are the main agents of law reform in Hong Kong, with particular roles in three areas: ensuring that the law of Hong Kong is compliant with Hong Kong's international obligations, especially major human rights instruments; ensuring that the law of Hong Kong is otherwise in line with major and developing international standards in such areas as financial law and regulation; and developing laws that are necessary to accommodate the increasing interaction with Mainland China.[27] If bureaux are to be judged as primarily responsible for keeping the law up to date in these areas, their record of achievement is, at best, patchy.[28]

The role of bureaux in law reform in no way diminishes the need for, or the role of, the HKLRC. A very important principle is at stake here, which is the independence from government of the body making recommendations

---

[22] See J Chan and C Lim (eds), *Law of the Hong Kong Constitution* (Sweet & Maxwell, 2011) [9.008]–[9.011].

[23] Ibid [7.133]–[7.134].

[24] See Basic Law of the Hong Kong Special Administrative Region of the People's Republic of China, art 64.

[25] See n 2.

[26] For examples, see Chapter 3 (Wong).

[27] See Chapter 3 (Wong).

[28] See Chapters 10 (human rights law) (Petersen and Loper); 9 (labour law) (Glofcheski); 8 (insolvency law) (Ng).

for the reform of the law. A government bureau or agency of any sort is part of the government. Recommendations that come from such a body run the risk of being perceived as no more than the views of a perhaps unpopular or distrusted administration, even where those recommendations have been arrived at after consultation with relevant stakeholders. Such stakeholders may, in any event, decide not to engage with a government agency in whose independence they have no confidence, thereby diminishing the value of reform proposals that come from that agency. The problem intensifies in politically sensitive areas over which the Chinese central authorities maintain a strong interest. We have seen many instances in which policies and proposals,[29] originating from the bureaux, were met with strong public objections, typically in the form of large-scale street protests, followed by the government's retreat, which ultimately results in little if any reform. Absent in these initiatives is the use of a credible and independent reform body to study and formulate options for public consultation. Such a strategy would also help to alleviate the public's concerns over Mainland Chinese intervention in matters reserved for Hong Kong's high degree of autonomy.[30]

The HKLRC is independent of government and regards this independence as one of its strengths, enabling it to present its recommendations "after an objective examination of the facts and the law".[31] Indeed, it is this independence that can be regarded as underpinning its mission "to engage the public in the law reform process, and to arouse public interest in that process by the dissemination of law reform material and by effective communication with the community."[32]

Moving beyond principle, practical reasons often favour law reform through the HKLRC rather than through a government bureau or department.

---

[29] For example, national security proposals to implement Article 23 of the Basic Law (2003); constitutional reform of the systems for electing the 2012 Chief Executive and LegCo members (2010); arrangements for filling LegCo vacancies (2011); moral and national education school curriculum (2012); arrangements on the inspection of directors' personal information on the Companies Register (2013).

[30] For the case for such a body in respect of security laws, see Simon N M Young, "Security laws for Hong Kong" in V Ramraj, M Hor, K Roach and G Williams (eds), *Global Anti-Terrorism Law and Policy* (2nd ed, CUP, 2012) 357.

[31] *The Law Reform Commission of Hong Kong, 2011* (Government Logistics Department, HKSAR Government, 2011) 4.

[32] Ibid 1.

The Hong Kong government itself realizes that the Commission plays a "particularly valuable" role in law reform in a number of circumstances.[33] First is "where the subject does not fall readily under the responsibility of one particular bureau of Government", an example being reform of the law of privacy.[34] Secondly, in situations that call for technical legal expertise that the government cannot provide, either because the subject matter is outside the government's day-to-day activities, or because that expertise cannot be provided on a full-time basis. An example of the former is the reform of the law of domicile; of the latter, reform of insolvency law.

Turning to the courts, we have already pointed out the general limitations that apply to piecemeal judicial reform of the law. There is, however, another important factor that ought not to be overlooked and that arises as a result of the way in which law reform commissions operate. In detecting any need for reform of the law, commissions place an emphasis on consultation with groups or people who know how the law operates in practice or who are affected by the operation of the law; and on research (including interdisciplinary research) that reveals how the law operates, or ought to operate, in practice. This distinguishes the task of law reform commissions from that of the courts, and makes them a more powerful locus for reform in appropriate cases. In the words of Sir Anthony Mason:[35]

> I do not doubt that there are some cases in which an ultimate court of appeal can and should vary or modify what has been thought to be a settled rule or principle of the common law on the ground that it is ill-adapted to modern circumstances. If it should emerge that a specific common law rule was based on the existence of particular conditions or circumstances, whether social or economic, and that they have undergone a radical change, then in a simple or clear case the court may be justified in moulding the rule to meet the new conditions and circumstances. But there are very powerful reasons why the court should be reluctant to engage in such an exercise. The court is neither a legislature nor a law reform agency. Its responsibility is to decide cases by applying the law to the facts as found. The court's facilities, techniques and procedures are adapted to that responsibility; they are not adapted to legislative functions or to law reform activities. The court does not, and cannot, carry

---

[33] Ibid 5.
[34] See further Chapters 11 (Chiang), 12 (Bacon-Shone) and 13 (Tilbury).
[35] *State Government Insurance Commission v Trigwell* (1979) 142 CLR 617, 633 (Mason J).

out investigations or enquiries with a view to ascertaining whether particular common law rules are working well, whether they are adjusted to the needs of the community and whether they command popular assent. Nor can the court call for, and examine, submissions from groups and individuals who may be vitally interested in the making of changes to the law. In short, the court cannot, and does not, engage in the wide-ranging inquiries and assessments which are made by governments and law reform agencies as a desirable, if not essential, preliminary to the enactment of legislation by an elected legislature.

The courts, however, have been a great motivator for law reform in Hong Kong. Many decisions from the Court of Final Appeal (CFA), especially ones concerning unconstitutionality, have prompted comprehensive law reform from the Executive and LegCo.[36] The CFA's invention of the power of courts to suspend temporarily a declaration of unconstitutionality to allow government time to enact corrective legislation has been highly effective in bringing about reform that is both timely and progressive.[37] There have been instances where a court's judgment, sometimes with an explicit recommendation for reform or study, has led to the matter being referred to the HKLRC.[38] This ability of the courts to influence policy and legislative changes, where

---

[36] For example, *Secretary for Justice v Chan Wah* (2000) 3 HKCFAR 459, leading to legislation on village representation elections in Village Representative Election Ordinance (Cap 576), which entered into force on 21 February 2003; *Secretary for Security v Sakthevel Prabakar* (2004) 7 HKCFAR 187, leading to legislation on Convention Against Torture *non-refoulement* screening in Immigration (Amendment) Ordinance 2012, Ord No 23 of 2012, which entered into force on 3 December 2012. But compare the discussions over a new offence of persistent child sexual abuse following the criticisms of specimen counts in *Chim Hon Man v HKSAR* (1999) 2 HKCFAR 145; see further, Amanda Whitfort, "The Proposed Offence of Persistent Sexual Abuse of a Child" (2002) 32 *Hong Kong Law Journal* 13.

[37] For example, *Koo Sze Yiu v Chief Executive* (2006) 9 HKCFAR 441, leading to the Interception of Communications and Surveillance Ordinance (Cap 589), which entered into force in August 2006; *Chan Kin Sum Simon v Secretary for Justice*, unreported, HCAL79A/2008, 11 March 2009, CFI, leading to removal of all restrictions on the right of prisoners to vote, see Voting by Imprisoned Persons Ordinance, Ord No 7 of 2009, which entered into force in July and October 2009.

[38] See *Wong Wai Man v HKSAR* (2000) 3 HKCFAR 322 (criminal hearsay); but the Court of Final Appeal's suggestion to the HKLRC to study the common law offence of champerty and maintenance in *Winnie Lo v HKSAR* [2012] 1 HKC 537 (CFA) has yet to be taken up.

ordinary reform processes have been impaired, partly explains why there has been an influx of judicial review cases since 1997.[39]

Specialist law reform bodies, such as the Standing Committee on Company Law Reform or the Office of the Privacy Commissioner for Personal Data, may not only use the research and consultation techniques that have been pioneered by law reform commissions, but also generate successful law reform.[40] Generally, however, there is no evidence that specialist law reform bodies are more successful in generating reform than generalist law reform commissions. On the contrary, and compared to law reform commissions, such agencies have three weaknesses. First, their specialization may mean that they lack the perception of independence that attaches to a generalist law reform body. They are associated with a particular area of law and may be perceived to have a particular position when it comes to reforming the law in the area concerned; alternatively, they may be perceived to be captives of particular interest groups. Could a privacy commissioner, for example, be perceived to be other than in favour of laws that would give individuals greater privacy, perhaps at the expense of freedom of speech? Secondly, a specialist agency will almost certainly have among its members groups or individuals who have conflicting views about how the law should develop in the area of specialization. Those views will often be strongly held, leading to internal conflict that diminishes the ability of the agency to act as an effective agent of law reform, as has happened in the case of the Labour Advisory Board in Hong Kong.[41] Thirdly, at least to the extent to which they are ad hoc, specialist agencies are transient. In contrast, a permanent law reform commission should possess an institutional memory that is able to recall past debates to inform present ones. Only thus can a constant reinvention of the wheel be avoided. As Professor David Weisbrot has written:[42]

> An obvious disadvantage of the various ad hoc law reform arrangements is their transience. Unlike permanent law reform agencies, they lack established processes, quality control mechanisms, tried and true staff,

---

[39] See S N M Young and Y Ghai (eds), *Hong Kong's Court of Final Appeal: The Development of the Law in China's Hong Kong* (CUP, 2013) chs 10 and 16.

[40] For example, the Personal Data (Privacy) (Amendment) Ordinance 2012, which resulted primarily from the work of the Office of Privacy Commissioner for Personal Data: see Chapter 11 (Chiang).

[41] See Chapter 9 (Glofcheski).

[42] Weisbrot (n 20) 22.

established links or databases to facilitate effective consultation, and a track record of excellence. Ad hoc bodies are also unable to contribute to the reform process at a later date — in a field with long lead times — through the maintenance of documents and websites, submissions to parliamentary or other inquiries, and so on.

The considerations just discussed highlight the necessity for a permanent body with a generalist law reform brief, such as the HKLRC, to which we now turn.

The Law Reform Commission of Hong Kong

The HKLRC's establishment in 1980 is located in the general historical movement of law reform in common law countries from part-time to full-time bodies. The Commission replaced a small Law Reform Committee that had operated between 1956 and 1964 and that had issued five reports.[43] Its generalist brief was "[t]o consider such reforms of the laws of Hong Kong as may be referred to it by the Chief Justice and the Attorney General and to report to the Chief Justice and the Attorney General".[44] The Commission now describes its primary mission as being "[t]o present proposals for reform which make the law in Hong Kong more effective, more accessible, and more in tune with the community's needs".[45]

Two aspects of the Commission's objectives and structure stand out.[46] First, the HKLRC has never had a law revision function — a function that can variously be described as the identification for repeal of obsolete and spent statutes; the consolidation of statutes; and the simplification and modernization of statutes (for example, updating or clarifying the language of statutes). Most law reform commissions established after 1965 were expressly invested with this function, although, with the exception of the Law Commission of England and Wales,[47] few law reform commissions have, in practice, devoted

---

[43] See S Stoker, *A Comparative Study of Law Reform Implementation* (University of Hong Kong, M Soc Sc thesis, 1987) 7 <http://hdl.handle.net/10722/55706> accessed 31 January 2013.

[44] Ibid.

[45] *The Law Reform Commission of Hong Kong, 2011* (n 31) 1.

[46] For details of the structure of the HKLRC, see Chapters 3 (Wong) and 4 (Stoker).

[47] See Sir David Lloyd Jones, "The Law Commission and the Implementation of Law Reform" (Sir William Dale Annual Lecture, 22 November 2012) 5–10 <www.lawcom.gov.uk/publications/lectures.htm> accessed 31 January 2013.

resources to it.[48] It is, arguably, unfortunate that the HKLRC was not given this function in view of the real need for the modernization of Hong Kong's statute book.[49] Secondly, the HKLRC has never had full-time commissioners who are able to devote their time to pushing forward a law reform agenda in the territory, though there are full-time lawyers working within the Commission's secretariat. The full-time staff members are responsible, among other matters, for organizing consultations in which the Commission and its sub-committees engage.

In the absence of full-time commissioners, and in view of its limited resources, the HKLRC relies heavily on the work of expert sub-committees set up to examine almost all of the projects that the Commission undertakes. The members of the sub-committees volunteer their expertise and are not paid. The Commission regards this arrangement as one of its strengths, since "its members come from a range of backgrounds, enabling it to consider reform of the law from the point of view of the community as a whole, rather than solely from that of the legal profession".[50] Of course, the Commission is right to be proud of the contribution that these volunteers have made to the development of the law in Hong Kong.

As at the end of 2012, the HKLRC had produced 61 reports, of which some 32 had resulted in the enactment of legislation, or the introduction of administrative measures, that gave effect, wholly or partly, to their recommendations.[51] This represents an overall implementation rate of approximately 52 per cent. This is in contrast to the overall implementation rate of the Law Commission of England and Wales, which is about 69 per cent.[52] The figure for the HKLRC can hardly be regarded as satisfactory. At the same time, there is no suggestion that the HKLRC has failed to achieve its vision of attaining and maintaining a reputation for excellence in law reform, both internationally and in Hong Kong.[53] That vision is achieved by law reform work of the highest

---

[48] See generally E Caldwell, "A Vision of Tidiness: Codes, Consolidations and Statute Law Revision", in Opeskin and Weisbrot (n 7) ch 3.

[49] For examples, see L Ng, "Reforming Law Reform", *Hong Kong Lawyer* (December 2010) 18, 21–23.

[50] *The Law Reform Commission of Hong Kong, 2011* (n 31) 5.

[51] The figures in this paragraph are taken from the website of the HKLRC: see <www.hkreform.gov.hk/en/publications/chronological.htm> accessed 31 January 2013.

[52] Sir David Lloyd Jones (n 47) 10.

[53] *The Law Reform Commission of Hong Kong, 2011* (n 31) 1.

quality. The Administration itself attests to the excellence of the Commission's work.[54] So the reason(s) for non-implementation must be sought elsewhere. A significant factor that the overall implementation rate hides is that the level of implementation fell dramatically following the resumption of Chinese sovereignty over Hong Kong in 1997. Of the 33 reports published before the handover, 26 resulted in some implementation, a rate of 78 per cent. In contrast, of the 28 reports issued since August 1997, only 6 have provoked any implementation activity — a rate of 21 per cent. Of course, it is foolish to attribute the poor implementation rate after 1997 simply to the change in sovereignty. The period since 1997 also corresponds roughly with the period in which professional law reform has been in decline in many common law jurisdictions.[55]

Whatever the cause, it became apparent in the first decade of this century that the state of law reform in Hong Kong required investigation. In an article published in the December 2010 issue of the *Hong Kong Lawyer*, one of us urged that a review of the process of law reform in Hong Kong was essential if Hong Kong were to continue to claim its legal system as a competitive advantage.[56] The article pointed out that the failure to bring the law into line with modern conditions extended over many areas of law — among others, legal aid, patents, corporate rescue, child custody and access, consumer protection, regulation of the sale of residential property, product liability, surveillance, and privacy. The article drew attention to the long periods of time that it sometimes took the HKLRC, with no full-time commissioners, to bring reports to finality. It also pointed out that, once the Commission had reported, the Administration frequently failed to take timely action to implement, or even to respond to, the recommendations in a report. The article called for a commitment by the Administration to invest adequate resources in law reform. These concerns were echoed in a number of articles appearing in the *South China Morning Post* at around the same period.[57] Responding to these concerns, a Conference on Reforming Law Reform, organized by the Centre for

---

[54] See Chapter 3 (Wong).

[55] See text to nn 8–10 above. The implementation rate of the Law Commission of England and Wales fell to about 55 per cent in the first decade of this century: see Sir David Lloyd Jones (n 47) 10.

[56] L Ng, "Reforming Law Reform" (n 49) 18. See also L Ng, "Law for the Times", *South China Morning Post* (29 September 2010).

[57] See M Ng, "Treatment of Custody Overlooks Child's Rights", *South China Morning Post* (20 December 2010); A Wong, "Series of Law Reform Ideas Left to Gather

Public and Comparative Law at the University of Hong Kong and co-sponsored by ONC Lawyers and others, was held at the University of Hong Kong in November 2011. This book is the result of papers that were delivered at that conference.

The dominant issues emerging from these critiques and from the conference were, first, the length of time that it takes the HKLRC to bring reports to conclusion; and secondly, the failure of the Administration to respond, either at all or in a timely fashion, to such reports with a view to their implementation. These are, in fact, two timeless themes in the literature of law reform commissions.[58] Critics of law reform commissions have seized upon them, while law reform commissions themselves have worried about them incessantly — law reform commissions being notoriously self-critical institutions (as even a cursory glance at the literature on law reform will confirm). The issues then resolve themselves into how these two problems should be addressed in Hong Kong in the second decade of the twenty-first century.

Timeliness

The most obvious response to the perceived excessive length of time that it takes the HKLRC to complete its reports is to appoint commissioners who are engaged full-time in overseeing law reform projects and in driving the overall mission of the Commission. This expansion of the role of the Commission in Hong Kong would, however, run counter to the experience in Canada and Australia where the more recent trend has been to revert to downsized or part-time law reform commissions.[59] The expansion would, however, mirror the model of law reform represented by the Law Commission of England and

---

Dust", ibid (20 December 2010); J Man, "Failure to Invest in Updating Flawed Laws 'Hurting Hong Kong'", ibid (21 December 2010); A Wong, "Lack of Liability Law Actions Puts Consumers at Risk", ibid (21 December 2010); Editorial, "The Key to Finding a Level Legal Playing Field", ibid (27 December 2010); M Ng, "Government Always Finds 'Good' Reasons to Delay Law Reforms", ibid (10 January 2011).

[58] For timeliness, consider A Rees, "Strategic and Project Planning" in Opeskin and Weisbrot (n 7) ch 8; B Opeskin, "Measuring Success" in ibid 202, 211–12. For implementation, consider Hurlburt (n 7) ch 7; Opeskin, "Measuring Success" in Opeskin and Weisbrot (n 7) ch 14; M Kirby, "Are We There Yet?" in ibid 433, 437–441.

[59] See Chapters 6 (Hughes) and 7 (Warner).

Wales,[60] which, as we have already pointed out, is arguably the most successful, and certainly the most stable, law reform commission of the modern era.

Whatever the reasons behind the reversion to part-time commissions in Australia and Canada, they are not, we suggest, of relevance to Hong Kong. First, there are no economic reasons to suggest that the Hong Kong government, with its healthy surpluses, cannot afford properly to resource a full-time commission. Secondly, at this crucial juncture in its history, Hong Kong cries out for appropriate investment in its principal law reform agency. As pointed out above, a legal system of obsolete laws is always worthless. This is particularly so in today's Hong Kong. At a time at which the legal system in China is being modernized — at least ostensibly — the HKLRC should be examining the compatibility of the Hong Kong legal system with that modernized system with a view to maintaining Hong Kong's competitive advantage within the region.

In the end, we cannot, of course, guarantee that the appointment of full-time commissioners will improve the timelines within which reports are published, since criticisms about overdue reports have plagued all modern law reform commissions (including those with full-time commissioners).[61] We also appreciate that modern part-time law reform agencies have made real contributions to the development of the law within their respective jurisdictions.[62] We do not, however, believe that the future lies in maintaining, or returning to, part-time law reform committees.[63] Our instinct is that it is more likely than not that a properly funded law reform commission, with an appropriate number of full-time commissioners, is likely to be much more efficient, and to deliver more timely law reform proposals, than a commission comprising already over-worked volunteers who come to the task of law reform at the "fag end of the day".[64] The Administration could, indeed, secure the benefit of adequately funding the Law Reform Commission by requiring the Commission to complete its projects within specified time periods.

A well-resourced commission, with full-time commissioners, would have the additional benefit of being able to take advantage of its increased

---

[60] See Chapter 5 (Partington).
[61] See Lord Justice Munby (n 13) 9–11.
[62] See Chapters 6 (Hughes) and 7 (Warner).
[63] See Chapters 2 (Kirby) and 14 (Kirby).
[64] See K Sutton, *The Pattern of Law Reform in Australia* (University of Queensland Press, 1970) 15.

capacity by raising the profile of the commission in the community, indirectly by attracting the interest of the media in issues of law reform, and directly by engaging the community in the business of law reform through intense and effective consultation processes. This, in itself, would contribute to the democratic development of Hong Kong. Full-time commissioners, having had a more direct role in developing reform proposals, are more likely to champion them long after they have been published, and this serves as an important catalyst to timely implementation.

Implementation

Crucial to a law reform commission's successful and efficient discharge of its functions is the commitment of other actors in the political process to its work. Governments' lack of response to law reform commissions' reports is an indication of the lack of such commitment, perhaps even of hostility. Two strategies have been suggested for overcoming this problem. First, it is argued that there must be some mechanism by which the executive government responds to recommendations of a law reform commission. Without such a response, the work of the law reform commission is marginalized, and can even be seen to be worthless. Secondly, there must also be some process for requiring the easy implementation through the legislature of the recommendations of a law reform commission — recommendations that have been already been subjected by the law reform commission to extensive public scrutiny and discussion, as well as subsequent review by relevant government departments or bureaux.

These two factors undoubtedly present a real challenge for law reform in Hong Kong at this stage of its constitutional development. First, there is the lack of real democratic accountability of the Administration, making it easy for the Administration to ignore or stall recommendations of the Law Reform Commission. Secondly, the structure of LegCo itself, particularly its voting configuration, allows powerful constituencies, themselves subject to the pressure of influential lobby groups, to block reforms that do not suit them or those that lobby them, no matter how rational and well thought out the recommendations may be. It may be that meaningful reform of the law reform process will have to await the changes in the structure of LegCo that are promised in the foreseeable future, since any substantial reform of the Law Reform Commission will itself ultimately have to be considered by LegCo.

However, this does not mean that the ground cannot be cleared by now putting in place administrative processes to facilitate a sensible relationship between the HKLRC, the Administration and LegCo.

In this respect, the October 2011 Guidelines issued by the former Secretary for Justice and Chairman of the Law Reform Commission are to be welcomed.[65] These require relevant bureaux to respond publicly, and as soon as practicable, to Law Reform Commission reports, setting out which recommendations they accept, reject or intend to implement in modified form (with an interim response to be provided within six months following the publication of the report).[66] The success of these Guidelines will depend on their effective implementation in practice; and in particular, on the extent to which they generate meaningful responses to Law Reform Commission reports in which the Executive effectively sets out, and justifies, its attitude to the recommendations of the Commission.[67] In early 2013, it appears from the updates to the HKLRC website that these Guidelines are already having an impact and the Administration has been providing timely and detailed responses (and updated responses) to HKLRC reports.

This leaves the necessity for some procedure that ensures that the legislature will give expeditious consideration to the recommendations of the law reform commission that are put before it. A recent development in this respect occurred in England in 2010 when the House of Lords adopted a new procedure that facilitates consideration of non-controversial recommendations of the Law Commission.[68] Early indications are that the procedure is working well.[69] An analogous procedure should be considered in Hong Kong. There is already a practice of discussing HKLRC consultation and final reports in relevant LegCo panel meetings, but the practice is haphazard and not systematized. Even with controversial issues, the LegCo panel could be a constructive process for hearing diverse views and making progress in reform. For example, a white paper accompanied by draft legislation for the use of public deputations to a LegCo panel would be a useful vehicle for gauging public sentiments at an early stage. This would be followed by the introduction of a (substantially)

---

[65] See Appendix to Chapter 3 (Wong).
[66] See Chapters 3 (Wong) and 4 (Stoker).
[67] Failure, or inadequacy, of response may be emerging as a problem under a corresponding regime in the UK: see Lord Justice Munby (n 13) 6–8.
[68] See Chapters 2 (Kirby), 5 (Partington) and 14 (Kirby).
[69] Sir David Lloyd Jones (n 47) 21–23.

revised bill for first reading in LegCo. Further public deputations to a bills committee would be possible, though typically only minor amendments to the bill would be entertained at this stage. To help link the LegCo process with that of the HKLRC, it would be worth introducing a stronger legislative drafting component within the work of the Commission and its sub-committees.[70] With draft legislation appended to HKLRC reports, the trip to the LegCo panel for initial public vetting should be shorter, and hopefully faster.

Conclusion

Any improvement in law reform processes and procedures must, necessarily, come from within Hong Kong itself, taking into account Hong Kong's unique constitutional structure, institutions and legal culture, but learning, where relevant, from the experience of law reform in other countries.

The recommendations with which we conclude this chapter are that:

(1) An appropriate number of full-time law reform commissioners should be appointed to the Law Reform Commission of Hong Kong;

(2) Where appropriate, the Law Reform Commission of Hong Kong reports should include draft legislation so as to facilitate and expedite the implementation process;

(3) The Guidelines that govern the response of bureaux and departments to reports of the Law Reform Commission of Hong Kong should be kept under review to ensure that they are satisfactorily implemented in practice;

(4) Consideration should be given to the development of a procedure by which LegCo can consider, with the benefit of public deputations, recommendations (including draft legislation) of the Law Reform Commission of Hong Kong with a view to their implementation;

(5) Drawing on the experience of jurisdictions such as Ontario and Tasmania,[71] the Law Reform Commission of Hong Kong and the Administration should consider developing closer co-operative and collaborative relationships with law schools and universities on law reform generally and on specific reform projects.

---

[70] The Department of Justice's Law Draftsman is already an ex-officio member of the HKLRC.

[71] See chapters 6 (Hughes) and 7 (Warner).

These are modest proposals. They do, however, go some way to realize the enormously positive effect on the development of the common and statutory law that the creation of professional law reform commissions initially held out. That promise has never been fully realized anywhere in the common law world. It is, in our view, time for Hong Kong to take the lead and to exploit the potential inherent in the noble cause of law reform.

Chapter 2
Changing Fashions and Enduring Values in Law Reform

Michael Kirby

Law Reform in Hong Kong: Context

This chapter offers thoughts on the arrangements for law reform suitable to Hong Kong in the current age. An historical perspective is called for and is appropriate to the time and occasion. However, each society must create law reform institutions suitable to its needs. The insights of foreigners, however well intentioned, may or may not be relevant to local conditions. This is specially so in Hong Kong where the legal and constitutional position is unique and complex.

Soon after my appointment in 1975, to be the inaugural Chairman of the Australian Law Reform Commission (ALRC), I created a quarterly journal *Reform*. Virtually single-handed, I wrote every word of that journal until my retirement from the Commission in 1984. For me, it was a kind of diary, or blog, of my experiences and thoughts during that first decade.

In the first issue, published in January 1976, I recorded the link that the ALRC had already established with colleagues working on law reform in Hong Kong:[1]

> The five reports of the Hong Kong Law Reform Committee were recently sent to the ALRC. No report has been produced by the Committee since 1964. A law reform drafting section has been established in the Attorney-General's Department. This is now responsible for preparing the law reform programme of Hong Kong. It does not issue publications.

This somewhat gloomy record was brightened a little in 1980 with the following entry, which was published after the 1980 Commonwealth law

---

[1] "Overseas Developments" [1976] *Reform* 8, 10.

conference in Lagos, Nigeria, where I presented a paper on "Law Reform in the Commonwealth of Nations":[2]

> Scarcely a quarter goes by now but a new Commonwealth law reform agency is established. For example, it has been announced that a new law reform commission has been established for Hong Kong. The chairman of the Commission is the Attorney-General . . . Mr. John Griffith QC, who was in Lagos. The first meeting . . . occurred in June 1980. The first three topics referred to it for consideration are: commercial arbitration; crime: homosexuality laws; and laws of evidence in civil proceedings.
>
> It is envisaged that the Commission will work principally through sub-committees to which will be co-opted suitable experts . . . Considerations of proposals for reform advanced by the government or private sector will also be part of its function.

In 1983, the succeeding Commonwealth law reform conference was held in Hong Kong. An issue of *Reform* that year recorded that a "Law Reform Forum" was being organized to coincide with that meeting.[3] A report on the meeting followed in the next issue.[4] It contained extracts from a keynote paper delivered by the Chairman of the Hong Kong Law Reform Commission (HKLRC) and Chief Justice of Hong Kong, Sir Denys Roberts. With tongue firmly planted in cheek (I hope), he is recorded as saying: "One of the important objectives of law reform is to provide a comfortable life for substantial numbers of unemployable academics and draftsmen." He declared that the law reformer was a "bizarre blend of relentless enthusiasm, burning faith and detachment from reality". The chief characteristics of a law reformer, as then seen in Hong Kong, were said to be:[5]

- Dedication, which his critics describe as pig-headedness;
- Faith — on UNESCO figures, about 16% of law reformers have taken their own lives having lost faith;
- Insensitivity, of the kind "which you can observe at Protestant funerals in Dublin"; and
- Patience, of exactly the same kind as enables judges to resist the temptation to deliver judgment within a reasonable time.

---

[2] "Well Met In Lagos" [1980] *Reform* 109, 111.
[3] "Uniform Law — At Last" [1983] *Reform* 142, 143.
[4] "Legislative Logorrhea" [1984] *Reform* 19.
[5] Ibid 19.

In my note on the aftermath of this speech, I observed that the participants at the Hong Kong forum were seen stumbling out into the sunshine, led by "Lord Hailsham, LC, Lord Scarman and law reformers from all parts of the Commonwealth, reeling with mixed amusement and shock". A question mark was then hanging over the future of Hong Kong, concerning the survival of the common law system and its institutions. The top priority, as declared by the Chairman of the Hong Kong Bar Association (Mr. Henry Litton QC), was to "[e]nsure . . . the survival of [the] system in the event of changes in administration". The record reveals that the then Commonwealth Secretary-General, Sir Shridath Ramphal, had urged Commonwealth lawyers to abandon smug conceits; to escape the shell; and to aspire to being more than "merely . . . passive keepers of the seals".[6]

In present circumstances that inevitably turn our minds to the big picture and the historical perspective, we return to Hong Kong to reflect on what has changed and what is enduring. The University of Hong Kong was built on the vision of Lord Lugard of Nigerian fame. He had a bold aspiration for it and it took as its motto *Sapientia et virtus*: wisdom and virtue. We would do well to adopt the same principles in considering the role and future of institutional law reform in Hong Kong.

The HKLRC remains in operation today. The Secretary for Justice still refers matters to it for study, public consultation and the formulation of recommendations in a final report. Additionally, government bureaux develop proposals for reform in-house, with or without public consultation or expert input. Ad hoc bodies, mostly of officials, may be created by government as it decides to develop proposals on particular topics. The final decision after every report is delivered is left to government: whether to take any proposed legislative change to the Legislative Council or whether not to action it. The various mechanisms operate in a way that is rather haphazard and without a clear or logical system. The processes are often said to be ill-defined, and not evaluated against performance indicators or other standards. In this, the Hong Kong situation parallels that in Australia and many other Commonwealth countries. Our present task is to consider whether this somewhat disorganized way of achieving law reform is satisfactory. And, if not, whether something better and more comprehensive should be put in its place and, if so, what?

---

[6] Ibid.

Considering Hong Kong (and for that matter Australia) as a significant economic unit, it seems certain that an efficiency audit, studying the way in which laws essential to the success of the unit and those living and working in it happen, would conclude that the present methodology is intolerable. It should be replaced by stronger, better-resourced and bigger institutions; more effective inbuilt mechanisms of reform and renewal; and regular checks on the performance of those institutions to evaluate their outputs, monitor their outcomes, and adjust them when required.

Many forces are contributing to the increasing need for law reform today. They include:

- The many advances in technology (particularly informatics, biology, nano-technology and energy sciences) that render earlier laws obsolete or ineffective;
- The changes in social attitudes and knowledge, including advancing perceptions of universal human rights, that occasion different demands and expectations of law in a just society; and
- In the particular case of Hong Kong, there is the need to adjust changes in the law to meet local and global expectations, whilst at the same time adapting to the rapid advances in interacting regulations operating in the People's Republic of China. The recent review of the *Code on Corporate Governance Practices 2005 and the Rules Governing the Listing of Securities* by the Hong Kong Exchanges and Clearing, operator of the securities and derivatives market, produced a public consultation paper in December 2010. However, the "soft consultation" in Hong Kong was obliged, in practice, to "dovetail" with at least the main contours of the laws operating in China. This phenomenon at once presents a stimulus to, and check upon, reformist inclinations, simply because of the practicalities presented by the economic integration of this jurisdiction with that of the economic giant that is China.[7]

When I first became involved in institutional law reform, in 1975, it was at a time described by Professor Michael Tilbury as a "golden age" of institutional law reform, at least in Australia.[8] It was 20 years after the creation of

---

[7] Phil Taylor, "One Country, Two Systems: Hong Kong's Proposed Changes to Corporate Governance Rules and How They Fit with the Approach in Mainland China", International Bar Association, *Global Insight* (London, April 2011) 43.

[8] M Tilbury, "A History of Law Reform in Australia" in B Opeskin and D Weisbrot, *The Promise of Law Reform* (Federation Press, 2005) 1, 15.

the Law Commission of India, 10 years after the establishment of the English and Scottish Commissions and a mere two centuries after the moves began in France for the codification and simplification of the civil law.[9]

Lord Scarman, first chair of the English Law Commission, became a kind of evangelist for the law reform movement throughout the common law world, supported by those who did not share Lord Denning's faith, or skill, to achieve reform from the judicial seat or who, in any case, felt more comfortable with reform effected by a well-advised legislature rather than by unelected judges.[10] The result was the proliferation of many law reform agencies throughout the common law world and, as well, their establishment in several civil law jurisdictions, including Indonesia, Quebec, Rwanda and Thailand.

When I surveyed the legal horizon in 2005 on the thirtieth anniversary of the ALRC, there were at least 60 bodies around the world that answered to the description of a law reform agency. Every Australian jurisdiction was served by such a body, save South Australia. And since then, that state has established a Law Reform Institute, after the model of a similar body in Tasmania created in 2001.[11] South Australia had a part-time law reform committee from 1968 to 1987, when it was abolished. Thereafter, the Attorney General's Department took on the general responsibility for legal review. However, the legal profession was critical of the populist tendencies of some of the legal changes in that state (such as legislation found invalid by the High Court of Australia, to ban "bikie" organizations).[12] Hence the Institute.

I suspect that Lord Scarman would view the substantially part-time Institute as a reversion to the law reform committees that preceded the creation of full-time professional law commissions in 1965: under-funded, comprised of serious but over-worked lawyers, performing their law reform tasks at the "fag end" of a busy day.[13] Although some of the work of such bodies makes it into legislation, inevitably the output tends to be small. The pace is cautious. The research facilities (especially for social data) are tiny. The capacity for genuine public consultation is miniscule. And the ability to provide drafts of legislation to give effect to the reform ideas is generally non-existent. This is the danger

---

[9] M D Kirby, "Are We There Yet" in Opeskin and Weisbrot (n 8) 433, 433–34.

[10] M D Kirby, "Law Reform, Human Rights and Modern Governance: Australia's Debt to Lord Scarman" (2006) 80 *Australian Law Journal* 299.

[11] K Toole, "Law Reform Institute for South Australia" (2011) 36 *Alternative Law Journal* 67, 68.

[12] *South Australia v Totani* (2011) 85 ALJR 19.

[13] Australian Law Reform Commission, *Annual Report 1975* (ALRC 3) [14].

of the model substantially utilized in Hong Kong and increasingly coming into fashion again in Australia.

So what happened to the dreams of Scarman? When and why did they go out of fashion? Will the fashion return? Should it? These are the questions I want to explore in this chapter.

The Utility of Institutional Law Reform

By the fourth quarter of the twentieth century, if not before, it had become apparent in Australia that the assumptions of the political theory on which the representative democracy of the nation operated were not being borne out in practice.

The fact was, and is, that elected, democratic parliaments are not always attentive to the rights of minorities or to the multiple needs for law reform. In Australia, we do not need to present much proof of this assertion for it is evident in our history and even in contemporary instances. I refer to the denial of the native title rights of indigenous peoples until decisions of the High Court of Australia made towards the end of the century;[14] the White Australia laws that only began to change in 1966;[15] and the many legal disadvantages suffered by women,[16] children[17] and homosexuals.[18] Even today in Australia, there continue to be laws that are disadvantageous to refugees and asylum seekers.[19]

It was defects and problems of this kind that led Lord Scarman, in his Hamlyn Lectures, to propose the grafting onto our legal system of effective legal protections for fundamental human rights.[20] These ideas bore fruit in most

---

[14] *Mabo v Queensland* (No 2) (1992) 175 CLR 1; *Wik Peoples v Queensland* (1996) 187 CLR 1.
[15] For example, *O'Keefe v Calwell* (1949) 77 CLR 261.
[16] For example, *Garcia v National Australia Bank* (1998) 194 CLR 395.
[17] *Minister for Immigration and Multicultural and Indigenous Affairs v B* (2004) 219 CLR 365.
[18] Until the laws began to change, commencing with South Australia in 1974 and concluding with Tasmania in 1998: see *Croome v Tasmania* (1998) 191 CLR 119.
[19] See *Al-Kateb v Godwin* (2004) 219 CLR 562: Cf *Plaintiff M70/2011 v Minister for Immigration and Citizenship* [2011] HCA 32.
[20] L Scarman, *English Law: The New Dimension* (Hamlyn Lectures, 26th Series, Stevens & Sons, 1974) 16–18.

jurisdictions of the common law, in the form of Charters or Bills of Rights.[21] However, in Australia, this has not happened. The federal government rejected a proposal for such a measure in 2010 and postponed its further consideration until 2014. The given reason was that it would be sufficient to improve present laws and procedures and to rely on parliamentary vigilance. Unsurprisingly, commentators have likened this to putting the occasional poacher in charge of the game park.

Even more fundamental than the problem of protecting individual rights is the defect of the parliamentary system seen in its neglect of, and inattention to, small, particular, controversial or large, daunting, technical or boring tasks of law reform. These tend, all too often, to be ignored or put off to another day. All too frequently, democratically accountable legislators postpone such tasks and concentrate on popular priorities that will attract media attention and help them win elections and win government. It was for problems of this kind that Scarman's second idea of a permanent law reform body was advanced.

Occasionally, of course, court decisions will deliver beneficial reforms by the judicial fiction of "re-declaring" the common law. Thus, in Australia, this happened with the belated recognition of native title;[22] the effective demand for legal representation of indigent accused facing serious criminal charges;[23] the discovery of a constitutional implication prohibiting unreasonable legislative inhibitions on freedom of speech;[24] and the abolition of the immunity for non-feasance of local authorities.[25]

However, the path of judicial reform is highly problematic. It depends on many chance factors. These include:

- The presentation of a suitable case and the imagination and courage of advocates;
- The composition and inclinations of the appellate court constituted to hear the case;

---

[21] For example, New Zealand Bill of Rights Act 1990 (NZ); Human Rights Act 1998 (UK).
[22] *Mabo* (n 14).
[23] *Dietrich v The Queen* (1992) 163 CLR 500.
[24] *Lange v Australian Broadcasting Corporation* (1997) 214 CLR 1.
[25] *Brodie v Singleton Shire Council* (2001) 206 CLR 512.

- The willingness of the judges to face down complaints and criticisms of "judicial activism";[26]
- The inclination of the judges to overcome suggested problems of funding and costs; and
- The capacity to confine the issues for decision to manageable proportions.[27]

Anyone who thinks that judges in appellate courts have a general inclination, willingness and enthusiasm to fix up all the problems of law reform that are present in litigation has never participated as a judge in such courts. Although there are a few occasions for law reform in the judicial function, they are overwhelmingly exceeded by the number, size and complexity of the tasks of law reform requiring action. The same can be said of the part-time law reform committees and institutes. They too can occasionally perform useful work. However, generally speaking, they represent cosmetic tokenism. They are not an effective institutional response to the needs of systemic ongoing reform of the law. In such matters, legislators, lawyers, the media and other citizens have to be realistic. A legal system that is out of date, chronically unjust and unresponsive to social and technological changes constitutes a serious inhibition for the rule of law. It extracts a price in inefficiency, community resentment and individual loss of confidence in the capacity of law making institutions to deliver rational legal outcomes. It is in such an environment that corner cutting, evasion and even corruption tend to breed.

The common features of the well-established law reform agencies, as envisaged by Scarman and his successors, were well described by the then President of the ALRC, Professor David Weisbrot, explaining what he saw as the "future for institutional law reform" in 2005. His description provides a check-list for the essential attributes of a "modern" and even "post-modern" law reform commission.

The "modern" commission, after the Scarman model, was to be permanent; authoritative; full-time and independent. The "post-modern" law reform commission (after the ALRC model) was additionally to be generalist in its legal capacities; interdisciplinary in its composition and methodology; consultative

---

[26] M D Kirby, *Judicial Activism* (Hamlyn Lectures, 55th Series, Sweet & Maxwell, London, 2004).

[27] See *State Government Insurance Commission v Trigwell* (1979) 142 CLR 617, 633 (Mason J).

in its outreach and engagement with society and interested groups; and implementation-minded in its determination to be more than an academic think tank and rather to be an effective part of the machinery of legislative government.[28]

In fairness to Scarman, in his original vision he too saw how the annexure to law reform reports of draft legislation would constitute an important practical contribution to implementation. More than that, draft legislation allowed (and indeed required) the law reform commission to test broad generalities carefully by identifying the precise changes that would be necessary to give the proposals legal effect. The English Law Commission, and some others, have ordinarily annexed draft bills to their reports. These drafts have helped to secure parliamentary time and enactments. The ALRC invariably followed this course during my period as Chairman. But in recent times, funding levels and the unavailability of drafting personnel have led to abandonment of this facility. A parliamentary enquiry in 1994 recommended the provision of drafting support to the ALRC; but so far, it has not been forthcoming.

This notwithstanding, the ALRC remained, until recently, a relatively large, well-funded, productive, generalist law reform body. It received excellent and highly relevant references from successive federal governments in Australia of differing political complexions. It enjoyed a high level of success in the implementation of its proposals. More than two-thirds of its reform proposals have been implemented, one way or the other.[29] And this statistic was the more admirable because many of the ALRC's reports were addressed to large, complex and controversial areas of federal law (*Complaints against Police*; *Criminal Investigation*; *Human Tissue Transplants*; *Unfair Publication*; *Sentencing of Federal Offenders; Aboriginal Customary Laws*.) In several projects, powerful and opinionated economic interests were involved (*Defamation*; *Privacy* and *Insurance Contracts*). In other cases powerful and conventional or traditional views widely prevailed (*Foreign State Immunity*; *Admiralty*; *Contempt*).

In the time immediately after I departed the ALRC, many highly controversial tasks were completed by it. One of these, on the law relating to genetics, so impressed the lead scientist on the Human Genome Project (Dr Francis

---

[28] D Weisbrot, "The Future of Institutional Law Reform" in Opeskin and Weisbrot (n 8) 18, 29.

[29] Parliament of Australia, The Senate, Legal & Constitutional Affairs References Committee, *Inquiry into the Australian Law Reform Commission* (April 2011). The ALRC stated that it had an implementation rate of over 90 per cent in respect of its recommendations: ibid [3.30].

Collins) that it caused him to declare that it was "truly phenomenal" and that it put Australia at the forefront of global responses to the legal issues raised by genomics.[30]

A failure regularly to revise, modernize, re-examine and re-express the laws is not only a default in the adjustment of law to changing circumstances. It involves an acceptance that unjust and inappropriate outcomes do not matter much or must simply be tolerated because of the endemic weakness and inflexibilities of the law making system. These were the attitudes that, in earlier times, tolerated racism, apartheid, slavery and sexual oppression. They are the attitudes today that encourage tolerance of endemic poverty; widespread corruption; and irreversible damage to the biosphere. Sun Yat-sen did not accept that change in the world was impossible. Nor did later Chinese leaders. Nor should we. Human institutions can be improved. In my own life, I have witnessed many changes in the law and social attitudes. We can give these changes a help along by adopting, and sustaining, improved machinery of government. Modest investments in institutional law reform represent a step in the right direction. Yet it is a step that continually runs into powerful and opinionated resistance.

A New Vision of Efficient Law Making and Change

Before I turn to the sources of resistance, two other features of a rational modern law reform agency may be added to those stated by Professor Weisbrot. They are, perhaps, implied in his post-modern features of contemporary law reform. But they deserve to be identified specifically.

The first is the importance of effective use of the social sciences to ensure that law reform proposals are durable, comprehensive and likely to succeed in practice. This is the view expressed in a recent essay by Evert A Lindquist and John Wanna, who state that:[31]

> To achieve policy durability in the longer term might require far more research and front-end analysis, and more political and public service

---

[30] Dr Collins quoted in Don Chalmers, "Science, Medicine and Law in the Work of the Australian Law Reform Commission" in Opeskin and Weisbrot (n 8) 381.

[31] E A Lindquist and J Wanna, "Delivering Policy Reform: Making It Happen, Making It Stick" in E A Lindquist, S Vincent and J Wanna (eds), *Delivering Policy Reform, Anchoring Significant Reforms in Turbulent Times* (ANU E Press, 2011) 1, 10.

executive implementation during the implementation phase. In turn, this implies that we need to scan emerging challenges and ascertain how one aspect of policy reform might fit in with, or be traded off against, other government priorities. But scanning, scenario developing and selection of preferred options can take time and be administratively precarious. Policy analysts have to secure ministerial, executive and stakeholder buy-in so that the fruits of their labours are not wasted . . . Recognising the need to make policy reforms more durable often requires more thorough testing and strategising of proposed policy designs at the outset. This requires more resources, acknowledging that implementation is not simply project management, and recognising that if *ex ante* engagement of interests is not possible, alternative and credible ways must be found to anticipate the reactions and needs of affected interests and citizens. Many problems with policies are practically discovered in the processes of implementation rather than anticipated and averted beforehand. Where it is not possible to pre-test we might be able to devise better monitoring of the consequences of the policy in operation and make iterative changes.

It is in the thorough processes of consultation and engagement, typically undertaken by law reform bodies, that durable solutions to problems of law are likely to emerge from social research and dialogue. This is next to impossible (except in the smallest, most technical and usually insignificant projects) when these activities are conducted by part-time bodies that may be distracted by the primary duties of their members in their daily work.

In the same volume, Paul 't Hart drew attention to the special obstacle to lasting reform that exists today — one that was predicted a century ago by the German sociologist, Max Weber. Contemporary society tends to be such that:[32]

> Tradition, mysticism and even charisma simply do not cut it as foundational principles for state power and legitimacy. Democratic mandates today are more conditional and fleeting than ever before. We live in the age of value-for-money. In a value-for-money environment, citizens take the rule of law and the democratic authenticity of the state largely for granted . . . Instead they judge their rulers on their perceived contribution to their own prosperity and well-being. Public leadership in such a world becomes . . . transactional. Citizens pay taxes, vote in legislatures and, mostly, obey the law. They are perfectly willing to do all that, so long as they feel their efforts are met by governments keeping their part of the bargain: providing safety, prosperity, care, sustainability and all the many

---

[32] Paul 't Hart, "Epilogue: Rules for Reformers" in Lindquist et al (n 31) 201, 201–2.

other things they say they will. In a value-for-money society, we judge government first and foremost by its results.

If these are truths for a society like Australia, they are probably even more applicable to China and Hong Kong. Bandaids and patchwork, including in the field of law reform, do not deserve the name of "reform". The do not cut any ice. As Professor 't Hart elaborates:[33]

> While much of [our] attention is on how governments have selected, designed and implemented reforms. . . . they . . . require an investment in public communication: your language, your timing and your performances. A compelling narrative is essential in "selling" the reform to the mainstream of uncommitted "wait-and-see" public servants and stakeholders out there to have a guiding narrative to help them literally "make sense" of what is going on. This is not about spin; it is about building a *public case designed to make people face the need for major change.*

The very process of institutional law reform is much more likely to perceive and understand the basic problems and obstacles, and their potential enemies, than amateurish resort to a part-time committee model, left over from the nineteenth century. Law is a major business in a modern society. It is an essential lubricant for the just and effective administration of conflict and interaction of competing interests in society. And if you do not spend money on doing it well, with appropriate expert and public input, the failures will be measured in communal discontent and anger and a resorting to shortcuts that may border on illegality; or, to zones of life where the relevance of law is excluded. To some extent, the failure or inability of the courts to deliver their uncorrupted service efficiently and speedily has produced multiple varieties of alternative dispute resolution that effectively bypass the judge and substitute market power and assessments of interests for the traditional will of the courts to do justice according to law in a particular case.

If this is an additional reason for mobilizing effective and well resourced law reform bodies in the business of rendering law reform a routine and efficient feature of society, there is another advantage that such bodies bring with their social science research procedures,[34] expert participation and widespread public consultation. I refer to the gathering and monitoring of allies and

---

[33] Ibid 206 (emphasis added).
[34] See R Sackville, "The Role of Law Reform Agencies in Australia" (1985) 59 *Australian Law Journal* 151, 157.

supporters for the product that emerges at the end of the enquiry in the form of the law reform report with recommendations. True law reforms of any significance frequently have notable redistributive effects. They shake up the status quo in a market, an economy, in powerful institutions or a society. They will therefore tend to be opposed by those who benefit from, or are comfortable with, the status quo as well as by people who are deceived into thinking that they are its beneficiaries.[35] This is what happened in respect of many projects of the ALRC which otherwise might have ended up in tears and inaction.[36]

Take the major project on reform of the law of insurance contracts. The Australian Federal Parliament, from the foundation of the Commonwealth, had enjoyed wide powers to enact laws on the subject. However, those powers were still substantially unused in the early 1980s. The insurance industry was almost incurably traditional and resistant to change. The precedents were mostly derived from England where the leading insurers and re-insurers had their headquarters. The landscape of federal, state and imperial law, and a wilderness of common law cases, were chaotic. Yet, by painstaking procedures of consultation and engagement with every section of the industry, the ALRC report on insurance contracts was ultimately produced, accepted and implemented, despite rearguard resistance.[37] The engagement of a large team of consultants from all sections of the industry ensured that their voices were listened to and considered — their expertise mobilized for improvement. The claims managers began to see that teaching personnel would be simpler if there were reform. The new provisions shifted some of the old balances between insurer and insured. But they did so justly, and not too far. When the Insurance Contracts Act 1984 (Cth) was enacted by the Australian Parliament, the courts had recourse to the ALRC report and gave the law a beneficial construction. Twenty-five years later, the English and Scottish Law Commissions used the ALRC report to advance many reforming proposals of their own.[38] And so have reformers in New Zealand.[39]

It would not have been possible for that task (or many others discharged by the ALRC) to have been performed in a few months; worked up by a part-time

---

[35] Paul 't Hart (n 32) 204–5.
[36] Ibid 205.
[37] Australian Law Reform Commission, *Insurance Contracts* (ALRC 20, 1980).
[38] The story is told in M D Kirby, "Australian Insurance Contract Law: Local Report with Global Relevance" (2011) 4 *Journal of Business Law* 309, 323f.
[39] Ibid 325.

committee of busy people; and pushed forward with minimum consultation and trivial public and stakeholder engagement. Those who hold to such views should go back and live in the nineteenth century. They have no place in the current more demanding and transparent age. And basically they have a contempt for the right of citizens, including corporate citizens, to have the most modern, well-informed, efficient system of law that the state can reasonably provide.

Effectiveness and Independence in Practice

It is against the background of these self-evident truths that we must address the current state of institutional law reform in Australia and Hong Kong. And measure that state against the fashions and aspirations that existed in the 1970s and 1980s and that exist now.

In Australia, despite the comparative success of the ALRC and its utility to successive governments, events have occurred in recent times that have endangered the effectiveness and capacity of that body to discharge its statutory functions as it should. In the financial year 2010–11, the Australian government reduced the ARLC's budget by $242,000, with an indication that in subsequent years, its budget would be reduced by $495,000 per year. This led the Australian Senate to refer an enquiry into the ALRC to the Legal and Constitutional Affairs References Committee, the first by the Australian Parliament since May 1994. The report of the enquiry, published in April 2011,[40] reveals a rather discouraging scene in terms of the real support being provided by the executive government and the Parliament for the ALRC:

- The budget cuts have had great impact on staff numbers and morale;
- Effectively, for an extended interval, the ALRC was reduced to a single full-time commissioner, the president, Professor Rosalind Croucher;
- The ALRC was effectively obliged to terminate its then current lease of its premises in Sydney and to move to other much smaller premises available to the Attorney General, abutting the Australian Government Solicitor's Office and sharing some of its facilities with that body, thus weakening the symbolic appearance of institutional independence from the executive;

---

[40] *Inquiry into the Australian Law Reform Commission* (n 29).

- The ALRC was also to be changed from decision-making as a collegiate body, which decided financial, staffing, priority and other questions by consensus, to a new model of questionable relevance to such a small institution directed by the president, in consultation with the Attorney General — a kind of duumvirate;
- Although ultimately a second full-time commissioner was proposed, this commissioner was to be assigned and designated to a particular reference project chosen by the government and not, as heretofore, by decision of the president or the ALRC as a whole;
- It emerged during the investigation that in 2009, the Federal Attorney General's Department had, without consultation, commissioned a review ("the Beale Review") of the ALRC. That review expressed a view, without any input from the ALRC itself, that the body was an unaffordable "Rolls Royce luxury operation" and that it should be wound up or rolled back into the Department. While this idea was rejected, and whilst government may, of course, take advice from whomever it wishes, the process was less than edifying, fair, well-informed or entirely rational;
- Complaints about delays are endemic in law reform. But for many years, the ALRC has worked to deadlines fixed by the Attorney General, which substantially have been observed;
- Budget cuts and changes in personnel have led to a dramatic reduction in the engagement of the ALRC with volunteers and in community outreach and educational activities;
- Two full-time commissioners' positions, at least, seem to have been lost;
- The journal *Reform*, which in different formats (print and electronic) for 30 years explained the work of the ALRC, has effectively had to be abandoned, and certainly in the way in which it was formerly published and distributed;
- The ALRC's dedicated law reform library, named after me no less, is to retreat into a shadow of its former self, rescued only at the last minute from complete disappearance;
- All of this has happened in a time when there has been a *huge* increase in the personnel of the Attorney General's Department, effectively a doubling of staff, ostensibly to perform duties responding to anti-terrorism legislation in the wake of 9/11;
- The institutional memory of the methodologies of law reform has suffered a serious blow from the changes in the composition of the ALRC;

the reduction in the numbers of commissioners; the loss of supporting staff; the narrowing of the available legal expertise; the inability to achieve outreach to stakeholders and social science research; and
- In particular, the engagement of the ALRC with overseas law reform bodies has, for budgetary reasons, become much narrower and more restricted — a measure of insularity has been imposed by government, which, in Australia, is never a good stance.

The majority of the Senate Committee enquiring into the ALRC (comprising members of the Liberal Party of Australia in Opposition and of the Australian Greens) was critical of the steps that had been taken by the government. They recommended a number of changes designed to restore the position before the budget cuts; to require the provision of a minimum of two standing, fixed term, non-enquiry specific commissioners; and the assignment of two or more ongoing reform enquiries. The Committee also recommended that the public information and service programme of the ALRC be resumed immediately and that face-to-face consultation should be resumed in place of the retreat to communication through telecommunications. The government (Australian Labor Party) members of the Committee, whilst affirming strong support for the ALRC, suggested that the changes introduced were designed to make it "more flexible" in its membership model and more capable of discharging many short-term references.

When the ALRC model is seen in the context of the wider issues of law reform, social change and national institutional arrangements, the current picture is discouraging, particularly when the very modest budget of the Commission in the first place is kept in mind. One can only assume that there are interests that are hostile to the ALRC model. And this is despite the repeated affirmation of appreciation, the objective evidence of considerable institutional success, and the criticisms that those now making decisions voiced regarding their predecessors' attempts to inflict the same pain on the Commission before a change in the Australian government in 2007.

When I was chairman of the ALRC, I was strongly advised by the then Secretary of the Attorney General's Department (Mr [later Sir] Clarrie Harders) to guard the independence of the ALRC with all my power; not to get too close to the department or its officers; but to safeguard that distance so that the advice given would be special, different and more engaged with stakeholders and external experts not so readily available within or to the public service. This conception appears not now to be in fashion, as may be seen in the close physical proximities secured with the change of premises effectively imposed on the ALRC in Sydney. Further, the model of corporate governance now required is very different from the collegiate, professional model that was in force in my time. I hope that Hong Kong law reformers will look at these developments and remember the wise advice of Clarrie Harders. He was a very insightful and experienced public servant. Essentially he was teaching me the lesson of product differentiation in a specialized market.

The loss of a real capacity to engage with the social sciences and to participate in public dialogue is also a serious departure from the innovations that the ALRC itself pioneered in the field of law reform. True, many lay participants cannot provide input of detailed legal advice of real utility to a law reform agency. However, quite often, lay submissions are a useful check. Occasionally, through individual stories, they give perspectives and insights that might otherwise be neglected. In any case, the process of consultation (which would necessarily be physically much simpler in Hong Kong than in Australia) raises expectations of adoption of reform. It stimulates participation by powerful interests. It encourages input from specialist consultants, academics, industry and experts. And it brings out the champions who can ultimately help ensure that distracted, hard working ministers and officials give attention to the often unsexy problems of law reform that are otherwise prone to be neglected.

Timeliness can undoubtedly be a problem in institutional law reform. For law reformers, the perfect is often the enemy of the good. I have to concede that in some of the earlier ALRC projects, drift sometimes occurred. It was this that led to the imposition of Attorney General deadlines. And these were generally observed by the ALRC. By the same token, if the work of institutional law reform is to be deserving of that name, it must strike a compromise between academic perfection and practical utility. It must undertake more than a formalistic, verbal and minimalist project of review. It must engage in a close examination of the way the applicable and proposed law actually works in practice. Only this is likely to reveal the real defects and imperfections of the law.

In that kind of disclosure, the voice of stakeholders and of ordinary citizens can be useful. Listening to those voices is right in principle. Modern governance cannot be a conspiracy of the powerful with the law-makers. Law reform is part and parcel of the modern conception of transparent governance —

accountable to the governed — which is what the founders of the Australian Commonwealth aspired to. And what Sun Yat-sen sought to secure a century ago in the place of the Chinese Empire.

Conclusion: Reviving the Cycle

A survey of law reform in the English-speaking world must go back at least to Jeremy Bentham and the moves in Britain, early in the nineteenth century, to follow the French codifiers and to bring more logic, modernity, accessibility and justice to the English law. The intermittent efforts of codification and modernization in the nineteenth century ultimately gave way, in the twentieth century, to looking to the concept of permanent, well-resourced institutions to reform, modernize and simplify the law. This idea is undoubtedly a good one; although the execution of the idea, it is true, has sometimes fallen short of the aspiration, as all human institutions do. But, in terms of per capita expenditure on the essential functions of reviewing and updating the legal system, the investment has been paltry and the returns substantial. Yet, even now, it has powerful antagonists and sceptics. Territorialism is never entirely absent from the thinking of many who wield power, including legal power.

Neither the judiciary nor the bureaucracy, unaided, can deliver the range of law reforms that are necessary to effective modern government. In principle, it is desirable that reform of any magnitude should be provided by the legislature. It can do so under the scrutiny of citizens. This is usually preferable to the judiciary, doing its best in a particular case. Law reform bodies can play a useful efficiency role in society. To regard the present law reform agencies as a "Rolls Royce luxury operation" is, frankly, laughable. There is something out of joint in many contemporaneous governmental responses to the needs of law reform. Responding to those needs is a manifest obligation of modern government. So that is why law reformers and their supporters must find legal champions who match the soothing words of praise with effective ongoing institutional and financial support.

The true defence against terrorism, disaffection, communal riots and social disharmony in a modern state includes efficient machinery to review, modernize and simplify the law where it is out of touch with those whom the law serves. This is not a Rolls Royce operation. It is a Volkswagen project. However, it still needs fuel and occasional care and constant maintenance by those with the power to provide this.

We must hope that fashion in law reform, like hairstyles, dress lengths and fashions in popular music, operates in cycles. The cycle may ascend once again. Anyone taking an historical view of the law and its institutional needs to serve a modern community will hope, and ensure, that it is so.

Chapter 3
Sources and Channels of Law Reform in Hong Kong

Wong Yan Lung[1]

Statutes, Bureaux and Specialist Law Reform Agencies

Any system of law requires constant review to ensure that it keeps pace with changes in society, whether technological, economic or social. The task of ensuring that our laws are kept up to date becomes both harder and more vital as ever more spheres of activity are permitted or regulated.

In Hong Kong, as in other jurisdictions with vibrant socio-economic activities, our statute book has expanded substantially in recent years. However, there are reasons peculiar to Hong Kong that account for the increase in legislation in the past decade or so.

First, our constitution, the Basic Law, and earlier the Bill of Rights Ordinance, have incorporated into Hong Kong the major international covenants on fundamental human rights protection. Coupled with the power of the courts to strike down local legislation in contravention of the Basic Law, we have to be very vigilant to make legislative changes to ensure that our law is compliant. Some changes have had to be effected expeditiously following specific adjudications by the Court of Final Appeal.

Secondly, rapid globalization, the need to maintain Hong Kong's competitive edge, and the need to bring local law in line with international standards, have also generated the need for new legislation in areas such as banking,

---

[1] This chapter is based on the opening address made by Mr. Wong Yan Lung at the ONC Conference on Law Reform on 17 September 2011, with some editorial changes by the editors of this book. The original and full version of Mr. Wong's speech can be found on the website of the Department of Justice of the HKSAR Government <www.doj.gov.hk/eng/public/pdf/2011/pr20110919e.pdf>.

shipping, corporate governance, public health, as well as international cooperation against terrorism and money laundering.

Thirdly, there are new laws necessitated by the reunification and the ever increasing interaction with the Mainland. For example, we have successive Adaptation of Laws Ordinances to adapt specific legislation so that it conforms with the Basic Law and with the status of Hong Kong as a Special Administrative Region of the People's Republic of China. Examples include the Mainland Judgments (Reciprocal Enforcement) Ordinance (Cap 597) to enable reciprocal recognition and enforcement of certain judgments between Hong Kong and the Mainland; and, the Shenzhen Bay Port Hong Kong Port Area Ordinance (Cap 591) dealing with certain legal issues to facilitate border crossing.

Most changes in the law are not brought about by law reform agencies such as the Law Reform Commission. The main agents of law reform are the government bureaux themselves, which often have to carry out detailed research and public consultation before introducing any bill into the legislature. For example, the Competition Bill was the subject of a very intensive specialist consultancy study and public consultation by the Commerce and Economic Development Bureau before being introduced.

The Department of Justice itself, apart from providing secretarial support to the Law Reform Commission, also plays a role in bringing forward law reform measures. In February 2011, for example, legislative provisions, promoted by the Department of Justice, were brought into force to relax the regime for applications for financial relief following a foreign divorce. In June, significant reforms to the Arbitration Ordinance came into effect, which have enabled Hong Kong to have a unified arbitration regime based on the UNCITRAL Model Law on International Commercial Arbitration. The new arbitration law of Hong Kong is the product of years of admirable joint efforts by members of the arbitration fraternity in Hong Kong and the Department of Justice, who worked together as an expert Working Group, and of the contributions of the Legislative Council, which carefully vetted the bill during numerous Bills Committee meetings, and, in particular, of the Honourable Margaret Ng who chaired that Bills Committee.

We have in Hong Kong another specialist law reform agency, the Standing Committee on Company Law Reform, which was set up in 1984 under the Companies Registry to advise the Financial Secretary on amendments to the Companies Ordinance and other related ordinances. The committee has played a leading role in the major review of company legislation, which is now well under way.

The Law Reform Commission of Hong Kong

Within Commonwealth jurisdictions, it is not difficult to find a variety of different models of law reform agencies. In some jurisdictions, law reform is subsumed within a unit of the government's legal department. In others, law reform agencies are independent but wholly part-time, while still others have a single full-time commissioner. Some are creatures of statute, or even incorporated into the constitution, while others are not. Some include non-lawyers in their membership, while others are exclusively the preserve of lawyers.

Here in Hong Kong, the Law Reform Commission (HKLRC) was established in January 1980 as a result of a joint initiative by the then Attorney General and the Chief Justice. After the reunification in 1997, its chairperson was the Secretary for Justice (who continued the role of Attorney General) with the Chief Justice of the Court of Final Appeal as an ex-officio member. Currently, the HKLRC is 12 members strong. Apart from the Secretary for Justice and the Chief Justice, other members include the Law Draftsman (also ex-officio), one Permanent Judge of the Court of Final Appeal, a senior counsel, experienced solicitors, eminent law professors, and other distinguished lay members.

The Commission may appoint sub-committees, drawing from an even wider pool of talent in the community and within the Administration, to study specific issues. At the end of 2011, the HKLRC had six sub-committees looking into different subjects. The following gives a feel of the calibre of these sub-committees: the Class Actions Sub-committee is served by, among others, two judges, one of whom is from the Court of Appeal, and two senior counsel. Membership of the Sub-committee on Review of Sexual Offences includes a criminal judge and two senior criminal silks and a law professor from the University of Hong Kong. The Sub-committee on Charities, which published, in mid-June 2011, a consultation paper proposing that a wider ranging regulatory regime for charities should be introduced in Hong Kong and that a charity commission should be set up as the regulatory body for charities, is chaired by the former chairperson, now vice-chairperson, of the Hong Kong Council of Social Service. Its members include lawyers and representatives from NGOs as well as from the Social Welfare and Inland Revenue Departments. Hence, it can be seen that the collective wisdom and experience within the HKLRC and its sub-committees are quite remarkable and probably not always found in other jurisdictions.

Although members of the Commission and its sub-committee members volunteer their services, part-time and unpaid, which means that some Commission projects may take longer to complete, it has the considerable advantage that those projects benefit from the wide range of expertise and experience represented by members of the Commission and its sub-committees which might not otherwise be available.

Further, because its composition comprises members of the judiciary and outside bodies most affected by the subject of the proposed reform, the independence of the HKLRC and its recommendations can hardly be questioned. Representation from the relevant stakeholders and government departments on the HKLRC and its sub-committees also ensures that discussion will not be divorced from practical considerations, hence strengthening the prospect of implementation.

It is also important to note that, despite the part-time nature of the HKLRC members and the sub-committee members, they are supported by a secretariat, including full-time counsel, led by the Commission Secretary. These lawyers carry out all necessary research and act as secretaries to the Commission and its sub-committees. Once the Commission has published a final report, counsel may be directly involved in assisting the relevant policy bureau of government to implement the Commission's proposals through amending legislation.

Public consultation is organized with the assistance of the secretariat. Such consultation can be very elaborate, as seen in the current consultation exercise on charity law. Since launching the consultation exercise in June 2011 with a press conference attracting extensive coverage, and the uploading of the consultation document on the HKLRC website, the sub-committee chairman and members have attended briefings with various stakeholders, and a special meeting of the Legislative Council's Welfare Services Panel, explaining the recommendations and exchanging views. The public has been enthusiastic in submitting responses to the HKLRC secretariat, which will be coordinated for the Commission's further consideration.

Hong Kong is a small jurisdiction. But we are indeed fortunate to have strong goodwill and support from the legal fraternity and those in other sectors who are ready to contribute their expertise and time for the public good. While we shall certainly consider how we can further strengthen the institutional set-up of the HKLRC, I do not think we should overlook the strengths of the present system.

No doubt, it is always possible to improve any law reform system. We do not shy away from the criticisms, as there is indeed room for improvement so far as our law reform process is concerned. However, while we must embrace criticisms and be ready to learn, for all of us who are committed to bringing real and lasting improvement, we would certainly not forget that any reform in the right direction cannot be achieved without appreciating the historical context, the legal system and the community in which our law reform body is developing and operating.

Implementation of Commission Proposals

One area where Hong Kong can do better is in the time taken to respond to HKLRC recommendations, and to implement them. The legal profession has, in recent years, quite legitimately expressed their concern about the implementation of the Commission's reports. As I stressed in my speech at the Ceremonial Opening of the Legal Year in January 2011, it is undoubtedly in the interests of the Commission, the government and the community that the Commission's hard work (including my own as Chairman) comes to fruition and that its reports are considered within a reasonable time frame. In this regard, when responding to a question in the Legislative Council in January, the Chief Secretary affirmed that the Administration attaches great importance to the recommendations of the HKLRC and agrees in principle that timely action should be taken to follow up on its recommendations. Of course, as one can appreciate, the complexity and scope of the subject matter of the reports vary greatly and some are likely to require longer than others for individual bureaux to consider.

For my part, as Chairman of the Commission, I have specifically impressed upon the responsible government policy bureaux the importance of responding to Commission reports and of speeding up their decisions and actions on implementation, and I will continue to do so.

The Administration has now agreed upon a new set of guidelines, set out as an appendix to this chapter, to improve the existing mechanisms and timeliness on response and implementation. For all new HKLRC reports, the relevant bureaux are required to provide a detailed public response, setting out which recommendations they accept, reject or intend to implement in modified form, to me as the Chairman of the Commission as soon as practicable. In any event, an interim response setting out the timetable for completion of the detailed response and the steps taken will have to be provided within six months following publication of the HKLRC reports.

Concluding Remarks

There is much in the process of law reform in Hong Kong that is right and needs preserving. However, as in any field, there is of course scope for improvement. Someone once said: "You can judge your age by the amount of pain you feel when you come into contact with a new idea." I can assure you that, in this regard, we who are involved in law reform in Hong Kong and elsewhere are by definition reformists and we are forever young and pleased to listen to new ideas.

APPENDIX

In October 2011, in response to concerns which had been expressed at delays in considering and implementing HKLRC proposals, the Administration issued a set of guidelines to bureaux and departments having policy responsibility over the subject matter of an HKLRC project.[2] The guidelines are as follows (note that the reference to "LRC" in the guidelines is a reference to the HKLRC):

(a) When a consultation paper is issued by the LRC, the Administration should at that stage decide (and resolve should there be any disagreement) which bureau (or bureaux) will take primary responsibility for consideration/implementation of the final report and should so notify the LRC.

(b) Bureaux/departments should provide the Secretary to the LRC with the contact details of the bureau's officer with responsibility for the LRC report within 14 days of receipt of the letter from the Secretary for Justice forwarding an LRC report to the responsible Policy Secretary and requesting his consideration of the report.

(c) Bureaux and departments having policy responsibility in respect of any LRC report should give full consideration to its recommendations and provide a detailed public response (setting out which recommendations they accept, reject or intend to implement in modified form) to the Secretary for Justice (as Chairman of the LRC) as soon as practicable. In any event, they should provide at least an interim response within six months of publication of the report which sets out a clear timetable for completion of the detailed response and the steps taken so far.

(d) Bureaux or departments having policy responsibility in respect of any LRC report should provide a detailed public response to the Secretary for Justice within 12 months of its publication, unless otherwise agreed by him as Chairman of the LRC.

To assist bureaux and departments to comply with these guidelines, the LRC will, four months after publication of an LRC report, remind the responsible bureau/department of the requirement under the guidelines for at least an interim response within six months of publication.

In appropriate cases, and subject to the availability of increased resources within the Department of Justice for this purpose, the Secretary

---

[2] The guidelines can be found on the HKLRC website at <http://www.hkreform.gov.hk/en/news/NewsArchive2011>.

for Justice (both in his capacity as Chairman of the LRC and as head of the Department of Justice) has undertaken to consider including draft legislation in the final LRC report.

While the decision whether or not to refer a subject to the LRC rests solely with the Secretary for Justice and the Chief Justice, the LRC through its Secretariat or Chairman may, without compromising the LRC's autonomy, seek and consider preliminary views from relevant bureaux and departments when starting a new LRC project. Bureaux and departments should provide their views or advice to the LRC where these are sought by the LRC (whether at the initial stage of the LRC project or in response to a consultation paper) on a project within their area of policy or expertise.

Part B

Law Reform Commissions

Chapter 4
Hong Kong's Law Reform Commission

Stuart M I Stoker

Introduction

Two of the principal strands of discussion that underlie this book address the Hong Kong Law Reform Commission's (HKLRC) structure and the implementation of its reports. In relation to the former, it is argued by some that the task of law reform would be more effectively accomplished by a body which consisted of full-time commissioners, while in relation to the latter, concern has been widely expressed at the government's delay in considering and implementing the HKLRC's proposals.

This chapter considers both these issues, beginning by outlining the historical context within which the HKLRC operates and setting out the HKLRC's key features that distinguish it from many other law reform agencies in the common law world. The advantages and disadvantages of the current model will be discussed before the paper considers the question of implementation and what improvements can be hoped for in future.

Historical Background

It is probably fair to say that it was the establishment of the English and Scottish Law Commissions in 1965 that gave impetus to the idea of having some kind of permanent, independent, machinery for wide-ranging review of the law. There had for years been criticisms of the state of the law in the UK (primarily of English law) and this culminated in 1963 in the publication of an influential collection of essays, entitled *Law Reform Now*, by a group of English Labour lawyers. Among the ideas put forward was a proposal that the Lord Chancellor's Office should be re-structured to take on the task of law reform:[1]

---

[1] Gerald Gardiner and Andrew Martin, *Law Reform Now* (Victor Gollancz, 1963) 8.

> Nothing less will do than the setting up within the Lord Chancellor's Office of a strong unit concerned exclusively with law reform, in that wide sense which also includes codification, so far as in the peculiar system of English law codification may be desirable and feasible.

One of the two co-editors of that collection of essays was Gerald Gardiner, QC. When the new Labour government was elected to office in 1964, Gardiner was made Lord Chancellor and he was instrumental in bringing forward the legislation to create the UK Law Commissions in 1965. In the ensuing years, law reform agencies of one sort or another have been established in most of the major common law jurisdictions.

In Hong Kong, prior to the establishment of the HKLRC in 1980, there had been a number of formal and informal committees and groups that had considered aspects of law reform. The first permanent machinery for law reform in Hong Kong appears to have been the Law Reform Committee, which was established by the then governor on 16 March 1956. Its terms of reference were restricted, however, to examining legislation enacted in the United Kingdom, "having regard especially to the reports of the Law Reform Committee appointed by the Lord Chancellor on the 16 June 1952." The Hong Kong Law Reform Committee issued five reports between 1957 and 1964, when it ceased to operate.

In 1965, a Law Reform Drafting Unit was formed in the then Attorney General's Chambers. It was concerned primarily with the drafting of approved law reform measures and to a lesser extent with identifying UK legislative measures that were suitable for adoption in Hong Kong. The unit was not in a position to go beyond that, however, and propose wider reform of the law.

In the late 1970s, a group of 14 lawyers drawn from government and the private profession formed themselves into an informal law reform committee under the chairmanship of a High Court judge, the then Mr Justice T L Yang.

The arrival of a new Attorney General in Hong Kong in 1979 coincided with calls for a more formal mechanism for law reform, and, in January 1980, the Chief Justice and the Attorney General presented to the Executive Council their joint views as to how law reform should be handled in the future. Their recommendation that a Law Reform Commission should be established was endorsed by the Executive Council on 15 January 1980, though with three significant amendments. The first was that the Attorney General should chair the Commission, rather than the Chief Justice; the second was that the members of the Commission should be appointed by the Governor, not the Chief

Justice; and the third was that the Secretary should be an Assistant Principal Crown Counsel in the Attorney General's Chambers, rather than an Assistant Registrar of the Supreme Court as envisaged in the proposal put to the Executive Council. A further minor adjustment was that references should be made jointly to the Commission by the Chief Justice and the Attorney General, rather than by one or the other. This last revision was subsequently reversed by the Executive Council some years later, but, in practice, every reference to the Commission has been made jointly by both the Chief Justice and the Attorney General/Secretary for Justice.

The Executive Council paper recommending the establishment of the HKLRC identified four broad areas of law reform:

(a) the identifying and making, preferably in an annual bill, of multifarious detailed minor corrections and improvements to the laws;

(b) the examination of more fundamental aspects of the reform of the laws or procedures in Hong Kong;

(c) the examination of aspects of law reform which overlap to a large extent with administrative or policy matters, particularly where the changes in law are incidental to the other aspects; similarly, detailed up-grading where a depth of expert knowledge is required (eg company law); and

(d) reforms which persons in Government or the private sector espouse in their personal capacities and wish to study or propose for legislative action.

Item (a) referred to matters of law revision, rather than reform, and would not be the concern of the HKLRC. It was envisaged that reforms in (b) would be dealt with by the HKLRC, while those at (c) would continue to be referred to ad hoc working parties with appropriate government and non-government membership. Proposals under (d) were likely to be sent to the Chief Justice or the Attorney General "who would, where appropriate, act upon them or refer them to the Law Reform Commission."

The membership of the new Commission was to consist of the Attorney General (as Chairman), the Chief Justice and the Law Draftsman (all as ex-officio members) and eight other unofficial members drawn from five categories:

(a) a member of the Hong Kong Bar Association;

(b) a member of the Hong Kong Law Society;

(c) two members of the Faculty of Law of the University of Hong Kong;
(d) two unofficial members of the Executive or Legislative Councils; and
(e) two or more other members.

It was envisaged that the last two categories would allow the appointment of non-lawyers to the Commission, which from the outset was seen as an important element in the Commission's composition. The three ex-officio members were entitled to have their places occupied by a representative and, in the Chief Justice's case, a member of the High Court was specifically named as representative. The inclusion of the Law Draftsman as a member was intended to provide the Commission with access to law drafting expertise, enabling the inclusion of draft legislation in the HKLRC's reports.

Though not spelt out in the Executive Council paper, it seems reasonable to suppose that the rationale for the structure and membership proposed for the HKLRC was that it built on existing expertise and could be established speedily with few resource implications.

Changes to the HKLRC since Establishment

The HKLRC today differs in a number of respects from the model established in 1980. Perhaps the most significant change relates to its membership, where a flexible approach has been adopted from the outset. Early in its life, the Chief Justice's representative morphed into a separate permanent seat on the Commission in addition to the Chief Justice, first as a High Court or Court of Appeal judge and later, since 1997, as a judge of the Court of Final Appeal. In contrast, neither the Attorney General/Secretary for Justice nor the Law Draftsman have availed themselves of the opportunity to appoint a representative in their stead, other than occasionally the individuals who have been temporarily acting in their posts. With the establishment of law schools at City University and the Chinese University of Hong Kong, the academic lawyers on the HKLRC are no longer restricted to those from the University of Hong Kong. Similarly, while there has never been an occasion on which at least one practising member of the Bar and of the Law Society have not been members of the Commission, it is usually the case that (certainly as far as the Bar is concerned) these numbers are exceeded. Over time, the view appears to have gained ground that the inclusion of members of the Executive or Legislative Councils brings more negatives than positives. In particular, it could be argued that their inclusion runs the risk of a perception of politicization of the Commission, with the concomitant difficulty of avoiding the appearance of favouring one political party over another. The last occasion on which a serving member of the Executive Council was appointed to the Commission was in 1989 and the most recent appointment of a serving member of the Legislative Council was in 1999.[2]

On an operational level, the Commission initially operated by having counsel from the Attorney General's Chambers "volunteer" to serve as part-time secretaries to the sub-committees set up to work on each reference. That was found unsatisfactory because of the competing demands on the secretaries' time and support is now provided by lawyers in the Department of Justice who work full-time in the HKLRC's secretariat. At the same time, not every Commission project has been referred to a sub-committee. In a number of instances, the Commission has itself undertaken the review without the involvement of a sub-committee, in part as an experiment in attempting to speed the reform process.[3]

A further minor change has been that references can now be made to the HKLRC by either the Secretary of Justice or the Chief Justice, rather than requiring joint referrals, but, as mentioned earlier, this has had no practical effect as every reference to date has been made by both the Secretary for Justice and the Chief Justice.

Contrary to the original expectation (and the express reason for the Law Draftsman's inclusion as an ex-officio member), only a very few of the reports issued by the HKLRC have incorporated draft legislation. That is unfortunate, as the advantages of the inclusion of such a draft are self-evident. Not only does a draft Bill provide a fuller picture of the effect of the report's proposals, and so facilitate consideration by the relevant policy bureau within government, but the process of drafting is likely to uncover shortcomings or gaps in the proposals which can be addressed before the final report is issued.

---

[2] Legislative Council member Sophie Leung was appointed to the Commission in September 1999 and served until August 2005. Maria Tam, who was then a member of both the Executive and Legislative Councils, served on the Commission from June 1989 to June 1992. Anna Wu was a member of the Executive Council during part of the period between January 2006 and December 2011 when she served as a member of the Commission, but her appointment to the Executive Council came after her appointment to the Commission.

[3] Examples include two projects reviewing aspects of the law relating to enduring powers of attorney and a report proposing the abolition of the "year and a day" rule in homicide.

No Single Model of Law Reform Agency

While almost every major common law jurisdiction has some kind of specialist body devoted to the task of law reform, their form and the resources available to them vary substantially. Some might regard the Law Commission of England and Wales as the "gold standard" or the model to aspire to, but there is no single "one size fits all" model of law reform agency in the common law world. The variations from one jurisdiction to another are considerable and relate to both structure and process:

Constitutional

- Some law reform agencies are statutory (such as those in England and Scotland), while others (including Hong Kong's) are not.
- Some (such as Malawi's) are even incorporated in the constitution.
- Some agencies are established in a formal partnership with a law school, the legal profession, or both.

Structural

- Some law reform agencies are formed within government (usually as a part of the Department of Justice or its equivalent) while others are separate.
- Resources differ substantially from one law reform agency to another. At one end of the spectrum, the Law Commission of England and Wales has considerable research and staff resources, including legal draftsmen and a full-time economist, while others operate without even the most basic Internet connectivity.

Membership

- The membership of a law reform agency may consist of full-time or part-time commissioners, or volunteers, or a mix of the two.
- It may be restricted to lawyers, or include those from other disciplines, or none.

Agenda

- A law reform agency may be restricted to areas of "black letter law" or it may be given (or carve for itself) a more expansive role and consider subjects which traditionalists might see as more policy than law.
- The agency may work to a series of programmes or adopt a more ad hoc approach. Such tasks as it undertakes may be given to it by the government or may be self-generated, perhaps in response to some kind of public consultation.

Despite the variety of their forms and operation, what most law reform agencies in common law jurisdictions have in common is that their output is an objective and independent review of the particular area of law in question, intended to be free from party political or sectional bias.

The Hong Kong Model and Its Strengths and Weaknesses

Though, as we have seen, there is no single model adopted for the structure and operation of law reform agencies in the common law world, each variation has its own strengths and weaknesses and Hong Kong's Commission, which is unusual in a number of respects, is no exception.

First, while the Commission itself is an independent body, which is not part of the government, the secretariat that serves it consists of lawyers within the Department of Justice who work full-time for the Commission and its subcommittees. Apart from that division between Commission and secretariat, the HKLRC has a number of other distinctive features, most of which have both advantages and disadvantages.

A non-statutory body

The HKLRC was created administratively as the result of an Executive Council decision, rather than statutorily. As was explained earlier in this paper, the advantage is that this has provided flexibility in, for instance, the appointment of members. The disadvantage is that the HKLRC is vulnerable to dissolution at the whim of the government, though political considerations could be expected to weigh against any such move.

Chaired by the Secretary for Justice

The fact that the Commission is chaired by the Secretary for Justice can be seen as both a strength and a weakness. The original proposal that the government's principal legal officer should chair the Commission no doubt reflected the Executive Council paper's intention that:

> [i]mplementation of the Law Reform Commission's recommendations would, it is envisaged, normally be a matter for the Attorney General who would have to take them forward through the appropriate [policy] Secretaries where necessary, in the same way as other legislative proposals.

It could be argued that the fact that the Secretary for Justice is both chairman of the Commission and a senior member of the government provides a useful two-way conduit which, on the one hand, can apprise the Commission of political practicalities on an issue and, on the other, provide a supporting voice for the HKLRC's proposals within the government. The countervailing argument is that the Secretary for Justice's position as chairman risks a perception that the HKLRC lacks independence and is but a mouthpiece for the Department of Justice or the government. In practice, however, this criticism has rarely been raised. On the contrary, on more than one occasion calls have been made for initiatives pressed by the government to be referred to the HKLRC for an objective and independent view.[4]

Part-time volunteer members

One of the significant features of the HKLRC is that it functions through volunteers who accept appointment to the Commission or its sub-committees. This again can be seen as both a strength and a weakness. On the one hand, it enables the Commission and its sub-committees to tap into expertise that would not otherwise be available, either because it would be too costly to

---

[4] One example arose in relation to the proposals in a report on the *Trial of Complex Commercial Crimes* put forward by the Attorney General in the late 1980s. The proposals were strongly opposed by, inter alia, the Bar and the Law Society and, even though the proposals were firmly identified with the Attorney General, there were calls from a number of Legislative Council members for the matter to be referred to the HKLRC.

the government or because the individuals concerned might be unwilling or unable to commit themselves to full or part-time engagement. On the other hand, there are obviously constraints on how much volunteers can be asked to do (and how quickly).

Non-lawyer members

Unlike many law reform agencies, the HKLRC includes non-lawyers among its members. The original thinking was that this would import consideration of the wider picture to the HKLRC's deliberations and avoid the risk of too academic an approach. The disadvantage, however, is that the inclusion of non-lawyers in its membership may render the HKLRC unsuited to references involving highly technical aspects of the law.

Sets its own agenda

The decision on which projects should be referred to the Commission rests with the Commission itself, in the shape of its Chairman and the Chief Justice (who is an ex-officio member). While the stance of the government on a particular issue is obviously relevant in assessing the chances of implementation of any reform proposals the HKLRC may make, the final decision on whether or not to refer a matter to the HKLRC rests solely with the Secretary for Justice and the Chief Justice.

A Change in the HKLRC's Structure?

There is no doubt that a legitimate case could be made for replacing the existing structure of the HKLRC with a commission comprised of full-time members, just as it could for revising the structure in a number of other ways. It is far from clear, however, that the proponents of change have made their case coherently.

First, the issue of implementation of the HKLRC's proposals appears to have been confused on occasion with the question of structure. Reference has frequently been made, for instance, to the HKLRC's unimplemented 1995 report on *Corporate Rescue and Insolvent Trading* as if the failure to implement the report's proposals was somehow a result of the part-time nature of the Commission. Not only is the structure of the HKLRC irrelevant in that regard, but in the particular case of the *Corporate Rescue* report legislation was brought forward by the government on two occasions but rejected by the Legislative Council. In the circumstances, that report is hardly the most obvious illustration of either Commission or government inadequacy.

Secondly, the HKLRC has been criticized in some quarters for not taking on tasks such as law revision[5] and consolidation which were never intended to be part of its remit, as the Executive Council paper establishing the HKLRC made clear. In addition, while there may be a sound case for wishing to speed up the process of law reform, the limitations of the legislative timetable render questionable the practical benefits of increasing the *volume* of law reform proposals issued by the HKLRC.

Thirdly, some who argue for an HKLRC of full-time commissioners appear to be unaware that, while the Commission itself consists of part-time volunteers, its secretariat is staffed by lawyers who work full-time on law reform.

Timeliness of LRC Projects

It is clear that, while the particular structure of the HKLRC has advantages, the downside is the length of time that projects can take. A commission consisting of full-time members and with greater resources might reasonably be expected to generate a speedier turnaround of the projects referred to it than one operating through specialist volunteer sub-committees. The average time that the HKLRC has taken to complete each of the 51 projects which have involved a sub-committee is just over 44 months from the date of the first meeting to the publication of the final Commission report (or, in the case of projects involving a series of reports, from the date of publication of the immediately preceding report). The figure drops to 41.52 months if the longest-lasting project is omitted. In contrast, the eight projects undertaken without a sub-committee have taken an average of 26 months from first referral to publication of final report.[6] The comparison should be treated with some caution, however, as some projects were chosen for review without a sub-committee because of the relatively straightforward nature of the issues involved.

---

[5] "Law revision" is essentially the correction of errors in the statute book, rather than reform: see, for example, Chapter 5 (Partington).

[6] The figures in this paragraph reflect the position as at September 2011.

The appointment of paid full-time or part-time commissioners might be expected to speed up the law reform process but there would clearly be significant cost implications of any such change. Additional factors that would need to be considered would be the availability of persons with the necessary expertise willing to take on the role of commissioner and whether the introduction of paid commissioners might deter some who currently offer their services to the Commission and its sub-committees pro bono. The contribution of those volunteers is considerable. As at 1 September 2011, some 458 members of the community had served on one or other of the Commission's various sub-committees since its establishment in 1980, and 68 had served on the Commission itself.[7]

If the review process is to be accelerated within the existing structure, it may be that the HKLRC should consider undertaking a greater proportion of its references without a formal sub-committee. One alternative would be for the HKLRC secretariat to produce preliminary reform proposals on the subject and to seek the views of selected individuals and groups on these before the Commission (via the secretariat) produces a detailed consultation paper for consideration by the community as a whole.

Implementation of LRC Proposals

The HKLRC naturally cannot expect that its reform proposals should automatically be accepted by the government but it is reasonable to expect that they will be given full and fair consideration within a reasonable time of their publication. It is in the interests of all concerned that a decision whether to implement the HKLRC's proposals should be made within a reasonable time frame so as to avoid the following problems:

- flaws in the legal system identified by objective HKLRC study remain uncorrected;
- the validity of the detailed research and consultation carried out by the HKLRC diminishes as it becomes out of date; and
- there is duplication of effort, with the Administration required to carry out further research and consultation the longer an HKLRC report is left unaddressed.

---

[7] That is in addition to the 16 official appointments to the Commission: six Attorneys General/Secretaries for Justice; four Chief Justices; and six Law Draftsmen as at December 2012.

The time taken for the government to reach a decision on whether or not to implement Commission proposals (far less actual implementation) has at times exceeded the time which the Commission took to complete the project itself. Governments have their own priorities and a law reform agency cannot expect to be top of the list. Nevertheless, the delays in the government's decision-making process in recent years have prompted widespread concern.

In some jurisdictions, administrative or statutory rules have been introduced which set out the time within which the government must respond to recommendations made by a law reform agency. In England, for instance, a protocol agreed between the Law Commission and the Lord Chancellor in March 2010 under section 3B of the Law Commissions Act 1965 (inserted by section 2 of the Law Commission Act 2009) provides, inter alia, that:

> 18. The Minister will provide an interim response to the Commission as soon as possible and in any case within six months of the publication of the report unless otherwise agreed with the Commission.
>
> 19. The Minister will provide a full response to the Commission as soon as possible after delivery of the interim response and in any event within one year of publication of the report unless otherwise agreed by the Commission. The response will set out which recommendations the Minister accepts, rejects or intends to implement in modified form. If applicable, the Minister will also provide the timescale for implementation.

In addition, section 3A of the Law Commissions Act 1965 (inserted by section 1 of the Law Commission Act 2009) requires the Lord Chancellor to report annually to Parliament on the extent to which the government has implemented Law Commission recommendations. The first such report was published on 24 January 2011.

In Hong Kong, in response to concerns widely expressed at delays in considering and implementing HKLRC proposals, the Chief Secretary's Policy Committee agreed in 2011 a set of guidelines for government bureaux and departments for the consideration of HKLRC reports.[8] The two key elements of those guidelines are:

> (c) Bureaux and departments having policy responsibility in respect of any LRC report should give full consideration to its recommendations

---

[8] The guidelines are set out in full as an Appendix to Chapter 3 (Wong). Note that "LRC" refers to the HKLRC.

and provide a detailed public response (setting out which recommendations they accept, reject or intend to implement in modified form) to the Secretary for Justice (as Chairman of the LRC) as soon as practicable. In any event, they should provide at least an interim response within six months of publication of the report which sets out a clear timetable for completion of the detailed response and the steps taken so far.

(d) Bureaux or departments having policy responsibility in respect of any LRC report should provide a detailed public response to the Secretary for Justice within 12 months of its publication, unless otherwise agreed by him as Chairman of the LRC.

The timetable set out in these administrative guidelines is similar to that imposed statutorily in England. Other practical measures incorporated in the Policy Committee guidelines include an injunction that, when the Commission issues a consultation paper, the government should at that stage decide which bureau (or bureaux) will take primary responsibility for considering and implementing the proposals in the HKLRC's final report, rather than waiting until the final report is issued. A further measure that may assist bureaux in assessing HKLRC proposals is an undertaking by the Secretary for Justice that he will in appropriate cases, and subject to the availability of resources, consider including draft legislation in the final HKLRC report.

It is to be hoped that the combined effect of the measures set out in the new guidelines will be to speed the decision-making process in future, and that the public nature of the commitment will enable the community at large to hold the government to account if it fails to comply.

Chapter 5
Law Reform: The UK Experience

Martin Partington

Introduction

In this chapter, I discuss the work of the Law Commission for England and Wales under the following headings:[1]

- Creation;
- Resources;
- Programmes;
- Procedures;
- Achievements;
- Lessons from the English experience.

Creation

The Law Commission for England and Wales was established in 1965. There had been law reform bodies in the UK before that date. For example, in 1868, the then Lord Chancellor, Lord Cairns, appointed the Statute Law Committee. Its remit was to produce a revised edition of the statutes and to supervise

---

[1] This is a personal account, based on my experience as a Law Commissioner between 2001 and 2005 (plus a further two years as Special Consultant to the Commission, January 2006–February 2008). It does not in any way represent the official view of the Law Commission. For an account of the principal project on which I was engaged, see my "Taking Renting Seriously: Reflections on the Law Commission's Housing Reform Programme" (2008) 37 *Common Law World Review* 277–298. In May 2013, the Welsh Assembly Government announced it intends to adopt the recommendations made by the Commission: <http://wales.gov.uk/consultations/housingcommunity/renting-homes-white-paper/?lang=en>.

progress on statute law revision and consolidation. There were 29 statute law revision acts passed over the next 40 years or so, based mostly on recommendations of that Committee. But its work was limited to the revision of statutes.

In 1934 a Law Revision Committee was created by Lord Sankey. This was the first standing law reform committee, concerned with reform of the law generally rather than merely the repeal and consolidation of existing statutes. It was, however, a ministerial committee — not an independent body — to which Sankey appointed judges, barristers, solicitors and legal academics. It worked on a part-time basis and ceased to function in 1939.

After the Second World War, in 1952, the then Lord Chancellor, Lord Simonds, established the English Law Reform Committee. This replaced the earlier Law Revision Committee. It also operated on a part-time and somewhat sporadic basis.

The case for the creation of a permanent law reform agency for the UK was developed in 1963 in a seminal work, *Law Reform Now*. This was a collection of essays edited by Andrew Martin and Gerald Gardiner.[2] The provenance of this book is very important. The two editors were leading lawyers and members of the Society of Labour Lawyers, a group of lawyers closely associated with the British Labour Party. They argued that the combination of the huge amount of law found in the common law system in cases decided in the top courts, plus the increasing amount of legislation coming from Parliament, had resulted in a body of law that was far too complex, lacked principle and was not fit for purpose in the modern world.

The timing of the book was perfect. The essays were written in the early 1960s. This was a period during which there was a growing sense of the need for, as well as a feeling that there was a real prospect of, political change after a long period of Conservative government. The book was ideally timed to influence the development of policy should a Labour government be created after the next general election.

The general election of 1964 did in fact elect a Labour government, under the leadership of Harold Wilson. However, the Wilson government had a much smaller majority than many people had anticipated. Thus, while it was undoubtedly in power, its grip on power was initially relatively weak.[3]

---

[2] Gerald Gardiner and Andrew Martin, *Law Reform Now* (Victor Gollancz, 1963).

[3] Wilson called a further general election in 1966, which gave him a much larger parliamentary majority and greater freedom to pursue his political agenda.

Paradoxically, this relative weakness provided an opportunity for the reforms proposed by Martin and Gardner to be taken forward. Debate on the creation of a body dedicated to the reform of the law was regarded as relatively uncontroversial, and one unlikely to generate the kind of political passion that might have undermined the slimness of the government's majority. In addition, and perhaps much more significantly, Wilson had appointed Gerald Gardiner as his Lord Chancellor. In his new role, Gardiner was able to use his considerable political clout to press for the creation of the institution he had been advocating before he arrived in power.[4]

As a consequence, one of the first decisions of the new government was to introduce the bill that would lead to the creation of the Law Commission. The Law Commissions Act 1965 was the final outcome. It created two Law Commissions: one for England and Wales, the other for Scotland. (Northern Ireland was not to have its own Law Commission until much later — in 2007.) The newly established Law Commission for England and Wales was the first body with full-time Commissioners and support staff, chaired not by the Minister but by an independent judge. For ease of exposition, I refer to this henceforth as the Law Commission, hoping that my Scottish colleagues will forgive the abbreviation!

Resources

There are four basic intellectual resources available to the Law Commission to enable it to carry out its work:

- The Commissioners;
- The Commission lawyers;
- Research assistants; and
- Specialist assistance.

In addition, there is a support staff, led by a Chief Executive (formerly known as the Secretary) who is a civil servant seconded to the Commission from the Ministry of Justice (formerly the Lord Chancellor's Department/ Department for Constitutional Affairs).

---

[4] A considerably fuller and more nuanced account of the history of the Commission's creation can be found in S M Cretney, "The Law Commission: True Dawns and False Dawns" (1996) 59 *Modern Law Review* 631.

The Commissioners

The legislation provides that the Law Commission for England and Wales should have five full-time Law Commissioners, including the Chairman. The persons who are appointed by the Lord Chancellor as Commissioners must, under the Act, either be the holder of a judicial office or be qualified by experience as a legal practitioner, or as a teacher of law in a university. Thus, unlike the position in some other countries, it is not possible to appoint a sociologist or economist to the position of Law Commissioner in the UK.

Although the policy has changed over the years, the current arrangements provide that Commissioner appointments are full-time appointments, but for a limited period. The Chair is usually appointed for three years; the other Commissioners are appointed for five years. There is a possibility of the renewal or the extension of an appointment, but it is rare to find any Commissioner serving more than two terms. This has two advantages: first, the Commission is being constantly refreshed with new energy and ideas; secondly, the system enables judges, practitioners and academics to be seconded to the Commission for a fixed period, before going on to a new challenge at the end of the period of office. Nearly all Commissioners have in fact gone to different jobs from those they had when they took up their appointments.

Furthermore, for many years the appointment process has been a transparent one. The private invitation to take up an appointment as Commissioner, which characterized the early years of the Commission, has been replaced by a system that depends on the advertising of posts and a rigorous selection and interview process.

From the outset, the chair of the Law Commission was always a judge.[5] The first Chairman was Mr Justice (later Lord) Scarman, who chaired the Commission for the first eight years of its existence. As regards the other four Commissioners, the informal rule was that the Commission should comprise two legal practitioners (one barrister and one solicitor) and two legal academics. This pattern has not always been achieved; for much of my time at the

---

[5] The requirement that the chair of the Law Commission should be a judge was never provided for in the original Law Commissions Act 1965, although as a matter of custom and practice, the chair was always a judge. The position was regularized by s 60 of the Tribunals, Courts and Enforcement Act 2007 which amends the original Act of 1965 to provide that the person appointed as chairman must either be a judge of the High Court or of the Court of Appeal.

Commission, there were two judges and three legal academics. But the current membership of the Commission has reverted to the two-practitioner, two-academic model.

A further bit of custom and practice resulted in the fact that, until relatively recently, successive Lord Chancellors were not willing to appoint a legal academic as the Commissioner in charge of questions relating to reform of the criminal law. It was thought that only practising lawyers would understand the practical implications of any reforms they might be proposing. The appointment of Professor Jeremy Horder as the criminal law Commissioner in 2005 broke that tradition, and his successor is also a legal academic.

Although section 3 of the Law Commissions Act requires the Law Commission "to take and keep under review all the law . . . with a view to its systematic development and reform", the reality is that the Law Commission does not do this literally. Rather it adopts programmes of work, in which particular areas of law are identified for analysis and proposals for reform.

The Commissioners in practice make a central contribution to these programmes of reform. The need to ensure that Commissioners are able to play a full part in the development work of the Commission has meant that throughout its history there have, in addition to a Commissioner taking the lead on criminal law reform, also tended to be Commissioners with an interest in property law and equity, in the common law, and in public law.

From time to time, there has arguably been a more direct linkage between the identity of particular Commissioners and the programme of work being undertaken by the Commission. For example, during the late 1980s and early 1990s the Law Commission engaged in a major programme of work on the reform of the Law of Children and of Family Law. During that era, the Commissioners included, at different times, Dr Stephen Cretney and Brenda Hoggett (now Lady Hale), both renowned family law experts.

When I was appointed, the advertisement for the post indicated that the Commission was intending — other things being equal — to appoint as a Commissioner either someone interested in company and commercial law (which were not my areas of expertise), or someone interested in housing law and administrative justice (in which I did claim some expertise). The reason for the job specification being drafted in this way was because the then Chairman, Mr Justice (now Lord) Carnwath, had reached informal agreement with the then government that there should be a major review of housing law — which over the years had become an area of law of extreme complexity.

My appointment was one of the factors that, as it transpired, encouraged the government formally to refer the issue to the Commission.[6]

The Commission lawyers

Each Commissioner is supported by a team of lawyers. Many of these lawyers are assigned to the Law Commission by the Government Legal Service (GLS).[7] These are lawyers who have experience of working within government, and have a particular understanding of how public policy is translated into legislative form. As they work within the overall framework of government, many GLS lawyers stay with the Commission for a time and then move back to the government department from which they originally came, or in some cases move on to a different government department.

By contrast, some Commission lawyers are hired directly on limited-term contracts for particular law reform projects. They are not appointed formally to the GLS and therefore do not have the same opportunity to move into other jobs within the Civil Service. A number of these lawyers are, in practice, seconded to the Law Commission for a specific project and who then move to another university appointment when their time at the Commission ends.[8]

In addition to the teams who work for individual Commissioners, there is a small team dedicated to the repeal of statutory laws that are no longer needed. Their work does not, perhaps, attract the same degree of attention as the work that proposes major changes to the law. But statute repeal was one of the objectives that the original designers of the Commission thought important. There is enough statute law on the books anyway without it being clogged by unnecessary provisions that are no longer of any practical utility. Much of the law repealed as a result of this team's work is of great antiquity, but some is

---

[6] A further statement of the circumstances surrounding my appointment can be found in the evidence of Sir Robert Carnwath to the Committee on Standards in Public Life on 13 July 2004: see <http://www.public-standards.gov.uk/Library/10th_Report_Inquiry___130704___Transcript.pdf> accessed 4 July 2012.

[7] More information about the UK Government Legal Service can be found at <http://www.gls.gov.uk/> accessed 22 July 2013.

[8] Details of the current teams and their work are found in the Annual Reports of the Law Commission. The report for 2012–2013 is available at: <http://lawcommission.justice.gov.uk/publications/annual-reports.htm> accessed 22 July 2013.

of surprisingly recent origin, reflecting changing political ideas, for example, on economic management.[9]

Research assistants

One feature of the Law Commission, which is certainly unusual if not unique internationally, is that it also employs on one-year (occasionally two-year) fixed-term contracts a number of research assistants. A highly competitive recruitment exercise is run annually which attracts outstanding young law graduates, often before they have completed their professional legal qualification training.

The research assistants undertake much of the basic research involved in developing law reform projects and play a full part in team discussions. These are posts that provide a demanding bridge between university and practice and/or teaching, and which have increased in importance during the life of the Law Commission. Many former research assistants have gone on to glittering careers in legal practice or in the academic world.

Specialist assistance

There are three other very important sources of intellectual input available to enhance the work of the Law Commission.

First, the Law Commission has from the outset had direct access to Parliamentary Counsel, specialist lawyers working within government, who are responsible for drafting legislation.[10] Each year a number of these are seconded to the Law Commission in order that, for projects where new legislation is called for, the reports of the Commission can be accompanied by a draft bill.

Secondly, and a much more recent innovation, the Commission now has available an economist who can undertake the impact assessments (cost-benefit) analysis that government — quite properly — insists should be carried out before new legislative proposals are put to Parliament. These used to be undertaken within the government department that would be sponsoring the

---

[9] For a recent statute repeals report published in 2012: see <http://lawcommission.justice.gov.uk/publications/19th_statute_law_repeals_report.htm> accessed 22 July 2013.

[10] For more information about their work, see <https://www.gov.uk/government/organisations/office-of-the-parliamentary-counsel>accessed 22 July 2013.

bill through Parliament. The Law Commission came to the view, however, that impact assessments would be better commissioned by those who had worked on particular legislative proposals.

Thirdly, and more generally, the Commission appoints consultants to work on specific projects, or particular aspects of projects, in relation to which the consultant in question has particular knowledge and expertise. These appointments are of particular value for projects, such as my housing law reform project or the adult social care law reform project, which benefit from the input of specialist social scientists and social policy experts.

Programmes

As mentioned above, the statutory function set for the Law Commission is to keep "all the laws under review". In practice, this is not possible. So the Law Commission operates by developing programmes of work. It is currently on its 11th programme (published in 2011).

Initially, programmes were both breathtaking in scope and published on a somewhat irregular basis. The first programme, published in July 1965 contained 17 items.[11] A second programme, published in July 1968, added

---

[11] Items listed were:
  1. Codification of the law of contract.
  2. Exemption by contract from common law liabilities, including (a) limits on exemption clauses; (b) regulation of exemption clauses; and (c) the doctrine of fundamental breach.
  3. Consideration, third party rights in contract and contracts under seal.
  4. Civil liability for dangerous things and activities.
  5. Civil liability for animals.
  6. Personal injury litigation including (a) jurisdiction and procedure; and (b) assessment of damages
  7. Civil liability of vendors and lessors for defective premises.
  8. Codification of the law of landlord and tenant.
  9. Transfer of land.
  10. Family Law, including (a) matrimonial law; (b) family inheritance and property law; and (c) jurisdiction in family matters.
  11. Financial limits on magistrates' orders in domestic and affiliation proceedings.
  12. Recognition of foreign divorces, nullity decrees and adoptions.
  13. Imputed criminal intent (*DPP v Smith*).
  14. Common law misdemeanours; crime of conspiracy.

three further items, including codification of criminal law and interpretation of wills. A third programme, published five years later in July 1973, added private international law.

It can be seen that, in those early years, there was a real enthusiasm, which reflected the interest, both of the original architects of and the initial appointees to the Law Commission, in codification. In addition to the items announced, there were other initiatives on the revision and codification of statute law (both of which functions are sustained to the present day).

In more recent years, publication of the Law Commission's programmes of work has evolved into a three-year cycle. The programmes are not discrete, but rather rolling programmes of work; some items are completed in one programme, others are carried forward into a new programme, and yet others are added to a new programme. From time to time, government asks the Law Commission to add a new item to a programme, for example, where an issue has arisen on which the government wants input from the Law Commission urgently, and cannot wait until the start of a new programme.

One of the questions that puzzles outsiders looking at the work of the Law Commission is: how do topics get chosen?

In the early years, as hinted above, it seems that programmes were very much the creation of the Commissioners themselves. Given the fact that there had been no such permanent body in existence before, the topics selected for those early programmes must have seemed obvious to the Commissioners. There would have been widespread agreement that these were the areas of the law that needed investigation with a view to reform.

More recently, the process of topic selection has become more open. First the Law Commission has itself articulated three criteria which underpin topic selection. These are:

- *Importance* — the extent to which the law is unsatisfactory (for example, unfair, unduly complex, inaccessible or outdated); and the potential benefits likely to accrue from undertaking reform.
- *Suitability* — whether the reform would be suitable to be put forward by a body of lawyers after legal research and consultation (this would tend

---

15. Miscellaneous matters involving anomalies, obsolescent principles or archaic procedures.
16. Judicature Act (Northern Ireland).
17. Interpretation of statutes.

to exclude subjects where the considerations are shaped primarily by political judgements).
- *Resources* — internal and external resources needed, and whether those resources are likely to be available; and the need for a good mix of projects in terms of the scale and timing so as to enable effective management of the programme.

Of these, the question of what is "suitable" is perhaps the hardest to pin down. Certainly the programme of work I led on the reform of housing law was only possible because the then newly elected New Labour government — which came to power in 1997 — decided to accept the major changes to the deregulation of the rented sector of the housing market that had been introduced in the Housing Acts of 1988 and 1996 by the Conservative governments of Margaret Thatcher and John Major. In short, there was political consensus that the broad regulatory approach should remain the same. The same political consensus was important for the new Law Commission project on adult social care.[12] For this reason, although extremely complex and in dire need of the sort of rationalization that the Law Commission could undertake, reform of social security law in the UK would not be a good topic for the Law Commission to undertake; nor would reform of employment law. Both these subjects are too politically controversial.[13]

With these three criteria in mind, the modern practice of the Law Commission is to build its programmes on a far more consultative and structured basis than used to happen in the early years. The process starts with consultation of government departments — asking them whether they have policy areas where a good look at the legal issues would be desirable. There is also a wider consultation with a large range of stakeholders — in the legal and commercial world, in the voluntary sector, in local government and the police, and amongst the academic community. Invitations to submit ideas are also sent to others already in touch with the Law Commission. The consultation period

---

[12] This desire to deal with important areas of law that were not politically very controversial is in contrast to the experience of a number of other law commissions around the world that have ventured into far more politically sensitive areas. It is noteworthy that some of these arguably bolder law reform agencies have since disappeared, whereas the Law Commission continues to exist.

[13] Consider further Chapter 9 (Glofcheski).

lasts for a minimum of three months (extended on the last occasion to accommodate the period of the summer vacation).[14]

Typically, these days, this will generate numerous ideas for matters that might go into a new programme. These are then distilled into a much smaller selection of items that the Law Commission assesses it can undertake within its available resources and within the sort of time table needed to sustain the momentum of its overall output.

The current 11th Programme of Reform contains, at the end, a summary of a number of ideas that were submitted to the Law Commission but which did not make it onto the finally agreed list. This shows the wide variety of sources from which these ideas came: legal practitioners; government departments; academic lawyers; pressure groups; and members of the public. It also gives a clear statement of the reasons why the ideas were not thought suitable for the Law Commission to investigate.[15]

Following enactment of the Law Commission Act 2009, statutory backing has been given to a protocol between the Lord Chancellor and the Law Commission, setting out how the government and the Law Commission should work together on law reform.[16] The protocol was agreed in April 2010.

The introduction to the protocol sets out the joint aims of the Lord Chancellor and Chairman of the Law Commission: to create law that is fair, modern, simple and accessible and to increase the momentum of law reform. The protocol lays down the procedure for deciding on projects to be included in a programme of law reform; and on projects referred to the Commission by Ministers.

Thus, the protocol requires consideration of: (1) whether project-specific funding is available (if relevant); (2) the degree of government department support; (3) whether there is a Scottish or Northern Irish dimension to the project that would need the involvement of the Scottish and/or Northern Ireland Law Commissions; and (4) whether there is a Welsh dimension that would need the involvement of the Welsh government.

---

[14] See <http://www.justice.gov.uk/lawcommission/docs/lc330_eleventh_programme.pdf> [1.14]–[1.18] accessed 4 July 2012.

[15] See <http://www.justice.gov.uk/lawcommission/docs/lc330_eleventh_programme.pdf> [3.12] accessed 4 July 2012. Consultation on the 12th Programme is currently being undertaken.

[16] *Protocol between the Lord Chancellor (on behalf of the Government) and the Law Commission* (Law Com No 321, 29 March 2010 (HC 499)).

The protocol has established a clearer system for ensuring that departments are supportive of the Law Commission's work in terms of future implementation. In other words, the Law Commission will not take forward proposals which the relevant government department has no intention of implementing. Some regret this development, arguing that it reduces the independence of the Law Commission to select those projects its regards as most important: it would not, I suspect, have been acceptable to the founding Commissioners. However, pragmatic considerations suggest that wilfully to expend resources on projects that have no chance of implementation would not, in times of austerity, be regarded as a sensible use of public funds.

Where the Law Commission is considering including a project in a programme of law reform, the protocol provides that the Law Commission must notify the Minister with relevant policy responsibility. In deciding how to respond to the Commission, the Minister must bear in mind that, before approving the inclusion of the project in the overall programme, the Lord Chancellor will expect the Minister (with the support of the Permanent Secretary) to agree that the department will provide sufficient staff to liaise with the Commission during the currency of the project (normally, a policy lead, a lawyer and an economist); and to give an undertaking that there is a serious intention to take forward law reform in this area (if applicable in the case of the particular project).

In discussion between the department and the Commission, the department will, insofar as is possible at that stage, provide views to the Commission on what it considers to be the most appropriate output for the project (for example, policy recommendations, a draft bill, draft guidance), the likely method of implementation, and any risks associated with that method of implementation which might lead to non implementation or significantly delayed implementation (for example, difficulties in obtaining legislative time if the method of implementation is legislation).

The 11th Programme is the first to be settled under the terms of the new protocol.

Procedures

Having considered how the Law Commission's programmes are settled, I turn now to discuss the procedures adopted by the Law Commission.

Setting the terms of reference

Although getting a programme item into the programme is obviously a key initial step, setting the terms of reference for the project is the first substantive step in the process. These emerge from discussions between the Law Commission and the relevant government department. The terms of reference define the scope of each project. They also determine the output from the project, whether there will be a bill, or simply a statement of recommendations, for example.

These days, and in accordance with the protocol, this initial stage also includes a statement giving the sponsoring department an opportunity for a particular project to be reviewed jointly with the Commission to ensure that the sponsoring department is still committed to it. In some cases this makes it possible to terminate a project prematurely.

At the outset of a project, the protocol also provides that "the departmental officials (to include, unless otherwise agreed, a nominated policy lead, a lawyer and an economist) and the Commission will agree a programme of regular communication, to include meetings which will normally be at least every quarter while the project is live."[17]

Research

The next substantive step is for the existing law on the topic in question to be thoroughly researched. This is fundamental work undertaken by the lawyers with assistance from their research assistants. Understanding the detail of the existing substantive law is clearly key to understanding the problems that the current law creates. This in turn informs the process of developing proposals for reform of the relevant law.

For some projects, the Law Commission will commission additional research, particularly empirical social science or economic research, which may not be readily available within the Commission itself.[18]

---

[17] See <http://www.justice.gov.uk/lawcommission/docs/lc321_Protocol.pdf> [10] and [11] accessed 4 July 2012.

[18] A particular example is the study by Professor (now Dame) Hazel Genn: "Personal Injury Compensation: How Much Is Enough? A Study of the Compensation

Consultation

The fundamental principle on which the Law Commission works is that of consultation.[19] Right from the beginning, the Law Commission consulted on ideas for reform of the law, testing those ideas in public, before coming to final recommendations.

In a normal project, therefore, having completed an analysis of the law in the research phase, the Law Commission formally sets out its proposals for reform in a consultation paper. In practice, however, the consultation process usually starts before any consultation paper is published. The Commissioners and their team of lawyers will have informal discussions with key stakeholders about how their thinking is developing and respond to the reaction of stakeholders to those ideas. In some projects, the Law Commission will establish an informal advisory or steering group, comprising representatives of key stakeholder bodies.

Once the consultation paper is published, the Law Commission is now more proactive than it was in the early years about ensuring that it gets a good response to its consultation papers. Depending on the nature of the project, the relevant Commissioner and team lawyers will address meetings of practitioners, of special interest groups and of the public. They will also meet politicians and civil servants to seek their views.[20] All these responses are collated by the Law Commission and considered by the project team.

Final report and bill

Having analysed all the responses, the project team will prepare a final report. In appropriate cases this will be accompanied by a draft bill. As noted above,

---

Experiences of Victims of Personal Injury" (1994) Law Com No 225. More general discussion of the commissioning and use of research by law commissions can be found in Martin Partington, "Research" in B Opeskin and D Weisbrot (eds), *The Promise of Law Reform* (The Federation Press, 2005) ch 9.

[19] See Martin Partington, "The Renting Homes Project" (2005) 23 *Windsor Yearbook of Access to Justice* 375, where I argue that the process of consultation should be seen as an aspect of access to justice in that members of the public are given the opportunity to help shape the laws that affect them.

[20] Regular meetings with relevant civil servants are now part of the protocol: see <http://www.justice.gov.uk/lawcommission/docs/lc321_Protocol.pdf> [12]–[17] accessed 4 July 2012.

bills are drafted by Parliamentary Counsel on the basis of instructions provided by the team lawyers. This is obviously a time consuming and testing period for the team.

The Commission also instructs its economist to undertake the impact analysis required for all legislative or other policy proposals, in which the costs and benefits of enacting those proposals are evaluated. The protocol states that the impact analysis should be undertaken in partnership with departmental officials, and the hope is expressed in the protocol that, in most cases, the impact analysis will be a joint report, agreed by both the Law Commission and the relevant government department.

The final report is then published.

Next steps

Historically, that used to be more or less the end of the process as far as the Law Commission was concerned. These days, however, there is a more formal process of follow-up and response that the government is required to pursue. The protocol provides that:[21]

- The Minister will provide an interim response to the Commission as soon as possible and in any event within six months of publication of the report unless otherwise agreed with the Commission;
- The Minister will provide a full response to the Commission as soon as possible after delivery of the interim response and in any event within one year of publication of the report unless otherwise agreed with the Commission. The response will set out which recommendations the Minister accepts, rejects or intends to implement in modified form. If applicable, the Minister will also provide the timescale for implementation.
- If the department is minded either to reject or substantially modify any significant recommendations, it will first give the Commission the opportunity to discuss and comment on its reasons before finalizing the decision.
- The Minister will send his or her final response to the Chairman of the Commission.

---

[21] See <http://www.justice.gov.uk/lawcommission/docs/lc321_Protocol.pdf> [18]–[22] accessed 4 July 2012.

- If the Minister intends to implement recommendations, the Commission and the department will agree what additional support (if any) the Commission will provide to the department to assist implementation and whether additional funding is necessary.

These provisions replace the formerly very unsatisfactory arrangements under which departments were supposed to give a response, but not infrequently failed to do so.

In addition, the Law Commission Act 2009 introduced a requirement for the Lord Chancellor to prepare and lay before Parliament an annual report setting out the extent to which Law Commission proposals have been implemented by government over the preceding year, including reasons why any proposal is not to be implemented or plans for future implementation. The first report was published on 24 January 2011.[22]

In some cases, Commissioners may also offer a more informal "after-sales service" by, for example, providing briefings on project outcomes to politicians — of all political parties — and others interested in specific reform proposals.

Achievements

The achievements of the Law Commission can be assessed in a number of ways. First, the published output of the Commission — its consultation papers and Final Reports — is a rich repository of high quality legal research and ideas for reform. With over 330 final reports and over 200 consultation papers, plus numerous other outputs, including scoping, discussion and issues papers, this is, of itself, a substantial achievement.[23]

However, what most people want to know is the extent to which proposals for reforming the law have in fact been implemented by successive governments. The Law Commission has produced data indicating that around

---

[22] See <http://www.official-documents.gov.uk/document/hc1011/hc07/0719/0719.pdf> accessed 4 July 2012.

[23] Details of the Commission's published output can be found by going to <http://lawcommission.justice.gov.uk/publications.htm> accessed 22 July 2013, and following the leads. Many of the earlier reports and papers of the Law Commission can be accessed through the British and Irish Legal Information Institute: see <http://www.bailii.org>.

two-thirds of its reports have been implemented either wholly or in part. (This figure is comparable to levels of outcome in other jurisdictions around the world.)

In order to try to improve the success rate of the English Law Commission, the House of Lords approved a new procedure for the handling of Law Commission bills. This procedure was adopted on a trial basis in April 2008 and used for the passage of two Acts deriving from Law Commission reports: the Perpetuities and Accumulations Act 2009 and the Third Parties (Rights Against Insurers) Act 2010. The House of Lords has now formally adopted the new procedure.[24]

The question of the success rate raises a broader more general question about the functioning of law commissions. Although lawyers may well regard the need for the reform of specific areas of law as a self-evident public good, this will frequently not be sufficient to secure law reform. There is always the need for *political* acceptance that the changes will be desirable. In addition, in order for a government to provide the required time to enable legislation to pass through the legislature, law reform proposals have to be sufficiently important for them to win a place in the legislative timetable. This political reality is often not sufficiently appreciated by commentators, particular legal commentators, on the work of the Law Commission.

Besides making proposals for reforming law, another important achievement — envisaged from the earliest days of the Law Commission — is the repeal and removal from the statute book of legislation that no longer has any modern relevance. This is an area of the Law Commission's work that does not attract much public attention, but is nevertheless an importance aspect of its work.

Lessons from the English Experience

In this final section I offer a few personal views on lessons from the English experience that might be of some relevance as authorities in Hong Kong decide

---

[24] See Procedure Committee, First Report of 2007–08 (HL Paper 63), <http://www.publications.parliament.uk/pa/ld200708/ldselect/ldprohse/63/63.pdf> accessed 4 July 2012, and Procedure Committee, Second Report of 2010–11 (HL Paper 30). These procedures only apply to non-controversial bills. They also apply to bills coming from the Scottish Law Commission.

how to take forward institutional arrangements for reforming Hong Kong law. In making these points I intend in no way to imply that everything about the English Law Commission is perfect. As with any institution, it is always evolving. Hong Kong's law commission will have to decide for itself what lessons it wants to take from other jurisdictions, and what innovations it thinks are sensible given the particularities of the local community it has been appointed to serve.

With these caveats in mind, I make the following comments:

First, it is hard, in a jurisdiction of any size, for the law reform function to be taken forward on the basis of a small number of part-time lawyers — however eminent and energetic — undertaking reform projects in their spare time. Effective law reform for all but the smallest countries requires, in my view, at least a core full-time leadership supported by a core full-time support staff. The practice, in England, of — in effect — seconding legal figures from the judiciary, from the legal profession and from the legal academic world for limited periods has worked well. The number of leaders and support staff will, of course, vary considerably between one country and another.

Secondly, in England the lack of any non-lawyer Commissioners has not prevented the Commission from ensuring that it takes account of the potential social and economic impacts of its reform proposals. There are, however, other jurisdictions in which suitably qualified non-lawyer members have been appointed. Depending on the issues that any law reform body in Hong Kong might wish to take up, this is perhaps an option that might be borne in mind.

Thirdly, the principle of consultation is, in my view, an essential feature of the law commission process. Sorting out difficult areas of law by getting advice from and building consensus with those likely to be most affected by proposals to change the law seems eminently sensible to me. In addition, the availability of new forms of communication media means that law reform bodies no longer need rely on written submissions in response to consultation documents. Many investigations are now carried on through questionnaires completed on line, with comments being received in a variety of modes of e-communication. These developments will become more and more commonplace.

Fourthly, it is important that law reform bodies are independent of government, in the sense that they are left to decide how they think particular areas of law should be reformed. This does not mean that law reform bodies should work in isolation from government. In my view, the engagement that is implicit between the Law Commission and individual government departments offers a sensible way of working. In fact, it may help a government from time to time to be able to distance itself from particular law reform proposals.

Fifthly, the sensible selection of topics is crucial to the success of a law reform agency. Although the experience of other jurisdictions might suggest otherwise, a focus on key areas of legal doctrine — particularly where they have become overcomplex and militate against sensible decision taking, whether in the public or private sector — gives law reform bodies a particular raison d'être which distinguishes them from other policy reform bodies.

Sixthly, I consider that law reform bodies need to take seriously their communications policy. I am not certain that, in the past, the Law Commission was as effective in its communications strategies as it should have been. It now has a small team devoted to promoting the work of the Law Commission, which has improved the Commission's profile. But there is much more that could be done. I suspect the average resident in the UK is unaware of the existence of the Law Commission, let alone its work and how it might impact the lives of ordinary people. On the other hand, successful communications have the potential for getting more people engaged in the law making process, which may mean that the resultant proposals for law reform have greater acceptance than they might otherwise have.

There are of course special political and constitutional issues existing in Hong Kong that are different from those which apply in the UK. These are, therefore, questions that need to be addressed specifically in the Hong Kong context.

Chapter 6
Lessons from Law Reform in Ontario and Elsewhere in Canada

Patricia Hughes

Introduction

There is no "one" way to organize a law reform agency, nor "one" way to "do" law reform. There are, however, some basic characteristics of law reform agencies that are more likely to make an arms-length law reform body successful as a law reform agency, including a mandate devoted to law reform, independence, "permanence", sufficient resources and a mature government open to reform.[1] These characteristics are required to avoid the charge that the law reform agency is simply a branch or agent of government. They are necessary regardless of the projects the law commission undertakes or how it approaches its work. Depending on how it does undertake its work, however, it may have other characteristics that David Weisbrot describes as "post-modern": generalist, interdisciplinary and consultative.[2] And if it is to have any hope of success, its recommendations, no matter how innovative, must also

---

[1] For characteristics, see Michael Kirby, "Law Reform — Ten Attributes for Success" (Address presented to The Law Reform Commission of Ireland, Dublin, 17 July 2007) <http://www.lawreform.ie/fileupload/Speeches/KirbyJ3rdProgAnnualConference.pdf> accessed 17 October 2011; Sandra Petersson, "Law Reform Agencies: The Essential Elements" (Paper presented to the Australian Law Reform Agencies Conference, Wellington, New Zealand, April 2004) <http://www.lawcom.govt.nz/sites/default/files/speeches/2004/04/ Petersson.pdf> accessed 17 October 2011.

[2] David Weisbrot, "The Historical Necessity of Law Reform" (The Alex Castles Memorial Lecture in Australian Legal History, delivered at Flinders University Law School, 24 August 2006) <http://www.alrc.gov.au/news-media/2006/alex-castles-memorial-lecture-2006-historical-necessity-law-reform> accessed 17 October 2011. In this paper, Weisbrot suggests that the "post-modern" characteristics are generalist, interdisciplinary, consultative and implementation-minded.

be feasible, whether in the short term or, given economic and other realities, in the longer term (Weisbrot's characteristic of "implementation-minded").

The Canadian Law Reform Experience: An Overview[3]

As in most other countries that eventually established "permanent" law reform agencies, initial efforts at law reform in Canada tended to involve committees composed of volunteer judges and lawyers, and sometimes academics, appointed by the Attorney General with the objective of reviewing a particular area of law for reform, usually "black letter" law.

The era of "modern" law reform in Canada began with the Ontario Law Reform Commission (OLRC), established by statute in 1964 and funded entirely by the government. The significant differences between it and prior bodies were that it was "permanent" (using that term judiciously) and benefitted from a permanent staff and stable financial resources. Its Commissioners were responsible for particular projects. It was expected to address matters referred to it by the Attorney General, although it could also review matters it self-selected. By the time its funding was eliminated in 1996, the OLRC had produced some 100 final reports ranging across the entire scope of legislation.[4]

The following decade was, of course, the heyday of law reform agency creation in a number of different countries. Canada was no exception and all the law commissions existing today had their origins in that period or are successors to commissions established at that time. Three other law commissions instituted then (in Prince Edward Island and Newfoundland [now Newfoundland and Labrador] and at the federal level), no longer exist.[5]

---

[3] A comprehensive overview of Canadian law reform agencies up to 2004 can be found in Gavin Murphy, Law Reform Agencies (Department of Justice, 2004) <http://www.justice.gc.ca/eng/pi/icg-gci/lr-rd/index.html> accessed 18 October 2011. The historical discussion of Canadian law reform agencies relies heavily on Murphy's description. A detailed history and discussion of their impact to the mid-eighties can be found in William H Hurlburt, *Law Reform Commissions in the United Kingdom, Australia and Canada* (Juriliber, 1986).

[4] A list of the OLRC's reports is found on The Open Library's website at <http://openlibrary.org/authors/ OL251484A/Ontario_Law_Reform_Commission> accessed 18 October 2011. The OLRC's mandating statute, the Ontario Law Reform Commission Act, was not repealed until December 2009, by the Good Government Act 2009, c 33 Sch 2 s 53.

[5] Prince Edward Island's law reform commission was established by statute in 1970, began work in 1976 and was no longer funded by 1983. Although legislation to create

There are six free-standing law reform agencies in Canada today, in British Columbia, Alberta, Saskatchewan, Manitoba, Ontario and Nova Scotia. Law reform in New Brunswick has always been carried out through a branch of government, and although Quebec enacted legislation to create a law reform commission, it has never done so.

Three of the current Commissions, in Manitoba, Saskatchewan and Nova Scotia, are more traditional commissions.[6] The Manitoba Law Reform Commission (MLRC) and the Law Reform Commission of Saskatchewan (SLRC) have continued in existence since they were first established in 1970 and 1971, respectively (although the SLRC did not begin work until 1973). The Nova Scotia Law Reform Advisory Commission was created in 1969, but did not commence operations until 1972. The Advisory Commission could not release reports except with the permission of the Attorney General. It stopped operating in 1981 (none of its members was reappointed or replaced), although the statute was not repealed until 1990 when the new Law Reform Commission of Nova Scotia (NSLRC) was statutorily created as an independent advisor to government.

As "traditional" commissions, the Manitoba, Saskatchewan and Nova Scotia Commissions are all creatures of statute and have part-time Commissioners appointed by order-in-council. The Commissioners reflect identified interests (such as the provincial law school(s), the Attorney General, the judiciary and sometimes the province's law society or community interests). While all three Commissions may inquire into any matter they consider appropriate, both the SLRC and the NSLRC are also required to address matters referred to them by the Attorney General. They all report to the Attorney General. Funding for all three Commissions (in all cases from the provincial law foundation[7] and the

---

a law reform commission in Newfoundland (now Newfoundland and Labrador) was enacted in 1971, the commission did not begin operations until 1981 and funding was eliminated in 1992.

[6] For information about the Manitoba Law Reform Commission, see <http://www.manitobalawreform.ca/index.html> accessed 19 January 2013; about the Law Reform Commission of Saskatchewan, see <http://www.lawreformcommission.sk.ca> accessed 19 January 2013; and about the Law Reform Commission of Nova Scotia, see <http://www.lawreform.ns.ca/introduction.htm> accessed 19 January 2013.

[7] Each provincial law foundation is responsible for the interest on lawyers' trust accounts which it invests; it distributes the income to various projects and organizations. See, for example, the Law Foundation of Ontario <http://www.lawfoundation.on.ca> accessed 25 October 2011. The different law foundations have different

provincial Department or Ministry of Justice) is not significant and they have small staffs.[8] The Chair of the SLRC has indicated an interest in breathing new life into the Commission and has been involved in discussions with the other Law Commissions.

The Commissions in British Columbia, Alberta and Ontario are structured differently from the traditional commissions. They are not based on statute,[9] created solely by government or required to report to the Attorney General.

The Alberta Law Reform Institute (ALRI) is now the longest continuous running law reform agency in Canada, as well as the largest and most stable (its Executive Director has held that position since 1988). In 1967, the Alberta government, the Law Society of Alberta and the University of Alberta agreed to establish the Alberta Institute of Law Research and Reform, with funding from the government and the university. Now known as the Alberta Law Reform Institute, ALRI was and is located at the University of Alberta and is currently primarily funded by the government and the Law Foundation of Alberta, with in kind contributions and a small cash grant from the university.[10] Its Board represents various interests, including the judiciary, the two Alberta law schools/universities, private practice and the government; the Executive Director is also a member. Its staff comprises six in-house lawyers, including two at the University of Calgary, and three administrative staff, a number of whom have been at ALRI for lengthy periods. ALRI also contracts out project work.

The Law Commission of Ontario (LCO) is the "youngest" law reform commission in Canada and to some extent follows the ALRI model. It was also created by agreement[11] rather than statute and is located at a law school,

---

approaches to the distribution of funding, although each funds the law commission in its province.

[8] The NSLRC staff consists of the Executive Director, Legal Research Counsel, an administrative assistant and the Special Counsel. The MLRC has one legal researcher and one administrator and the SLRC has a Director of Research.

[9] As indicated below, the British Columbia Law Institute is established under the province's Society Act as a non-profit corporation, but not by government or under specific law reform commission legislation.

[10] For information about the Alberta Law Reform Institute, see <http://www.law.ualberta.ca/alri> accessed 18 October 2011.

[11] Similarly to ALRI, the Ministry of the Attorney General, the Law Society of Upper Canada and Osgoode Hall Law School (not York University where Osgoode is located) are parties and funders; the Law Foundation of Ontario, also a funder, and

Osgoode Hall Law School in Toronto, which is a major funder and in-kind contributor. Its funding is diverse, coming from all the parties to the agreement, except the law schools (other than Osgoode). LCO funding is "block" funding and is not allocated for particular purposes, allowing the LCO flexibility. The reason given for the diverse sources of funding is that it is not possible for the government to "pull the plug" on the Commission, as occurred with the LCO's predecessor, the OLRC. However, realistically, one might question whether other funders would want to fund a commission to which the government had not indicated some kind of commitment. Each funder appoints a member to the LCO's Board of Governors and there are also appointees from the law deans (as a group) and the judiciary, along with at large members who are appointed by the Board members. Currently, the Board has 12 members, including the LCO's Executive Director who is an ex-officio member; only one is a government appointee, a function of the Ministry of the Attorney General's status as a funder. All but one of the Board members is legally trained and their professional work is in some way related to the law; one member was selected for her expertise in social science research. The Chair is not a member of government. The first Chair was the dean of Osgoode Hall Law School,[12] the second a lawyer in private practice and the third a former dean.

Originally established in 1969 by statute as a traditional commission funded by government, the British Columbia Law Reform Commission had its funding cut in 1997. The current British Columbia Law Institute (BCLI) was incorporated shortly afterwards under the British Columbia Society Act.[13] BCLI's funding is derived from a number of sources, including the Law Foundation of British Columbia and the Ministry of the Attorney General (the government did not contribute funding until 2003). It receives core funding, but is also required to obtain funding on a project-by-project basis; funding for projects may come from the Law Foundation, and also from professional foundations, federal or provincial government ministries or law firms, for example.

---

the other six Ontario law deans as a group (other than Osgoode, Ontario has five law schools, one of which has both common law and civil law sections) are also parties.

[12] An interesting "historical" note is that this same individual was recently appointed to be the Deputy Attorney General of Ontario and has returned to the Board in that capacity. There is no formal past chair position, although there is talk of one, and the most recent chair was recently reappointed as a member at large.

[13] For information about the British Columbia Law Institute, see <http://www.bcli.org> accessed 18 October 2011.

The members of its Board of Directors represent the two universities in British Columbia, the Ministry of the Attorney General, the BC Law Society, the Notary Foundation and the CBA (BC).[14] It is the only Commission that has an executive committee. Unlike both the LCO and ALRI, the BCLI Board does not have a judicial member; however, a separate group of three judges provides judicial liaison. Along with the Executive Director, there are three full-time lawyers, one of whom is the Director of the Canadian Centre for Elder Law (CCEL) which is affiliated with BCLI. CCEL is dedicated to researching the law particularly relevant to older adults. It also contributes to education for professionals whose responsibilities extend to older adults, including the preparation of practice manuals.

The provincial law commissions belong to the Federation of Law Reform Agencies of Canada (FOLRAC), established in 1990.[15] Its members have considered how "active" FOLRAC should be (whether it should undertake semi-lobbying activities, for example) and to date have decided not to do more than hold a symposium about every 18 months or so for education and networking. Over the years, there has been an attempt to include more and more staff members and to bring practical experience to bear in the sessions. FOLRAC usually holds its annual general meeting at the Uniform Law Conference of Canada (ULCC) meeting (ULCC is discussed below).

The first federal law reform commission (the Law Reform Commission of Canada) was established in 1971 by statute. It developed its own research programme, which the Minister of Justice tabled in Parliament, along with a statement of any areas to which the Minister was opposed. It was disbanded in 1993. Its successor, the Law Commission of Canada (LCC), created by statute in 1997 (never repealed)[16] did not have its funding renewed in the federal budget of 2006. The government in office at the time has been re-elected since and has shown no inclination to re-establish a commission.

The LCC was to be guided by several principles that were reflected in the work that it produced. Its work was to be "inclusive", "understandable" and use a multidisciplinary approach "that views the law and the legal system in

---

[14] "CBA (BC)" is the British Columbia branch of the Canadian Bar Association, effectively a lobbying group for lawyers.

[15] See FOLRAC's website <http://www.folrac.com/index.html> accessed 27 October 2011. ALRI developed and maintains the site. When there was a federal commission, it also was a member of FOLRAC.

[16] Law Commission of Canada Act 1996, SC 1996, c 9.

a broad social and economic context". The LCC was to develop partnerships with "a wide range" of groups, use modern technology, be innovative in all reports, and consider "cost-effectiveness and the impact of the law on different groups and individuals in formulating its recommendations".[17]

The principles governing the LCC reflect the characteristics of "postmodern" commissions Weisbrot identified, some of which I will discuss in greater detail below in considering the LCO's approach to law reform. The Law Commission of Canada did not generally address specific legislation but rather looked at some of the big challenges facing Canadian society today. For some, this seemed to be not sufficiently practical, yet perhaps the first lesson of the Canadian experience is that that kind of commission is no guarantee against its demise: the OLRC and the LCC could not have been more dissimilar in philosophy and approach, yet funding for both was eliminated, even though the statute creating them in each case remained on the books.

The Uniform Law Conference of Canada's mandate is to propose uniform statutes intended to harmonize provincial and territorial law.[18] Delegates from all provincial and territorial governments and the federal government, the law commissions and bar associations meet once a year to consider new, on-going and "final" statutes. Most of the work goes on through the year, relying mainly on volunteers.

It is possible to make a few initial observations about the differences in structure and related factors among Canadian law commissions. First, no Canadian commission has been structured in the way many commissions elsewhere have been structured. Lawyers or former academics (or academics on secondment) head every Canadian law reform agency, rather than judges.[19] All commissions recognize the importance of having a link with the courts and therefore judges do play a formal role in the structures of all of them, primarily through representatives on the boards. The three traditional commissions

---

[17] Ibid, Preamble.

[18] Information about the ULCC and a listing of uniform statutes developed and those enacted are available at <http://www.ulcc.ca/en/home> accessed 19 January 2013.

[19] Compare the Law Commission of England and Wales: see Chapter 5 (Partington). It is arguable whether having persons other than judges heading commissions results in governments treating them with disrespect and a greater willingness to reduce a commission's resources: see Chapters 2 (Kirby) and 14 (Kirby) where note is made of recent changes to the Australian Law Reform Commission's resources at a time when a judge was not at the head of that Commission.

have the fewest resources. Both Manitoba and Saskatchewan have historically been able to participate less often in FOLRAC symposia or at the ULCC, for example, and have limited in-house resources for undertaking extensive projects, although Manitoba appears to have the capacity to retain consultants.

The Work of Law Reform

Introduction

In this section, I discuss the nature of law reform work and the kinds of activities that might be included under this rubric, as well as the extent to which resources and philosophy affect a law commission's decision about the nature of law reform activities.

It is common for law reform bodies to undertake "black letter law" or "lawyer's law" projects, focused around legislation, although they can be narrow (even a review of one section of a statute, for example), or broad, being the review of an entire statute or group of related statutes. Other projects may address emerging social, technological or, for example, medical developments, or consider an innovative approach to an "old" problem. Of course, legislation may be recommended in these projects, but they are likely to involve consideration not only of the law, but also of other disciplines and non-legal matters as they relate to the law (I call these projects "law in context" or "social justice" projects, as appropriate).[20] Projects might relate to process, to substantive law or to policy. Final recommendations may be directed entirely at government or quasi-government agencies or may also target the private sector.

The type of project is likely to affect the type of consultation that occurs. The minimum form of consultation today is to post a consultation paper or interim report on the commission's website and invite feedback from anyone or any organization interested in commenting. More pro-active consultation may also occur. Depending on the subject matter of the project, consultation

---

[20] The LCO's Board of Governors has recently concluded that this distinction is possibly no longer useful, since the subject matter of projects in reality flows along a continuum with those dealing only with legislation at one end and social context (or social justice) projects at the other. This is surely the preferable normative and more realistic characterization of projects. In short, there is no longer any need to justify the LCO's undertaking social justice projects as it seemed necessary to do when it began its mandate.

may be primarily (although perhaps not exclusively) with the legal community or may extend to other professionals and the broader community. Project advisory groups provide on-going consultation.[21] The form of consultation is also likely to be reflective of the commission's philosophy of law reform and its relationship with the public (I discuss this further below).

Law commissions may also engage in outreach primarily meant to raise the commission's profile, independently of particular projects (although certainly projects may be discussed during outreach sessions). To some extent, outreach or lack of it may reflect a commission's understanding of whether it is "of" or "in" society. Traditionally, law reform bodies were insular, rarely reaching out beyond the legal and academic worlds. In this, they reflected the notion that the law itself is somehow above or transcends society, and not part of the pull and tug of opposing societal forces or one of several orders of authority to which people consider themselves subject.[22]

Finally, law commission activities may include conferences and symposia, both those in which staff members participate and those they organize or co-organize. I also include in this category of activity writing for different kinds of journals, newsletters or the like, as well as social media. These activities, too, may involve experts in areas other than law and those whose knowledge of a law is experiential.

Projects: the core responsibility

Most projects undertaken by Canadian law reform agencies have been focused on legislative reform, the traditional bailiwick of law reform agencies, although they may be very large projects. For example, ALRI undertook a review of

---

[21] See, for example, BCLI's advisory committees: <http://www.bcli.org/sites/default/files/2011-02-09_List_of_BCLI_Committees.pdf> accessed 28 October 2011. An example of the LCO's advisory groups is for the older adults project: <http://www.lco-cdo.org/en/older-adults-advisory-group> accessed 28 October 2011.

[22] This is, by necessity, a simplistic description of the perception of law. It ignores, for example, the role institutional religion has played as a force competing with secular law to constitute itself as the source of authority for the populace. My comment is merely to make the point that, traditionally, law reform bodies did not see the need to hear from the people about how the law affected them, or to obtain a conceptual and empirical understanding about how the issue they were considering might be informed by other disciplines.

the civil rules of procedure at the request of the Rules of Court Committee that took many years and involved many people.[23] Most "black letter" projects are considerably smaller, such as the study of the Stable Keepers' Act by the Manitoba Commission or the revocation of wills by the Saskatchewan Commission. Regardless of the topic, "black letter" legislative projects tend, in the normal course, although not always, to be contained, manageable and possible to complete with little pro-active consultation and at low cost.

Larger or law-in-context or social justice projects are far less frequent for obvious reasons. They can be costly, take a great deal of time and require extensive consultation if they are to be meaningful and accepted by those affected by them. Law commissions must have adequate resources, both financial and human, to undertake or commission multidisciplinary research, reach out to affected communities, including travelling to meet them, and have the time and skills to write reports that add to the sum of knowledge in the area. Not all law reform bodies are able to do this. For example, the SLRC began an ambitious project in collaboration with the Law Commission of Canada on aboriginal self-government issues; with the demise of the LCC, it would be almost impossible for the SLRC to undertake the project alone, given its resources, and it appears the project came to a standstill over five years ago. This does not mean that law reform bodies with less extensive resources cannot undertake solid and useful work. Of course, they can when they use their resources to focus on one or two projects at a time.

The LCO has undertaken a mix of smaller and larger projects and projects focused on legislation and law-in-context projects. Not surprisingly, it has been able to complete several small or legislative projects, and has taken

---

[23] Alberta Law Reform Institute, *Rules of Court Project* (Final Report No. 95, October 2008) <http://www.law.ualberta.ca/alri/docs/fr095.pdf> accessed 27 October 2011. The Final Report describes in great detail the process developed for the project. Just one example of the degree of work: 12 topic-related working committees (in addition to a steering committee) produced 21 memoranda and produced draft recommendations for further consideration. Although the Final Report does identify new rules, there are only two recommendations: (1) enact the proposed legislative framework for the creation, validation, and maintenance of the Rules; and (2) enact the proposed rules in their entirety and in the format in which they appear on the attached CD. A project of this complexity, both in topic and process, and high cost (it was estimated that it would cost CDN$2.6m) could be undertaken only by a relatively large and mature law commission with access to considerable volunteer resources.

longer with large law-in-context projects.[24] Two new "small" projects are underway. A review of the Forestry Workers Lien for Wages Act is almost completed.[25] This is a "classic" law reform project, since it deals with a statute enacted in 1891 which has failed to keep currency with the nature of logging and legal processes. It raises the big question of whether it should be amended or, indeed, repealed, with the matters it addresses incorporated into another statute or regime. The other small new project is a simplified procedure for small estates that is in the earliest stages. A much larger project focusing on legislation is a review of class actions in Ontario.[26] In addition, the Ontario government has requested that the LCO make recommendations with respect to increasing accessibility for adults with developmental and related disabilities to the federal Registered Disability Savings Plan programme.[27]

Two of the large projects have been somewhat innovative; these are two frameworks for law, policy and practice composed of principles, steps in applying the principles and questions to assist in doing so. One framework relates to older adults and one to persons with disabilities.[28] It is anticipated that the

---

[24] The first two projects the LCO completed were on division of pensions on marriage breakdown and the charging of fees by the alternate financial sector for cashing government cheques: see <http://www.lco-cdo.org/en/pensions> accessed 21 January 2013; <http://www.lco-cdo.org/en/content/fees-cashing-government-cheques> accessed 21 January 2013. The third small project was on joint and several liability under the Ontario Business Corporations Act; see <http://www.lco-cdo.org/en/content/joint-several-liability> accessed 21 January 2013. The LCO has also completed a larger legislative project: see the Final Report on the Modernization of the Provincial Offences Act: <http://www.lco-cdo.org/en/content/provincial-offences-act> accessed 21 January 2013. The POA is a provincial regulatory statute that governs the procedure in many different provincial statutes, from those dealing with parking and highway traffic act offences to those addressing serious environmental offences.

[25] Law Commission of Ontario: <http://www.lco-cdo.org/en/forestry-workers> accessed 21 January 2013.

[26] Law Commission of Ontario, Class Actions: <http://www.lco-cdo.org/en/class-actions> accessed 24 July 2013.

[27] Law Commission of Ontario, Capacity of Adults with Mental Disabilities and the Federal RDSP: <http://www.laco-cdo/en/rdsp> accessed 24 July 2013.

[28] *A Framework for the Law as It Affects Older Adults: Advancing the Substantive Equality of Older Persons through Law, Policy and Practice* (April 2012); and *A Framework for the Law as It Affects Persons with Disabilities: Advancing the Substantive Equality of Persons with Disabilities through Law, Policy and Practice* (September 2012). Both are available at http://www.lco-cdo.org.

frameworks can be used by government, public bodies, courts and the private sector. The final reports of both these projects include a great deal of background material, examples of how the law or a practice does or does not satisfy the principles and a lengthier example of how to apply the principles. In each case, the framework itself has been released separately and the LCO intends to produce a "plain language" version that will be easier to apply. These frameworks have been well received, with the older adults framework warranting an invitation from an advisory group member to attend a United Nations working group on older adults, and the persons with disabilities framework already being used in classrooms and by relevant groups in their own work.

The LCO has most recently completed the final report of a project that looks at ways to increase the effectiveness and responsiveness of the family law system at its entry points to Ontario's cultural and other forms of pluralism.[29] The final report of a project on precarious work and vulnerable workers, which recognizes the impact of this kind of work on the lives of workers outside the workplace, was released in the early spring of 2013.[30] These projects illustrate the difficulties with more complex projects when there is staff turnover and other delays. In each case, it was important that the LCO was able to make "new" recommendations that had not been made in other studies that have been published in the time since the project was undertaken.

The LCO has also completed a different kind of initiative: the development of law school curriculum modules on violence against women for which it received a grant from the Ontario Women's Directorate.[31] This initiative is somewhat related to the family law project and also to the LCO's relationship with Ontario law schools. The curriculum modules have been made available to the law schools and faculty members interested in using them as segments of existing (or new) courses, intensive programmes or full courses.

In 2012, the LCO Board of Governors approved what can be termed "a second generation" project that arose from the two framework projects.

---

[29] See Law Commission of Ontario, *Increasing Access to Family Justice through Comprehensive Entry Points and Inclusivity*: <http://www.lco-cdo.org/en/family-law-reform-final-report> accessed 24 July 2013.

[30] See Law Commission of Ontario, *Vulnerable Workers and Precarious Work*: <http://www.lco-cdo.org/en/ vulnerable-workers-final-report> accessed 24 July 2013.

[31] *Curriculum Modules in Ontario Law Schools: A Framework for Teaching about Violence against Women* (August 2012): <http://www.lco-cdo.org/en/violence-against-women-modules> accessed 21 January 2013.

Unlike the latter, the new project relates to a particular area of law, the law of capacity, consent and guardianship. It allows the LCO to build on expertise and relationships developed in the framework projects. We are applying the frameworks relating to older adults and to persons with disabilities to the analysis of this new area.

Commissions may have little choice but to address relatively narrowly defined legislative issues. To the extent that their project agenda is determined by references from the Attorney General, the references, especially to a small commission, are likely to be narrow. It is true, however, that a commission may limit itself to "black letter law" projects, small or large, because that is what it believes its role to be. If the resources are small and the projects narrow, there is a risk that the commission becomes little more than an arm of government, but it does not need to be and much can be accomplished even with a focus on legislation.

The types of projects a commission undertakes and its philosophy of law reform will influence the process of consultation in which it engages, as well as more general outreach and other activities.

Consultation and outreach

All commissions consult: it is the "with whom" and "how" that distinguishes them. Consultation can occur at different stages of a project and for different reasons: it may be to involve those who are likely to be affected by the project to learn about the way the law affects them and what is needed, from their perspective, to make it effective and responsive to their needs; it may be to learn from the legal community how they view the law and the problems they face in working with it to represent clients or in applying or implementing it; it may be to obtain academic or other professional expertise.

Consultation can occur at the earliest stages of a project with the goal of determining its appropriate scope: what should this project actually address? Before determining the scope of its family project, for example, the LCO held a roundtable with various participants in the family law system to learn which issues they felt needed to be addressed and issued an "options" paper with the two main options identified by most of the participants. It, as do other commissions, might engage in some preliminary consultations with a small group before preparing an initial discussion or issues paper for feedback. The LCO has now instituted a process by which small groups of experts assess potential projects to provide input on whether the matter needs to be addressed and, if so, what are the main issues, concerns and controversies before the Board makes a decision to approve the proposal or not.[32]

The LCO consults on all projects. However, smaller legislatively focused projects usually involve less consultation, and primarily (but not only) with professional experts from legal and other professions (for example, the LCO consulted with actuaries for the pension project). Larger law-in-context projects involve extensive consultation with focus groups, individual interviews, perhaps web based discussions, telephone interviews, or whatever method may permit people to respond. The LCO attempts to meet with community groups, advocates and service providers. In the disability project, staff met with 17 focus groups in five cities in Ontario, ensuring participation by racialized persons, aboriginal persons and francophones. We post all documents on our website and encourage feedback; we have also tried surveys on our website in some projects. In our older adults project, we held a day-long "stakeholder" event involving over 30 representatives of advocacy and service organizations. We recently held a symposium that highlighted both the framework projects and included a panel designed to introduce the important issues in capacity and consent, as a beginning for our current project in the area. (There were also panels addressing the relationship between academia and law reform, and the importance of inclusivity in the law reform enterprise, both of fundamental importance as to how we undertake law reform).

Because the LCO views itself as part of the community and wants to be known, we also undertake more general outreach not specifically part of a project. These are meetings across the province with professional groups, obviously including legal groups, but also of other professionals (such as engineers, for example), community groups and others. There are six law schools in Ontario and we make visits to each every 18 months or so, meeting with the deans, faculty members and students. These visits usually include meetings with community or professional groups in the same city.

The LCO's commitment to consultation in the community is pro-active to the extent it is able. Its outreach arises from the LCO's view of its relationship

---

[32] This new "small expert group" process replaces the process in the first mandate under which project proposals were reviewed by a Research Advisory Board comprising members with fixed terms, who might or might not have had subject expertise in the area of a proposal. The new system was used for the first time for the capacity and guardianship project.

with the community, that the public should be part of the law reform process and that the LCO is "of" the society and not merely "in" it. At the same time, it must maintain its independence and impartiality and too close a connection with a particular group can be as inappropriate as too close a relationship with government.

Other activities

Although the LCO organizes or takes part in conferences or symposia that relate to a particular project or projects, from time to time it will do so to meet its mandate to stimulate critical debate about the law, sometimes in conjunction with other organizations. Occasionally these events will lead to a project, as may be the case with a symposium on multidisciplinary approaches to community safety, currently in the planning stages.

The LCO has held roundtables and conferences to widen the audience exposed to the areas we are addressing in our projects. The Canadian Centre for Elder Law (CCEL), of the British Columbia Law Institute, annually holds an elder law conference; in 2010, the LCO co-organized it with CCEL when it was held in Toronto, along with the Advocacy Centre for the Elderly. Staff members have spoken at both scholarly conferences and practice-oriented events. Again, these events reflect the LCO's view that it is desirable to participate in activities outside the immediate law reform world, not only to raise its own profile but to contribute to and engage with the broader community.

Staff members have also been invited to participate in events organized by others. One example reflected the LCO's emphasis on inclusivity, a symposium addressing how to balance "competing rights" organized by the Ontario Human Rights Commission and the York Centre for Public Policy and Law, with resulting publications. Other publications have appeared in academic journals, another way of linking the LCO to the academic world and emphasizing the importance it places on scholarship, as well as on feasible recommendations. The Commission as an institution may be invited to co-host or contribute in a substantial way to a conference. It is tempting to accept such an invitation, particularly when it is relevant to the Commission's on-going or future work. However, it takes a great deal less time to say "yes" than it does to undertake the work required, and here a judicious consideration of how far resources can stretch is in order.

There are times when staff are invited to participate in events or organizations independently of their association with the LCO or only peripherally because of it.[33] They may not formally represent the LCO, but their participation should contribute to the LCO's reputation. These may be academic conferences on constitutional law, for instance. As an example of a different kind of activity, I am a member of the Friends of Community Legal Clinics, a group brought together to advise clinics about dealing with the various issues they face. The clinics also engage in law reform and they also have helped the LCO with consultations.

The Lessons of the Canadian Law Reform Enterprise

Challenges and lessons in juggling projects

Here I will refer only to two significant challenges that most law commissions face, related to timely completion of projects and staffing, and to one other more amorphous quality that is easy to mention but hard to maintain in the hurly-burly of everyday work.

Lesson one about selection of projects is that "black letter law" projects are a safe bet, while law-in-context projects are risky. Although projects that avoid multidisciplinary approaches and wide-ranging consultations may be lengthy and resource intensive (as ALRI's Civil Law Rules Project shows), they generally are easier to manage and take fewer resources. Law commissions devoting themselves to them for whatever reason are doing what is traditionally expected of law commissions. The relatively short period from the beginning of the LCO's work to when it needed to address renewal of its founding agreement affected the nature and number of its projects.[34] It considered it important to show that it had the capacity to undertake both short "black letter" and broader projects in different areas of the law. In the event, it was able to

---

[33] The Executive Director and other staff of LCO have participated in domestic and international law reform conferences to talk about law reform. This is true, too, of the Executive Director and staff at ALRI.

[34] Although the parties to the Founding Agreement dated it 1 January 2007 to 31 December 2011, for a five-year mandate, they did not sign it until June 2007 and the LCO was not actually "launched" until September 2007. Project work began when the Staff Lawyer joined in February 2008. The LCO was renewed for a further five-year term beginning January 2012.

show that it could complete projects (and indeed, have government take up its recommendations, specifically in the division of pensions final report), and that it could make progress on larger, more complex projects, even though it could not complete them. The LCO began, as it hoped to continue, with this approach to project selection, and this has now become part of how it is defined. Nevertheless, there is no gainsaying that the larger, complex projects can be challenging and can take several years to complete. This requires understanding by funders and a plan that permits the law reform body to show that it is progressing with outputs of various kinds, whether consultation documents, reports to funders, or through some other mechanism.

Lesson two is that it is difficult to select staff who are able to undertake a complex law reform project with its multilayered elements and its integration of innovation and feasibility. Staff turnover can result in serious project delays. Secondments can be a wonderful resource (and in the case of the LCO, secondments of Ministry of Attorney General counsel have made a significant contribution to the work), but can result in delay when they are for a specified time and not for the duration of a project. Building in cushions to time schedules is crucial, as is matching the project with the availability and skills of the researcher responsible for it.

Lesson three, related in part to the first two, is that law reform agencies need to be nimble. Ministers change, governments change, members of the agency's governing board will change, new staff will join, and other actors will undertake work in the same area as a law reform project. All of these can affect the progress of projects or require a shift in focus. The trick for law reform commissions is to maintain consistency while continuing to distinguish itself, to maintain ongoing relationships, even while it develops new ones, orienting new members to the commission's methods, yet benefitting from the new ideas they may bring.

What form consultation?

Consultation can be relatively easy or it can be a bit "messy" and costly. From the beginning, the LCO has said that widespread consultation is crucial to its work, particularly in the law in context projects.[35] We are continuing that

---

[35] One might argue that pro-active consultation among community groups should be conducted in all projects, but this is not feasible.

practice, agreeing with Neave that consultation contributes to the development of civil society, and of democracy, because it involves citizens in the law reform process.[36]

Consultation also serves several other functions, most obviously learning how the law affects particular members of society; what might be required for the law to be effective; and to obtain the views of experts or those who argue about (lawyers or paralegals) or apply the law (administrators, judges and tribunal adjudicators). Consultation or feedback on documents may correct errors or indicate an issue that should have been addressed, but was not; it may help develop support for the final recommendations[37] and even promote lobbying by those who wish to see the recommendations implemented. Some of this can be ascertained through the feedback to distributed and posted documents, but some is difficult without personal contact.

For commissions with few resources, widespread pro-active consultations are not feasible; they must rely on technological means of promoting a public response to discussion papers or interim reports. For commissions whose commitment is to "black letter law" projects but which do have sufficient resources, there might be pro-active consultations with experts or representative groups. Regardless, the days are long gone when law reform bodies can be insular, not only because, in many places, modern scholarship and government practices recognize the need to hear from those affected by the law, but for "public relations" purposes (as discussed in the next section). An important lesson of law reform, however, is that this is no guarantee of continued funding, as the experience of the LCC shows.

As indicated above, the LCO's extensive in person consultations involve travel and related expenses to different parts of Ontario for the staff involved, and travel costs for those coming from outlying areas; venue costs; accommodation; honoraria for some participants; and specialized facilitators when necessary, such as interpreters for the deaf or personal attendants or persons

---

[36] Marcia Neave, "The Ethics of Law Reform" (11 August 2004) <http://www.law-reform.vic.gov.au/wps/wcm/connect/Law+Reform/Home/Newsroom/Speeches/LAWREFORM+Ethics+of+Law+Reform+speech> accessed 23 October 2011.

[37] David Weisbrot, "What's the Value of a Full time Standing Law Reform Commission?", paper presented at the Australasian Law Reform Agencies Conference (ALRAC), 20 June 2002, cited in Patricia Hughes, "Law Commissions and Access to Justice: What Justice Should We Be Talking About?" (2008) 46 *Osgoode Hall Law Journal* 774, 799.

from particular language communities. They are resource intensive, both in organizing them and in implementation.

The other major factor to consider is raising expectations, and this applies to general outreach and project-related consultations. Extensive outreach to promote the LCO's profile has to be tempered by the reality that the LCO can undertake only a very limited number of projects, for example. The Commission must be clear that not all views will be reflected in recommendations. In project-related consultations, there may well be disagreements about how to address an issue, defining what really matters or what the impact of recommendations will be. In this, the law reform body must stand apart from the fray and make recommendations based on evidence and its best understanding of an issue, gained from several sources.

The expectations associated with so-called "consultation" have changed a great deal over the past few years in some academic quarters and communities. Action research involves both the researchers and the community at the heart of the study as peers in the process.[38] Community participants may act as facilitators because they know the community better than do the academic researchers, or because members of the community are more likely to respond to them or for reasons of language.[39] Action research explicitly integrates the concept of critical reflection in its process, meaning that later stages of the research benefit from the lessons learned from earlier stages.[40] Many communities,

---

[38] "Action research" is also referred to by many other names, including participatory research. It refers to a process that combines systematic study of the problem and the involvement of those affected by it as partners in the process, including helping to define the problem and the approach: see, for example, Rory O'Brien, "An Overview of the Methodological Approach of Action Research" (1998) <http://www.web.ca/robrien/papers/arfinal.html#_Toc26184651> accessed 21 January 2013. It has been used in the education context, and in this context, there is a journal devoted to this practice: The Canadian Journal of Action Research <http://cjar.nipissingu.ca/index.php/cjar> accessed 21 January 2013. As the CJAR's website explains, "To some, action research signifies individual, reflective practice; to others, group empowerment. Action researchers use it as a means of professional development, curriculum reform, and even democratic institutional change. Regardless of the reason, the shared goal of all these approaches would appear to be the mending of the rift between the researcher and the practitioner."

[39] Bob Dick (1997), *Participative Processes* <http://www.scu.edu.au/schools/gcm/ar/arp/partproc.html> accessed 28 October 2011.

[40] B Dick (2000), *A Beginner's Guide to Action Research* <http://www.scu.edu.au/schools/gcm/ar/arp/guide.html> accessed 28 October 2011.

therefore, now expect to have a decision-making role in deciding what will be studied and what the recommendations will be.[41] The approach is based on the premise that the project should benefit the community in a way that has been defined by the community.[42]

Notions of self-reflection, or "reflexive practice", are quite consistent with law reform work. Law reform bodies should try to sit back from time to time to assess what they are doing, why they are doing it and whether they should continue to do so. What new processes of consultation should they be employing? Exactly how are they interacting with those who are affected by the law they are studying? To what extent have they fallen into "bad habits" of various kinds? However, other aspects of action or participatory research are not compatible with law reform by independent and "impartial" law reform bodies.[43] Specifically, these aspects relate to the involvement of the community in designing the problem and in determining the recommendations. Community members should no more have authority over the recommendations than should government. The views of others, including communities and government, play a major role in shaping the project and the recommendations because they can inform how these will play out "on the ground" or in practice; however, the nature of the recommendations will be the law commission's decision.[44] Yet, as this pattern of research develops, the expectations surrounding it may well extend to bodies such as law reform agencies.

The lesson here is that law commissions should be self-reflective and capable of change, but they must also retain the integrity of their mandate.

---

[41] Brenda Roche, "New Directions in Community-Based Research" (Wellesley Institute, 2008) 2.

[42] Maritime Centre 4 Excellence in Women's Health, "Community-Based Research Ethics", *Moving Towards Women's Health* (October 2000).

[43] I have placed quotation marks around "impartial" because law reform bodies do not act on behalf of a particular group; their recommendations should be their own best understanding of an effective way to address a problem. However, law commission staff and governing boards, as judges, are not insulated from what goes on around them and may have a predisposition to improving the situation for disadvantaged groups, for example.

[44] See Patricia Hughes, "Competing Rights Policy: The Law Commission of Ontario Approach" (2010) 8 *Canadian Diversity* 54 (where I discuss the challenges of the LCO's consultation process).

Necessary and helpful relationships

There are many relationships that a commission is required to satisfy. The most significant is with government, but they may also be with diverse communities and with other commissions.

The relationship a commission has with government is crucial to its success and very likely to its existence. Every commission struggles to maintain independence while responding to government expectations, many of which may be communicated "behind the scenes" and indirectly. Even where the commission receives referrals from government there is no guarantee that government will implement its recommendations. By the time reports are released, the government's agenda and even the government itself may have changed. Or the government may simply not accept the commission's recommendations. There are many reasons why recommendations do not come to fruition or come to fruition only at a much later date. Nevertheless, the agency does well to maintain an ongoing relationship, discussing its research agenda, being aware of the government's own initiatives (to the extent it can) and otherwise maintaining regular contact. Knowing what the government is doing or planning and how it affects the commission's work (the direction of a project, for example) is at least helpful. There is no magic solution other than ongoing dialogue and ensuring that the commission does not exist in isolation, that it has "friends" who support it and will speak for it. Most commissions have only one government to consider, but the issue can obviously be compounded when there is more than one.

It is worth noting, perhaps, that the LCO's relationship with government is somewhat different from that of many commissions (although similar to that of some other Canadian commissions). Since it is not created by statute, government does not have a formal referral power, and there is no provision for reporting to the Attorney General or for the Attorney General to table reports in the legislature (or to explain to the legislature how it is responding to the report). The LCO releases its reports itself and is not reliant on government's doing so.

In the LCO's case, the relationship with the community means releasing all documents in both English and French, since Ontario is meant to be a bilingual/bicultural jurisdiction. In reality, the LCO operates in English and translates its documents (and website) into French. This is costly and was not adequately accounted for in the initial budget. The LCO has now looked into different ways to reduce the cost. More difficult is oral communication with members of the francophone community at large and with lawyers, the French-language law school and the francophone media. The small size of the LCO and the difficulty of finding bilingual staff with the requisite combination of other relevant skills makes the objective of operating in both official languages a challenge. We have also been less effective in involving francophone groups in consultations than we need to be, despite our efforts and ensuring that there are French speakers in attendance.

While some communities are eager to be involved in law reform, others are less so, no doubt because of previous experiences. I have mentioned, for example, the francophone community, its reluctance likely related to the LCO's own limitations. The LCO has also had mixed success in developing relationships with aboriginal communities in Ontario. The lesson here is that there is no reason anyone should necessarily respond to a law commission's overtures and that it should expect to prove its bona fides. In part, to assist it in "making connections", the LCO has created a community council, with members from diverse communities, as well as those with professional expertise. Here we have learned to be realistic about what can be achieved, to begin slowly and to maintain ongoing efforts, a lesson that can be learned about many aspects of law reform.

The relationship with other commissions can run from conducting joint projects to assisting each other with ideas on how to carry out projects, how to work with government, and so on. ALRI, as the "senior" Canadian commission, has been very helpful to other commissions. The western commissions have undertaken one joint project, but generally efforts to do so have not been successful. The commissions work differently, have different resources, operate on different timelines and have different relationships to their governments, all of which have to be managed carefully.[45]

Law commissions may be located on government premises or in law schools, for example. The commission must learn how to work with its "landlord". Both ALRI and the LCO are located in law schools, yet are not research centres but independent bodies. Universities generally are not familiar with this concept, however, and are likely to treat the commission as a unit of the university more or less like any other. The LCO's arrangement with York University, which has significant advantages for the LCO, has been

---

[45] See further Chapter 13 (Tilbury).

complicated by York's (not surprising) assumption that the LCO is a "unit". As with much else in life, the lesson is that the nature of the relationship should have been determined more clearly at the beginning.

Some Canadian law reform bodies have explicit relationships with the province's law schools. All six Ontario law schools are parties to the agreement creating the LCO, although one, Osgoode, has a quite different relationship from the others, since it provides funding, space and other in-kind assistance. It is necessary, therefore, for the LCO to maintain ongoing relationships with six different entities, a process assisted by representatives from all the law schools who form a group whose "tasks" are reflected in their name, the Law School Research and Liaison Group.

Finally, I include under this heading the ensuring that interactions with others, no matter how they occur, are meaningful and reflect the LCO's mission of advancing access to justice. The LCO has made accommodations, such as closed captioning and ASL/LSQ,[46] to name only two, that are central to consultations. For ongoing accommodations, the costs can be significant and need to be treated as an integral part of operating a commission today.

Post-report: what is a commission to do?

It can be frustrating for a commission (and the person or persons responsible for producing a report) when the government ignores it. How active should a commission be about promoting its recommendations to government? There are different views about where a commission should fall on a continuum from lobbying to passivity. The LCO does not lobby. It considers that its job is to provide advice and it is the government's to decide whether to implement it. Not "lobbying" does not mean it cannot offer itself to assist with additional work that may be required on a project or to meet with interest groups that do want to lobby the government in order to explain the report. During its first five years, the LCO had little time to follow-up its final reports. Now, however, post-release dissemination is being included as part of the initial planning, subject to development as the project progresses. The better the relationship with government, the more likely informal contacts can have an effect. As all commissions know, it may be some time before a commission sees its recommendations implemented. If the implementation matters, however, the lesson

---

[46] "Langue des signes québécoise" is French sign language.

is that repeated failures of government to respond positively to recommendations should encourage a commission to reconsider its objectives, its selection of projects or the kinds of recommendations it makes.

Claiming success

Inevitably, a commission wants to show that it is successful. Its funding relies on it, as does being able to take pride in its work and others being willing to contribute to its activities. This is particularly difficult in an age of "bean counting" and so-called "objective" measures.

Seeing the law reform agency's recommendations enacted in whole or in part or having recommendations translated into policy may seem to be the most obvious and easily measured criteria of success. Even a commission limiting itself to references from the government and "black letter law" projects cannot guarantee satisfying these criteria, however. Thus, the temptation for a commission is to give the government what it says it wants, even though the commission would not otherwise make such recommendations. To do so, however, diminishes the value of the commission as an independent and impartial body.

A broader view recognizes that law commissions play a bigger role than proposing legislative amendments and that there are other ways it can contribute consistent with its distinctive function. It is incumbent on law commissions themselves, as well as those who support them, to make these criteria an integral part of law reform discourse. For example, judges may find commission reports helpful in their decision-making or academics may use the material in their courses or to contribute to their own research. As indicated above, we know that our older adults framework has attained some currency at the international level and that the disabilities framework is being used by groups working in that area. These results need to be taken into account in considering a commission's success. It remains, though, that a law reform agency is not merely a think tank, but a body that is meant to give advice to government.

If a public profile matters (and it does not for all commissions), law reform commissions must compete for media space but, unless they release a controversial document, they are unlikely to receive a great deal of coverage in the traditional media in a large city. Access to social media is relatively easy, since these media are usually looking for content, and the LCO regularly receives references or commentary on relevant blogs. As Executive Director,

I post a blog and issue tweets on an irregular basis about the LCO's processes and work. Reports can also be posted on the websites of other organizations (ranging from law-related to community-based). Traditional media coverage is more difficult to obtain; for the LCO, there has been an increase, but in only a limited fashion to date. Furthermore, coverage can be positive or negative, and, of course, sometimes incorrect. The lesson here is that coverage can be hard to control, requiring the kind of relations with media that only a professional can develop.

A crucial measure arises from the obligation of the commission to produce work of high quality consistent with the values its Board has articulated as governing it.[47] It must, accordingly, be prepared to be assessed on both quality and consistency with its values by third parties. This is also measured indirectly by the extent to which others use the work, and to which the commission is invited to participate in the activities of others.

The last and most important lesson of the Canadian experience — and of law reform commission experience elsewhere — is perhaps this: that the commission must decide how to fulfil its mandate in a way that respects its mandate and is consistent with its resources. But equally, governments that establish law commissions as independent impartial law reform bodies must recognize that adequate resources are required, that the commission may not always give it what it wants and that ignoring its reports without serious consideration is antithetical to the reason it established the commission in the first place.

---

[47] The LCO has articulated its values, its method and its philosophy in its Strategic Plan: see <http://www.lco-cdo.org/en/strategic-plan-2012-2016> accessed 21 January 2013.

Chapter 7
Lessons from a Small University-based Law Reform Body in Australia

Kate Warner

Introduction

In the second decade of the second millennium, law reform in Australia remains a "crowded field".[1] It is by no means the exclusive domain of law reform agencies: law reform proposals emanate from Royal Commissions and other ad hoc inquiries, from parliamentary committees and specialist agencies. The website of the Australian Law Reform Commission (ALRC) lists 16 Australian law reform agencies. They include the generalist law reform agencies; independent statutory agencies such as the ALRC; ministerial law reform bodies such as the Northern Territory Law Reform Committee; and parliamentary law reform committees, such as the Victorian Parliamentary Law Reform Committee. In addition there are specialized statutory agencies, for example the Family Law Council, the Administrative Review Council and Queensland's Crime and Misconduct Commission, which have law reform functions in their particular area. Two noteworthy developments are the emergence of a new form of specialist law reform agency, namely Sentencing Advisory Councils and a new form of generalist agency, university-based law reform institutes. In this paper the birth of Sentencing Advisory Councils is first briefly considered, together with the possible implications of this development for generalist law reform bodies. More detailed consideration is then given to the university-based law

---

* I would like to thank Simon Rice, the Chair of the ACT Law Reform Advisory Council, and Helen Cockburn, Executive Officer of the TLRI, for their helpful comments on an earlier draft of this chapter.

[1] David Weisbrot, "What's the Value of a Full Time Standing Law Reform Commission?", paper presented at the Australasian Law Reform Agencies Conference, Darwin, 20 June 2002.

reform model with a particular focus on the Tasmania Law Reform Institute. Its work is described and a number of case studies and examples are used to demonstrate both its shortcomings and advantages. Despite its size and meagre financial resources, it is argued that the story of the operation of this small and lean university-based institute provides some lessons for other law reform bodies operating at a time when reform of law reform is a pressing issue and survival is a major challenge for even the most prestigious of our law reform bodies.[2]

Specialist Law Reform Agencies: Sentencing Advisory Councils

A new development in Australia is the emergence of sentencing advisory bodies, which have the functions of a specialized law reform agency as well as other functions such as public education, and gauging public opinion. They may be either statutory or non-statutory ministerial bodies. The best resourced is the Victorian Sentencing Advisory Council which was established in 2004. It has been described by its Chair as "an innovative organization performing the functions of a specialized law reform commission, bureau of statistics, sentencing guidelines panel and public education body combined".[3] Sentencing reform has been a fertile source of law reform references for generalist law reform bodies in Australia and at first it seemed likely that these bodies would take over from the generalist bodies in this area of law reform. As well as Victoria, there are now sentencing councils in New South Wales (2003), Tasmania (2010), South Australia (2012) and one is in the process of being established in the Northern Territory.[4]

The emergence of specialist sentencing law reform bodies raises two issues. The first is the risk of weakening general law reform agencies by diluting and

---

[2] Anne Susskind, "Absolutely Stretched ALRC Must Maintain Independence", *New South Wales Law Society Journal* (June 2011) 20, 20–22.

[3] Arie Freiberg, "The Victorian Sentencing Advisory Council: Incorporating Community Views into the Sentencing Process" in A Freiberg and K Gelb (eds), *Penal Populism, Sentencing Councils and Sentencing Policy* (Hawkins Press, 2008) 15.

[4] Delia Lawrie, "New Sentencing Council for the Territory", Media Release, 26 August 2011 <http://www.newsroom.nt.gov.au/index.cfm?fuseaction=print Release&ID=8535> accessed 4 July 2012.

diverting resources from them. The Victorian Sentencing Advisory Council had around 17 support staff in 2011, a similar number to the Victoria Law Reform Commission. And the Tasmanian Sentencing Advisory Council, while meagrely resourced in comparison, receives about twice the funding support from the government as does the Tasmania Law Reform Institute.[5] Recent developments suggest that the threat to generalist bodies from sentencing advisory councils has diminished. Queensland's Sentencing Advisory Council, which was established in 2010, was well-resourced and probably better resourced than the Queensland Law Reform Commission. However, following the State election in 2012, it was abolished as part of a series of funding cuts by the Liberal National Party government early in its term.[6] But the Queensland Law Reform Commission survived. The New South Wales Sentencing Council does not appear to have attracted funds away from the New South Wales Law Reform Commission and the latter has continued to receive significant sentencing references from the Attorney General.[7]

The second issue relates to the risk of compromising the independence of institutional sentencing law reform. This is not inevitable but will be a continuing challenge for the sentencing councils. It is demonstrated by the context in which the announcements relating to sentencing councils have been made in Queensland, the Northern Territory and South Australia. For example, in the Northern Territory, the Attorney General stated: "While Territory courts are the toughest in the nation, with people convicted four times more likely to go to jail than elsewhere in Australia, we understand the community has concerns about sentencing. This is why we are establishing a Sentencing Council."[8] While the Attorney General's comments may be populist media hype, it does suggest the potential for sentencing councils to be used by the government to implement a particular sentencing agenda rather than offering independent advice. In the Victorian Sentencing Advisory Council's racial

---

[5] In its first year the Sentencing Advisory Council received $150,000 plus accommodation. In comparison the TLRI has, in most years, received between $50,000 and $75,000 in cash per annum from the Government.

[6] Criminal Law Amendment Act 2012 (Qld) s 17.

[7] The New South Wales Law Reform Commission has been asked to review the Crimes (Sentencing Procedure) Act 1999 (NSW) and the two bodies have been working together on the standard non-parole periods section of the reference, see NSWLRC, *Sentencing: Interim Report on Standard Minimum Non-parole Periods* (May 2012).

[8] Lawrie (n 4).

vilification reference, the Council was asked how the sentencing legislation could be amended to make racial hatred or prejudice an aggravating factor in sentencing, rather than asking the Council the broader question of whether it should be amended, and if so, how.[9] Similarly, in the baseline-sentencing project, the Council's brief was to advise on the structure of a baseline-sentencing scheme given the government's commitment to introduce one.[10] In an area such as sentencing, which is so susceptible to populist policies, maintaining independence and avoiding co-option by governments seeking to be seen to be tough on crime will be a challenge. While it may be better to be bypassed than co-opted, reluctance to embrace a populist topic could lead to the Council losing the opportunity to argue against a punitive outcome which may in fact not be supported by informed public opinion or evidence-based research. Despite the challenges, the Victorian Sentencing Advisory Council has managed to maintain its independence.

University-based Partnership Models

There are now three university-based law reform institutes in Australia. All are modelled on the Alberta Law Reform Institute in that they are university-based and are the creatures of partnership agreements rather than statute.[11] The Alberta model has spawned another university-based law reform body in Canada, the Law Commission of Ontario, which was established in 2007 as a result of a partnership agreement between the Attorney General of Ontario, the Law Foundation of Ontario and the Law Society of Upper Canada and the Law Deans of Ontario Law Schools. It is based at Osgoode Hall Law School and is funded by the Law Foundation, the Attorney General and the Law Society.[12] This chapter will focus primarily on the longest established Australian university-based institute, the Tasmania Law Reform Institute. The reasons for its establishment and how it works in practice will be described and its operational problems and issues discussed. In assessing the strengths

---

[9] Victoria, Sentencing Advisory Council, *Sentencing for Offences Motivated by Hatred or Prejudice* (July 2009) 1.

[10] Victoria, Sentencing Advisory Council, *Baseline Sentencing* (May 2012).

[11] For a description of the Alberta model, see K Warner, "Institutional Architecture" in B Opeskin and D Weisbrot (eds), *The Promise of Law Reform* (Federation Press, 2005) 55, 62.

[12] See Chapter 6 (Hughes).

and weaknesses of the Institute, an assessment will be made of whether this is a worthwhile model for law reform or merely "cosmetic tokenism" that involves the exploitation of dedicated amateurs by a government which can claim to have a law reform body without properly resourcing it or being committed to implementing its recommendations.[13] Is it a bandaid and patchwork approach to law reform that does not deserve the epithet "reform" and a convenient receptacle for controversial issues which the government never seriously intends to implement?[14]

The Tasmania Law Reform Institute (TLRI)

The TLRI was created by an agreement between the Tasmanian government, the University of Tasmania and the Law Society in 2001. It was the brainchild of the then Dean of Law, Donald Chalmers, who was impressed by the possibilities of the Alberta model for a small jurisdiction like Tasmania which had first abolished its statutory law reform commission in 1987 and then, in 1997, allowed the legislation creating its replacement, the Law Reform Commission, to lapse. These developments between 1987 and 1997 occurred during a period when independent statutory bodies were out of fashion in Australia and elsewhere in the common law world.[15] Chalmers was a former Law Reform Commissioner and worked for a number of years to bring the agreement to establish the TLRI to fruition. The 2001 agreement was renewed in 2005 and then again at the end of 2008. The current agreement is due to expire in 2014.

The founding agreement provides for a Director, who is to be an academic member of staff of the University appointed by the Vice Chancellor, and five members, namely the Dean of the Faculty of Law and appointees of the Chief Justice, the Attorney General, the Law Society and the University Council. There is also provision for two co-opted members. The Board has co-opted an appointee of the Bar Association and a non-legal member from the community.

---

[13] Consider Chapter 2 (Kirby) and Chapter 14 (Kirby).
[14] Ibid.
[15] See further Michael Tilbury, "A History of Law Reform in Australia" in Opeskin and Weisbrot (n 11) 3; Neil Rees, "The Birth and Rebirth of Law Reform Agencies", Australasian Law Reform Agencies Conference, Vanuatu, 10–12 September 2008; Patricia Hughes, "The Importance of Developing the Law: The Part Law Commissions Can Play" (2010) 3 *Journal of Parliamentary and Political Law* 407.

The functions of the Institute are consistent with a standard list of functions for a generalist law reform body, namely to review an area of law with a view to:

(i) Modernization of the law;
(ii) Elimination of defects in the law;
(iii) Simplification of the law;
(iv) Consolidation of any laws;
(v) Repeal of laws that are obsolete or unnecessary; and
(vi) Uniformity between laws of other States and the Commonwealth.

Unlike many law reform agencies, the TLRI can accept projects from members of the public and community groups as well as from the Attorney General, Parliament, the judiciary, the Legal Aid Commission and the legal profession. It can also initiate its own projects. Proposals for projects must be in writing and presented to the Board. If considered suitable, a project plan is presented to the Board with time-lines and a budget. The Board is free to reject any proposal including the Attorney General's proposals.

The annual budget allocation from the Tasmanian government is $50,000 although there is a scope for additional allocations for specific projects. The University undertakes to provide up to $80,000 including in-kind support, which includes the provision of office space, equipment and access to library facilities. In the University's organizational structure, the TLRI is an institute within the Law Faculty and is accountable to the Dean of Law. The agreement provides that the Law Society will support the Institute by the provision of advice on research projects from the legal profession and by monetary support on a case-by-case basis. It also provides that the Law Foundation may make annual grants for the operation of the Institute and that the Institute shall investigate other funding sources from competitive grants and donations. In practice, no money has been provided by the Law Society, nor have annual grants been received from the Law Foundation. However, a number of successful grant applications for specific projects have been made to the latter.

In its twelve years of operation the TLRI has completed twenty projects, nine of which have been references from the Attorney General. Two resulted from references from the Children's Commissioner; one from the Vice Chancellor; one from a member of the public; three from the Board itself; two from law students; one from a legal practitioner and one from a Law Society committee. Many more projects have been considered but rejected by the Board, including proposals from members on topics as diverse as the correct classification of budgerigars under Tasmania's Nature Conservation Act 2002. In some cases briefing papers have been sent to the Attorney General with suggestions for change rather than the Institute's accepting a project on the topic. In 2010, for example, two proposals from members of the public (on indefeasibility of title and vicarious liability indemnity) resulted in the preparation of detailed briefing papers with recommendations for reform that were forwarded to the Attorney General.

How the Board manages to complete its work with such a small annual cash input from its partners is illustrated by the case studies considered below. First, a brief description of the other two Australian university-based bodies will be given.

The Australian Capital Territory Law Reform Advisory Council (LRAC)

The ACT Law Reform Advisory Council was established in 2009 as a collaboration between the ACT Government and the Australian National University (ANU) College of Law. Its role is to provide expert advice and recommendations to the Attorney General on terms of reference dealing with law reform matters referred to it by the Attorney General. The Council does not have the power to instigate its own inquiries, and reports are not published until they are tabled in Parliament by the Attorney General. It comprises a wide panel of expert members who are selected from time to time by the Attorney General for a period of three years. Currently there are 16 members. The chairperson is a staff member of the ANU College of Law (currently Associate Professor Simon Rice) and the Council is based at the ANU College of Law. The Council establishes a sub-committee to oversee a reference and ad hoc committees of invited members to consult on a reference. The ACT government provided $50,000 per annum as research funds for the first three years, 2009–2012, after which the terms of the agreement will be renegotiated. The government funding is used to fund part of the time of the chairperson, research assistance and the cost of an inquiry. The ANU College of Law contributes administrative and organizational support services, as well as access to the expertise of its academic staff. The Council has completed projects on suspended sentences and legal recognition of sex and gender diversity. The Attorney General has also requested the Council to inquire into the scope and operation of the Territory's anti-discrimination legislation.

An interesting facet of the Council is its links with the undergraduate program at the College of Law. The College offers a unique unit on law reform which uses discussion and case studies to examine theories and processes of law reform. This unit was the initiative of Michael Coper, the Dean of Law, and was part of a model to bring together the separate worlds of law reform and legal education.[16]

The South Australian Law Reform Institute

The South Australian Law Reform Institute was established in 2011 making it the first independent law reform body in South Australia for over 20 years. Like the TLRI, it is formed by an agreement reached between the government of South Australia, the University of Adelaide and the Law Society of South Australia. This followed lobbying for some years for the introduction of a law reform commission or institute. The Institute is based at the Adelaide Law School and the composition of its Board closely mirrors that of the TLRI. Members include the Dean of the Adelaide Law School. Its function is to conduct reviews and research on proposals from the Attorney General but it also appears to have the power to initiate its own projects. It has six projects listed on its website and published its first final report in January 2013 dealing with the modernization of evidence law to deal with new technologies.[17]

Case Studies from the TLRI

As well as explaining how the TLRI manages on such a tight budget, the case studies below also illustrate the extent to which the Institute's projects involve engagement with the community by consultation and soliciting community views. The case studies will also inform the assessment of the value of the Institute, demonstrate its strengths and weaknesses and perhaps help to inform responses to some of the questions addressed in this book.

---

[16] Michael Coper, "Law Reform and Legal Education: Uniting Separate Worlds" in Opeskin and Weisbrot (n 11) 388, 398.

[17] South Australian Law Reform Institute, *Computer says no*, IP 1 (May 2012).

The Charter of Rights project

This has been the most ambitious project undertaken by the Institute to date. It was referred to the Institute by the then Attorney General of Tasmania, Judy Jackson, in 2006.

To assist with the project an additional $50,000 was provided by the government. This funded teaching relief for one semester to allow for a staff member (Terese Henning) to focus on the project and it also helped fund research assistance and community consultations. An issues paper was released in August 2006. Widespread community consultations then took place over a four-month period involving presentations to approximately 70 groups. Four hundred responses were received to the issues paper. This easily exceeded the number of responses received in any other project — the adoption by same sex couples issues paper attracted 196 original submissions,[18] male circumcision 126 submissions, and the physical punishment of children attracted 56 submissions. A team of two to three recent graduates assisted Terese Henning with research, consultations, analysing submissions and writing up the final report. This was presented to the Attorney General in October 2007.

Given the size and scope of the project, 22 months was a respectable time frame in which to complete the final report and recommendations. Engagement of the public in the consultation process was a success. It achieved its two major purposes, namely to gain responses and feedback and to promote a sense of public ownership of the process of reform.[19] Although the recommendation for a Charter of Rights has not yet been implemented, the issue is still on the government's agenda, although current budget problems are creating an obstacle to implementation in the short term. The report has been widely praised and cited.

Sentencing

The Institute was requested to undertake this project by the Attorney General in November 2001 and further terms of reference were added in April 2002.

---

[18] There were many duplicated: 957 submissions in total were received and a petition with 45 signatures.

[19] R Atkinson, "Law Reform and Community Participation", in Opeskin and Weisbrot (n 11) 160, 166.

An issues paper was released in August 2002, covering sentencing trends, crime reduction, sentencing options, the role of victims, the role of the community, and parole. The terms of reference were again extended in December 2006 to include sentencing of sex offenders. The final report was presented to the Attorney General in June 2008. In the absence of published or easily accessible sentencing data, the data collection required for this report was an onerous undertaking. However, it was facilitated by the work of two law students in particular. Rohan Foon, an undergraduate law student, completed a supervised research project on parole and this provided valuable background material for the purpose of assessing the impact of changes to the parole legislation on sentence length. He also created a sentencing database of all Supreme Court sentences from 2001 to 2006, a task that was a necessary first step to answering the first question in the terms of reference on sentencing trends. As explained above, the founding agreement envisaged that the Institute would apply for competitive grant funding where appropriate to help finance projects. In 2002, two Board members (Warner and Henning) successfully applied for an Australian Research Council Linkage Grant to obtain funding support for a postgraduate scholarship to evaluate the use of suspended sentences in Tasmania. The successful applicant, Lorana Bartels, completed her PhD in June 2008. Her thesis included the first reconviction study of offenders in Tasmania to explore the outcomes of different sentencing options. Her research was heavily relied upon in Part 3 of the final report on sentencing options and her data was also used in various other parts of the final report.

Easements

This project was recommended by a member of the public and approved by the Board in 2007 for commencement in March 2008. The project plan required the Institute to review the current law of easements and analogous rights to determine whether it currently meets community expectations and needs. The issues paper for the project was based upon a supervised research project completed by Kirsten Murkett, an undergraduate student. A grant of $13,000 from the Law Foundation was obtained to fund a graduate research assistant to complete the project under the supervision of Lynden Griggs, a senior lecturer in the Law Faculty, who had also supervised Murkett's research. The final report was completed in 2010.

Non-therapeutic male circumcision

This project was proposed by the Commissioner for Children and accepted in February 2008. One of the reasons the Institute agreed to accept this project was that a preliminary analysis indicated that it was a suitable topic for a postgraduate research degree. The law in relation to the legality of non-therapeutic male circumcision of incapable minors is uncertain. This is a concern to medical practitioners who are requested to undertake this procedure. In addition, in the absence of a medical indication, doctors have ethical concerns about conducting the procedure, and children's rights advocates object to it on the grounds that is contrary to the rights of the child. Moreover, we had a suitable honours graduate who was both eligible for a postgraduate scholarship and willing to work on the project. Given the complexity and uncertainty of the law in this area and the interesting policy issues it raised, it was a suitable thesis topic. Warwick Marshall completed an issues paper for the Board in June 2009. Then, supported by a postgraduate scholarship, he completed his Masters thesis in early 2011. He continued to work for the Institute in 2011, writing up the final report for the Board which was published in 2012. The consultations with community groups (including doctors and the Jewish and Islamic communities) were conducted by the postgraduate student. He also analysed the 126 original submissions and a number of supplementary submissions and was engaged in an ongoing dialogue with some of the respondents to the issues paper who continued to forward information on the topic until the final report was released. At least in part on the strength of his work on the project, he was offered a number of policy jobs in the Commonwealth government.

The TLRI: Its Strengths and Weaknesses

Generalist and interdisciplinary

A desirable attribute of a modern law reform body is that it should be both generalist and interdisciplinary. Rather than confining itself to traditional "black letter law", it should embrace multi/interdisciplinary research to inform its discussion of issues and recommendations. A university-based body has the advantage of access to a broad range of disciplines. Moreover, legal academics now commonly engage in research outside narrow doctrinal issues and they frequently have cross-disciplinary expertise relevant to their field. To take two examples from the University of Tasmania's Law Faculty, criminal lawyers commonly research and write on criminology and have some quantitative and qualitative social science research skills. And specialists in biotechnology law use their legal disciplinary skills in medical law, intellectual property, privacy, and discrimination law to explore the legal, ethical and social issues in genetic technology. The TLRI has employed social science methods in a number of its projects. In the sentencing project, for example, the doctoral student working on suspended sentences combined qualitative research (interviews with judicial officers) with quantitative research methods to examine the use and effectiveness of suspended sentences.[20]

Implementation and success

While implementation of reports is regarded as a key measure of a law reform agency's success, it is also acknowledged that there are problems in measuring implementation, such as defining it (substantial or partial implementation; percentage of recommendations or percentage of reports), and issues of time intervals. Moreover, implementation is itself a narrow measure of success.[21] Nevertheless, it remains a measure that continues to be used as a means of demonstrating relevance. The TLRI has had rather limited success in terms of implementation. The same sex adoption recommendations have been implemented and the recommendations in the vendor disclosure final report were adopted in the Property Agents and Land Transaction Act 2005 (Tas) Pt 10. The Charter of Rights recommendations have not been implemented, although they are still on the government's agenda. Some of the 96 recommendations in the 2008 sentencing report have been adopted, including the establishment of a Sentencing Advisory Council and changes in relation to suspended sentences. The recommendations in the 2007 report in relation to warnings about delayed prosecution in sexual offence cases were largely implemented in the 2010 amendments to the Evidence Act 2001 (Tas), which came into effect in early

---

[20] See Lorana Bartels, *Suspended Sentences in Tasmania*, PhD thesis, University of Tasmania, 2008. This was extensively relied upon in Tasmania Law Reform Institute, *Sentencing*, Final Report No 11, 2008, particularly for the data from 151–173.

[21] For a discussion of success measures, see Brian Opeskin, "Measuring Success" in Opeskin and Weisbrot (n 11) 202, 216.

2011. In one report, following a reference from the Attorney General, which investigated the need to change the law in relation to the criminal responsibility of drivers who cause death by falling asleep at the wheel, no legislative changes were recommended although advice was given in relation to prosecutorial practice. So, in the case of five reports, at least some of the recommendations have been adopted and others remain on the agenda.

As Opeskin has explained, the multiple reasons for a government's failure to implement a law reform report do not necessarily indicate a lack of success or quality. Some reports with recommendations that are perceived to be politically unappealing have been ignored and may not be implemented, at least in the short term. Nevertheless, a report may have influence in the way it shifts popular thinking on an issue[22] or at the very least encourages debate. This is particularly the case with a law reform body that determines its own projects. It is free to undertake projects that do not necessarily accord with the agenda of the government of the day, knowing that its research and recommendations may not have an immediate impact. The recommendations in relation to the physical punishment of children are an example of this. The report recommended the abolition of the defence of domestic discipline and it attracted national and international media coverage and community debate. In time it may shift thinking. A less emotive but nevertheless controversial report examined the defence of intoxication. The Institute reviewed this area of the law because of confusion and uncertainty in the law relating to this defence and because there are three different rules depending on whether the offence is a Commonwealth or State offence, and, if a State offence, whether indictable or summary. The report's recommendations have not been implemented but at the very least there is an authoritative and clearly reasoned overview of the law, which has helped to clarify it. The Ontario Law Commission's founding agreement includes as a function the stimulation of critical debate about the law and the promotion of scholarly research. While this is not explicit in the TLRI's agreement, it is an accepted role of the Institute and is particularly apposite for a university-based law reform body. This function is well illustrated by the TLRI's current project on same sex marriage. In this instance, the Institute has undertaken to produce a discussion paper outlining the constitutional and legal issues to inform debate rather than to make recommendations.

---

[22] Ibid.

Timeliness

Timeliness is a real problem for the TLRI. Some projects have taken too long to complete. It is a real problem for law reform agencies that lack a reasonable complement of full-time staff, including full-time commissioners. Relying on part-time volunteers inevitably means that there are delays. The problem is accentuated if the person primarily responsible for drafting a paper is trying to fit this in with other commitments. Even if there are paid, full-time experienced research officers, problems can arise when the person supervising or overseeing the project is part-time or primarily employed in some other capacity. Academics can be overwhelmed by teaching and other research commitments causing delays in providing feedback. Judicial officers and other board members can hold up projects when they are unable to devote time to reviewing drafts. In a quickly changing area of the law, such delays can create the need for updating research thus exacerbating delays. This is illustrated by one of the TLRI's recent projects on tendency and coincidence evidence in sexual offence cases with multiple complainants. This project was proposed to the Board of the Institute by the sole judicial member on the Board. He was concerned that applications for separate trials in sexual offence cases were leading to the necessity for complainants to give their evidence a number of times. The project was accepted by the Board in November 2006 and the issues paper was released in September 2009. A draft final report was ready for the Board's consideration in early 2011. While there was no dearth of expertise in evidence law on the Board, which included a well-published evidence scholar, a backlog of judgments and cases in the Supreme Court meant that the judicial member who proposed the project was not able to focus on reviewing the final report for publication. His "paid-work" properly took priority. In the meantime, the survey of trials used to demonstrate the nature of the problem became dated and had to be revised. There was a danger that the very capable post-doctoral legal officer who was primarily responsible for drafting the report would be unable to see the project through to completion. The final report was released in February 2012.

Consultative

Weisbrot has observed that "a deep commitment to undertaking extensive community consultation as an essential part of research and policy development is the sine qua non of a law reform commission".[23] The fact that law reform bodies are independent of government is what sets the consultation process apart from community consultations conducted by governments. It provides a level of confidence, which is essential to achieving wide community input. While the nature and extent of community engagement depends upon the subject matter of the reference, it is no longer considered enough for a law reform body to publish a discussion or issues paper, schedule a public hearing or two and wait for the submissions to flow in. Greater creativity is expected. Weisbrot recommends carefully crafting a consultation program appropriate to the particular project, which might include use of the mass media, surveys, telephone hotlines, public opinion polling and focus groups.[24] Interactive social media such as Facebook and Twitter are now used as part of community consultations by some law reform bodies.[25]

The TLRI has primarily relied upon releasing an issues paper, together with a press release and media interviews, and circulating the paper to individuals and groups who are likely to be interested in the topic to solicit responses. This has been supplemented by consultations and presentations. Occasionally talkback radio has been used. In the case of the Charter of Rights project the TLRI consulted widely and intensively over a four-month period at some 70 community meetings, presentations, consultations and government briefing sessions. A Human Rights Community Consultation Committee was established to assist in the consultation process and interstate and local human rights experts assisted with both consultations and advice. In addition to the issues paper, which was reprinted a number of times, a brochure was also published briefly outlining the issues to be considered. While developments in online media present creative and intensive ways for the consultation process to be carried out by law reform bodies, they can be beyond the reach of the small under-resourced agencies.

Concluding Comments

In determining an appropriate model for a law reform body, local conditions are of fundamental importance. For many jurisdictions the model of a properly

---

[23] David Weisbrot, "The Future for Institutional Law Reform" in Opeskin and Weisbrot (n 11) 32.
[24] Ibid.
[25] See the web site of the Victorian Sentencing Advisory Council.

resourced, permanent, statutory full-time body is not something a government is willing or able to support, at least as the sole financial contributor. Tilbury has described the TLRI as an "interesting experiment with new law reform machinery".[26] Twelve years after its creation it is appropriate to reflect on the effectiveness of this experiment. Although modelled on the Alberta Law Reform Institute (ALRI), the TLRI and the other two Australian university-based institutes are very much poor cousins of their Canadian counterparts. The two Canadian university-based bodies are full-time models with permanent research staff. The ALRI has from five to ten full-time "counsel" in addition to its Director and support staff. It receives funding from the Department of Justice and the Law Foundation as well as in-kind contributions from the University of Alberta. The Ontario Law Institute has two to three full-time research lawyers in addition to the Executive Director and administrative support staff. It also has the benefits of secondments (scholars or counsel-in-residence). It receives funding from its four partners.

Neither the TLRI, nor the ACT LRAC, nor the South Australian Institute has a full-time in-house research capacity. And yet the TLRI has managed to complete 18 projects in twelve years. As a university-based institute it has the benefit of easy access to academic staff for advice, assistance and supervision, excellent library resources, physical space and a stimulating work environment. These are not the only advantages. While the lack of permanent full-time researchers is a deficiency and timeliness is a problem, both academics and students can benefit from having a law reform body based at their institution. Academics have the capacity to engage in major research, and this is increasingly expected and encouraged. But in many cases they do not have the ear of government that engaging in a law reform project provides. Having a law reform body based in a law school also provides an opportunity for instilling a law reform ethos into the curriculum. This can be done explicitly by making a law reform unit available to students, as is the case at the ANU College of Law. But it can also be achieved by adopting a law reform focus in individual courses and giving consideration to how the functions of the law in a particular area might be better served.[27] As Coper argues:[28]

---

[26] Tilbury (n 15) 16.
[27] Coper (n 16) 398.
[28] Ibid, 400.

> [A] focus on law reform and social justice is consistent with the traditional role of a university in asking questions, submitting dogma to scrutiny, and exposing alternatives. The small step from a critical perspective to thinking about a constructive case for change, and the positive mindset that this encourages, has vast potential to provide lawyers, throughout their careers, with a wonderful pathway to add value to the society they serve.

The TLRI has provided many students with the opportunity to be directly engaged in law reform. As a prerequisite for honours, students are required to enrol in a supervised research project. Additionally, students enrolled in the law review unit are also required to do a research project which can be law reform based. The TLRI's projects or potential projects have provided research topics for students. Two projects have been initiated by students and adopted by the Board. At the same time the Institute has benefited from the students' research. The Institute has also benefited greatly from the work of postgraduate students, as described in the case studies on sentencing and circumcision. And the Institute has provided temporary research positions for recent graduates, giving them valuable employment experience for the future.

There are, however, some disadvantages in a university-based model, particularly one that is insufficiently resourced to employ permanent full-time research staff. While academics are often able to spend more time drafting and supervising papers than practitioners because it is at least in some degree part of their job, there are competing demands. Research quality exercises (such as ERA 2010 and ERA 2012 in Australia) have meant that research outputs are carefully audited and classified. Outputs such as refereed journal articles and research books are highly valued. While there is now the ability to record law reform publications, such as issues papers and final reports, as "non-traditional research output" under the sub-heading "original creative works" they have an inferior status, although they can also be used in assessing research impact. However, in the competitive world of research quality assessment, which determines the status of a law school and its funding, it is inevitable that less priority will be given to law reform publications. Timeliness of output is therefore a problem. Large-scale reviews such as the comprehensive reviews of the criminal and civil justice systems undertaken by the Law Reform Commission of Western Australia are not possible. The inability of a small institute to meet the community's and stakeholders' expectations, not just in relation to timeliness but also in its capacity to widely consult in creative ways, can give rise to criticism which detracts from the standing and authority of the body.

There is also the real possibility that without a great financial stake in its performance, a poorly resourced university-based law reform body is simply "cosmetic tokenism" and a convenient receptacle for controversial issues that the government wishes to pigeonhole. With this in mind, it is important that such bodies remain relevant and, to some extent at least, "implementation minded" in their choice of projects. A balance is needed. It is appropriate to adopt some projects that are not on the government's own law reform agenda and to make recommendations that may not have an impact until some time in the future. The two projects the TLRI accepted from the Children's Commissioners provide examples: physical punishment of children and male circumcision. Whether or not the government accepts the recommendations in these reports, the Institute has performed the important function of promoting scholarly research and stimulating critical debate on these topics. The final report on intoxication is another example. It has not been implemented but has an independent and enduring value as an authoritative text on the law of intoxication. The Charter of Rights report is also a first class piece of scholarship which has done much to win respect for the TLRI. It has laid the groundwork for the adoption of a Charter of Rights in Tasmania. Producing high quality research and independent advice to the government is something that the TLRI has successfully done. It has also produced reports that have stimulated debate on controversial issues. At the same time, if it is to remain relevant as an agent of change, it must couple its high quality scholarship with a degree of pragmatism and accept a range of projects, and to this end it is important that the government's interest in a proposed project is a factor in project selection.

Despite the size and meagre resources of the TLRI there are some valuable lessons to be learnt from its first twelve years. The most important relates to the benefits of being based in a law school. The advantages of having excellent research staff cannot be underestimated. A law school has the advantage of a ready supply of not only academics with a broad range of expertise capable of providing advice and counsel, but also experienced supervisors. Research training can be provided to undergraduate and postgraduate students and there is a congenial and stimulating environment for postgraduate and postdoctoral researchers. The benefits of this research training are not all one way. The reform body, students and staff can all benefit. Reform projects can provide a worthwhile and interesting project for students and also stimulate research ideas among academics. The competing demands on academics in the university research environment mentioned above are real. However, the TLRI, at least, has benefited greatly from the admittedly small number of academics who have been prepared to assist in the work of the Institute. Hosting a law reform institute also has the potential of instilling a law reform ethos into legal education, and the fact that it is resourced by a number of partners who have an interest in its continued existence provides some security against the prospects of decimation or demise which seem an ever present risk for standing law reform commissions.

Part C

Law Reform in Diverse Contexts

Chapter 8
Tortoise in Coma: Reform of Hong Kong's Insolvency Law

Ludwig Ng

Professor Charles Booth, an insolvency law expert, graphically described the reform of insolvency law in Hong Kong and China as a race between two tortoises.[1] In November 2006, when he was able to declare that the China tortoise had finally reached its goal, he said that the Hong Kong tortoise "if not dead . . . is in the midst of a long-term stupor." Fast-forward six years and where is the Hong Kong tortoise? Answer: it is still in a coma.

Reform in the 1990s

Rewind twenty years to the 1990s and one would not say that reform of Hong Kong insolvency law is a tortoise, at least not one in a coma. In September 1990, the then Attorney General and Chief Justice referred the topics of individual bankruptcy and winding-up provisions of the Companies Ordinance (Cap 32) to the Hong Kong Law Reform Commission (HKLRC).[2] The reference specifically mentions that the review should take "into account existing and proposed legislation in other jurisdictions, and in particular the UK Insolvency Act 1986 and Chapter 11 of the U.S. Bankruptcy Code" and that the HKLRC was required to "submit an early interim report on . . . any other aspects of insolvency law or practice which the Commission considers should be introduced in advance of the Commission's final report". It is

---

[1] Charles Booth, "The Race of Two Tortoises: Insolvency Law Reform in Hong Kong and China" 2(2) *ABA China Law Reporter* 3, 3.
[2] The HKLRC's terms of reference provide that it "considers such reforms of the laws of Hong Kong as may be referred to it by the Attorney General or the Chief Justice". See Law Reform Commission of Hong Kong, *Report on Bankruptcy* (Government Printer, May 1995) 3 <http://www.hkreform.gov.hk/en/docs/rbankrupt-e.pdf>.

apparent that a sense of urgency in regard to corporate rescue was already felt at the time of the reference. At that time, the Bankruptcy Ordinance (Cap 6) of Hong Kong was basically a copy of the UK Bankruptcy Act 1914, which, in 1986, was replaced by the Insolvency Act 1986; whereas the Companies Ordinance was based largely on the UK Companies Act 1948.

At that time, the Standing Committee on Company Law Reform (SCCLR), a committee under the Companies Registry, was already in existence. There was no logical reason why the corporate insolvency law review was not referred to it. It was possibly because the government preferred to have one body consider both individual and corporate insolvency law, and the SCCLR was not considered to be suitable to deal with individual insolvency law.[3]

As a result of the hard work of the sub-committee, chaired by Professor Edward Tyler and with Mr Jeremy Glen, a senior officer seconded to the HKLRC from the Official Receiver's Office, as secretary, a report on individual bankruptcy was published in May 1995.[4] The report recommended fundamental changes to the then bankruptcy law of Hong Kong, including the abolition of the ancient concept of "act of bankruptcy", the four years automatic discharge mechanism and the introduction of the procedure of individual voluntary arrangement. Legislation was quickly drafted and the Bankruptcy (Amendment) Ordinance was duly enacted in December 1996 and came into operation in April 1998, just in time for the Asian Financial Crisis!

The benefits of a modernized bankruptcy law can hardly be overstated. Before the reform, bankruptcy was, in the great majority of cases, a life sentence.[5] Now bankrupts could turn over a new leaf after four years. Also, tens of thousands of people were saved from bankruptcy due to the newly available procedure of individual voluntary arrangement, greatly benefiting both debtors and creditors.[6] It could be said that the Bankruptcy (Amendment) Ordinance is the crowning achievement of the HKLRC. No other piece of substantial legislation, either before or after 1997, has ever been enacted so swiftly following

---

[3] The SCCLR was established in 1984 and its terms of reference include: "To advise the Financial Secretary on amendments to the Companies Ordinance as and when experience shows them to be necessary."

[4] *Report on Bankruptcy* (n 2).

[5] Ibid 156.

[6] Up to July 2011, around 17,000 people have entered into approved individual voluntary arrangements. See statistics of the Official Receiver's Office at: <http://www.oro.gov.hk/eng/stat/stat.htm> accessed 4 July 2012.

a report from the HKLRC. Sadly, the fate of the other subject, corporate insolvency law, referred to the HKLRC at the same time, is completely different.

Glitches in the Reform

Before reviewing the progress of reform of corporate insolvency law, let me first mention a well-known problem unwittingly caused by the Bankruptcy (Amendment) Ordinance. One of the reforms contained in the Ordinance is the replacement of the concept of "fraudulent preference" by "unfair preference".[7] Under s 50 of the Bankruptcy Ordinance, a preference to an "associate", which basically means a relative of the bankrupt,[8] is presumed to be motivated by a desire to put him in a better position, and if effected within two years of bankruptcy, can be set aside. In the case of a non-associate, there is no presumption of the desire to prefer and the relevant twilight period is only six months.[9] Since at that time, the Companies Ordinance also had provisions dealing with "fraudulent preference", a consequential amendment was made to the Companies Ordinance by deeming references to "fraudulent preference" to mean "unfair preference". In a word, the provisions of "unfair preference" in the new Bankruptcy Ordinance were transplanted to the Companies Ordinance, without any thought being given to whether the concept of "associates" fits well in the corporate context. As a result, unlike the position in England,[10] the spouse of a director of the company could not be treated as an "associate" and any preference to her beyond six months from the commencement of winding-up would not be caught as an unfair preference.

In fact, there is the even more fundamental problem of whether a director could be treated as an "associate" for the purpose of the presumption of desire and extension of the twilight period to two years. A director could not be so treated if a literal interpretation were applied to the relevant sections of the Bankruptcy Ordinance.[11] It is only through a purposive interpretation of these

---

[7] Bankruptcy Ordinance s 50.
[8] Bankruptcy Ordinance s 51B.
[9] Bankruptcy Ordinance s 50(5), s 51.
[10] See Insolvency Act 1986 ss 243 and 435, which deem the spouse (and also "civil partner") of a director to be a person connected with the company.
[11] There is no specific provision in the Bankruptcy Ordinance or Companies Ordinance that deems a director to be an associate. Section 51B(4) of the Bankruptcy Ordinance deems a director to be an employee and provides that an employee is an associate.

provisions by the court that a director could be held to be an associate for the purpose of the presumption and the longer twilight period.[12] It is not impossible that such an interpretation could be overruled by a higher court in future if the relevant provisions are not amended.

Further, under s 51B(6) of the Bankruptcy Ordinance, "a company is an associate of a debtor if that debtor has control of it . . .". Applying this in the corporate context, it means that a subsidiary is an associate of the wound-up company, but the holding company is not. Hence, preference to a subsidiary, which is relatively rare, is caught, whereas preference to the holding company (or major shareholder), which is much more common, is not.[13]

The above anomalies have been clearly recognized ever since the enactment of s 266B of the Companies Ordinance in 1997.[14] It is not an overly complicated piece of law and the solution to it is already there: just adopt the relevant English provisions.[15] Yet for so many years, no legislative measure has been taken to remedy it.

The Fate of the 1999 Winding-up Provisions Report

The second part of the September 1990 reference to the HKLRC required it to report on the winding-up provisions of the Companies Ordinance. Probably appreciating that corporate rescue was in more urgent need of reform, the HKLRC first published the *Report on Corporate Rescue and Insolvent Trading* in October 1996 (the 1996 Report), then the *Report on Winding-up Provisions of the Companies Ordinance* in July 1999 (the 1999 Report). Both reports made very important proposals to reform the corporate insolvency law of Hong Kong. In the 1996 Report, reform along the lines of the English system of administration and wrongful trading was proposed. As the Companies Ordinance did not then, and does not now, contain any effective corporate rescue provisions, the 1996 Report was meant to plug a substantial gap in our corporate law. The 1999 Report is an overall review of all the provisions in the Companies Ordinance concerning winding-up and the Companies

---

However, ss 50(5) and 51(1)(b) of the Bankruptcy Ordinance provide that, for a person who is an associate merely by reason of being an employee, the presumption and the extension of the twilight period do not apply to him or her.

[12] *Re Phantom Records Ltd* [2006] HKEC 2233 [81] (Kwan J).

[13] Compare Insolvency Act 1986 (UK) s 435.

[14] Philip Smart, "Unfair Preferences", *Hong Kong Lawyer* (June 1997) 15.

[15] See n 10.

(Winding-up) Rules. It contains over 200 recommendations. Important proposals put forward include: proper funding of the Official Receiver's Office for insolvency administration; a licensing regime for professional insolvency practitioners; streamlining and unifying procedures for compulsory and voluntary liquidations; proposals to remedy the "associate" problem discussed above; and the adoption of "transactions at undervalue" provisions as in the Bankruptcy Ordinance.[16]

What happened to these two reports? In short, apart from some technical changes enacted in 2003 and 2005, none of the significant proposals in the 1999 Report were implemented. As regards the 1996 Report, the road for the tortoise has been very tortuous, it rolled over a few times and the light at the end of the tunnel is still nowhere in sight.

It is not clear why almost nothing had been done to implement the substantive recommendations of the 1999 Report up to mid-2006.[17] By then, the 1999 Report seems to have been overtaken by another bigger project — the Companies Ordinance rewrite, which was launched in mid-2006 by the Financial Services and Treasury Bureau (FSTB), the government bureau under which the Companies Registry and Official Receiver's Office, and a lot others, operate. The Companies Ordinance rewrite project is meant to be an overhaul of the whole Companies Ordinance, to modernize it to meet present day social and economic needs of our society. Broadly speaking, the project is divided into two major parts. The first concerns the "general provisions" of the Companies Ordinance: the second concerns the winding-up provisions. After rounds of consultation, the bill for the first part of the rewrite project was introduced into the Legislative Council (LegCo) in January 2011. It proceeded to the stage of examination by LegCo's Bills Committee, clause by clause, with officials from the Companies Registry, Department of Justice and FSTB. There were 909 clauses and 10 schedules to be reviewed. After more than 40 meetings of the Bills Committee, the new Companies Ordinance was passed on 12 July 2012.[18]

---

[16] Bankruptcy Ordinance s 49. Up to now, s 49 of the Bankruptcy Ordinance has had no equivalent in the Companies Ordinance. Hence, unlike the position in the UK, "transactions at undervalue" has no application in corporate insolvency.

[17] One possibility is that priority has been given to the work on the corporate rescue bill, as described in the next section, and FSTB had no more spare capacity for the winding-up provisions review.

[18] Companies Ordinance, Ord. No. 28 of 2012.

Whilst the FSTB is planning to revive the review of the winding-up provisions, it was always unlikely that legislative work for the winding-up provisions could commence before the general part was finished.

The Fate of the 1996 Corporate Rescue Report

The 1996 corporate rescue report suffered the same fate of non-implementation, though there have been two attempts to push it through the legislature, and a third attempt is now being planned. In January 2000 the Companies (Amendment) Bill 2000 was introduced mainly for implementing the recommendations of the 1996 Report. The 2000 Bill differed from the 1996 Report in an important aspect regarding employee protection. In the 1996 Report, when a company goes into provisional supervision, its employees could lodge a claim for their unpaid wages with the Protection of Wages on Insolvency Fund.[19] Under the 2000 Bill, the company had to set up a trust fund or make payment in full of wages and benefits in arrears before it could go into provisional supervision. Apparently the Bills Committee did not consider that the solution proposed by the government was acceptable and those parts of the bill concerning provisional supervision were excised as it was thought that a workable consensus could not be reached before that term of LegCo ended in July 2000.

The government came back with the Companies (Corporate Rescue) Bill in May without any significant changes on the issue of employee protection from the 2000 Bill (that is, full payment of employees' arrears of wages is still required). The debate languished until 2003, when the government proposed a cap on workers' entitlements and sought comments from the public.[20] A new proposal was presented to LegCo in 2004, but corresponding amendments to the 2001 Bill were never tabled. No workable consensus was reached and the bill lapsed again due to expiry of the then LegCo term in July 2004.[21]

---

[19] The PWIF was set up by the government in 1985 under the Protection of Wages on Insolvency Ordinance (Cap 380). It provides limited protection to employees for arrears of wages and other benefits upon insolvency of their employers.

[20] See <http://www.legco.gov.hk/yr00-01/english/bc/bc12/papers/bc12cb1-2185-1e.pdf> accessed 14 June 2011.

[21] For details of the controversies and the respective roles of LegCo and the FSTB in the failed attempts, see Edward Tyler and Angus Young, "Provisional Supervision in Hong Kong: Third Time Lucky?" (2001) 8(1) *International Corporate Rescue* 19.

Legislative initiatives were revived once more thanks to the global financial crisis, which again exposed the deficiency of the law.[22] In October 2009 the FSTB put forward another consultation paper. Nineteen questions regarding provisional supervision were put forward for comment, including one specifically on how to deal with workers' entitlements. Although the conclusions of the consultation were published in July 2010, no new bill was introduced into LegCo in 2010–2011 as promised in the consultation paper.[23] It is still unknown when the bill supposedly incorporating the consultation conclusions could be introduced into LegCo. It was not introduced before the conclusion of the previous LegCo term and as of May 2013 has yet to materialize under the new C Y Leung Administration. However, recently, FSTB began yet another consultation on legislative proposals, ending in July 2013, with a view to introducing an amendment bill in the 2014 to 2015 LegCo session.[24]

The Tortoise in Coma Syndrome

It is more than 25 years since the UK Insolvency Act 1986 was passed and 22 years since the HKLRC was asked to report on the insolvency law of Hong Kong. Yet, apart from the Bankruptcy Ordinance, there has been no progress at all on the reform of Hong Kong's corporate insolvency law. As a rough comparison, the UK Cork Report was commissioned in 1977, published in 1982, and the relevant legislation, the Insolvency Act, was enacted in 1986.[25] In Australia, the Australian Law Reform Commission Report on Corporate Insolvency was commissioned in 1983, published in 1988, and its

---

[22] FSTB, *Review of Corporate Rescue Procedure Legislative Proposals (Consultation Paper)* (Government Printer, October 2009) [1.8].

[23] Ibid [9].

[24] See FSTB, "Improvement of Corporate Insolvency Law", paper for LegCo Panel on Financial Affairs, 16 April 2013, CB(1)876/12–13(01); FSTB, *Improvement of Corporate Insolvency Law Legislative Proposals Consultation Paper*, April 2013, accessible at <www.fstb.gov.hk>.

[25] See Insolvency Law Review Committee of Great Britain, *Report of the Review Committee on Insolvency Law and Practice* (Cmnd 8558, 1982). The Cork Committee was an independent commission set up by the UK government and chaired by Sir Kenneth Cork, a renowned insolvency practitioner and Lord Mayor of London from 1978 to 1979.

major recommendations became law in 1992 in the Corporate Law Reform Act of that year.[26]

What does this tortoise story tell us about the problems of law reform in Hong Kong? Many reasons could be put forward to account for the Hong Kong tortoise syndrome. However, I would like to first rule out the suggestion that the people involved are incompetent or not working conscientiously. Quite the contrary. All the individuals I personally know who were involved in the reform process are first rate professionals or civil servants.

When a job is not done or done well with such a group of first rate professionals and civil servants, I suggest that two major factors are at play: the first is an organizational/structural problem and the second is one of resources. As mentioned above, in the UK and Australia, a dedicated commission was set up to take up the task. In Hong Kong, the HKLRC, the FSTB, the Official Receiver's Office and the Companies Registry all played a part. It is a well-known phenomenon in organizational behaviour that when the lines of responsibility are not clearly drawn, effort and resources can never be utilized effectively. A related issue is whether the tasks were assigned to the right persons. Since the publication of the 1996 and 1999 Reports, the HKLRC has no longer been involved in the reform process. The FSTB seems to have taken over the helm. With no disrespect to the FSTB officials, insolvency is not only a technical but also a fast changing subject. A reasonably intelligent non-lawyer may be able to learn it. But it is totally unrealistic to expect that he or she could lead the reform process as effectively as a practising professional or an academic of several decades' experience.

Another facet of the organizational/structural problem is that of continuity. Administrative officers of government bureaux taking leadership roles change posts every few years. LegCo has a term of four years. And, of course, no one ever attempts to synchronize LegCo terms and government officials' postings. Such instability is hardly conducive to the efficient use of resources for law reform. Substantive reforms that take more than a few years to implement become almost impossible.[27]

---

[26] See Australian Law Reform Commission, *General Insolvency Inquiry* (ALRC 45, 1988). This inquiry was chaired by Mr R W Harmer, a Commissioner of the Australian Law Reform Commission.

[27] This is an argument that leadership for substantive law reform projects should be assumed by a much strengthened Law Reform Commission.

The second problem is one of resources. I have argued elsewhere that the resources given to the HKLRC should be vastly increased so that not only could it produce better reports faster, but also it could have the resources to follow up and assist in the implementation of its reports.[28] I shall not repeat my arguments here. Suffice it to point out that at present, with its part-time membership and a secretariat of six lawyers, the mission assigned to it, namely, to "attain and maintain a reputation for excellence in law reform, both internationally and in Hong Kong"[29] seems unattainable.

Corporate insolvency law is an integral and important part of every developed economy's rules for corporate governance and regulation of economic activities. Academics and professionals are in consensus that our corporate insolvency law is in urgent need of reform. The tortoise in coma is symptomatic of the ills in our law reform process, and the position of insolvency law reform is not unique. I urge the government to devote sufficient resources to the important task of law reform.[30] I also urge the government to look into the structural problems that put the reform tortoise into a coma. Without such reform of the reform mechanism, many reform tortoises will continue to languish without making any real progress, a scene that would no doubt tarnish the good reputation of Hong Kong's legal system.

---

[28] Ludwig Ng, "Reforming Law Reform", *Hong Kong Lawyer* (December 2010) 18.

[29] See HKLRC web site: <http://www.hkreform.gov.hk/en/about/mission.htm> accessed 4 July 2012.

[30] In March 2011, the Hong Kong government decided to pay HK$6,000 to every Hong Kong citizen over the age of 18 as a way to deal with the "problem" of its budget. It lies ill in the mouth of our Government that it does not have sufficient resources to quicken our much needed reform.

Chapter 9
The Dynamics of Labour Law Reform in Hong Kong

Rick Glofcheski

Introduction

When social and economic conditions change, so do the expectations of the workforce. Processes must be in place to ensure that labour and employment law keeps abreast of the times and reflects changed conditions. At a minimum, labour law reform should be timely, transparent, and should take into account the views of stakeholders and, where possible, experience elsewhere. However, because of institutional shortcomings, including the absence of universal suffrage, a fully accountable government and a unified and effective trade union lobby capable of pushing for needed labour law reform, labour law reform in Hong Kong falls rather short of these basic requirements. Rather, it is uneven, sporadic, politicized, with the agenda ultimately in the hands of and controlled by the Administration.

This chapter will review some of the factors, forces and institutions that influence or impede labour law reform in Hong Kong. It will begin with a brief assessment of the state of Hong Kong labour law today, identifying some key areas in need of reform. This will be followed by a review of some aspects of Hong Kong's government and economy that are essential to an understanding of how labour law reform takes place or is impeded. Thereafter, consideration will be given to the influence on labour law reform of relevant institutions, structures and processes, including the role of judicial decision-making. The recent experience with the Minimum Wage Ordinance will provide a case example. It will be seen that much of Hong Kong labour law is in need of reform, but that labour law reform is a very political process, limited by Hong Kong's conservative economic philosophy as much as by its under-developed system of government. Labour law reform does take place, but when it does it is usually piece-meal, reactive, and modest, with only occasional examples of substantive reform, leaving the state of Hong Kong's labour law far behind that of most developed jurisdictions. On this assessment, any hope for real progress in substantive labour law reform, and in a more rational system of law reform, will have to wait until the introduction of universal suffrage and a more accountable government in 2017 and 2020.

Labour Law in Hong Kong

The Hong Kong government cannot be accused of having ignored labour law reform altogether. Recent years have witnessed some welcome, albeit overdue, reforms,[1] in particular a minimum wage law, in the form of the Minimum Wage Ordinance (Cap 608), enacted in 2010. Moreover, the government can point to a credible record of legislative activity over the past decade. Of 346 bills introduced since the year 2000, 30 were labour-law related.[2] However, all but three of them[3] consisted of amendments to older enactments some of which,

---

[1] See R Glofcheski and F Aslam, *Employment Law & Practice in Hong Kong* (Sweet & Maxwell Asia, 2010), Preface: "Hong Kong is and has been experiencing a particularly dynamic period in the evolution of its employment laws, triggered by a number of factors and conditions, including an increasingly impatient working population demanding more in the way of a decent quality of life . . . Important reforms to Hong Kong's statutory employment laws have been introduced in the past number of years . . . including, for example, an extensive (though not yet comprehensive) anti-discrimination package, a mandatory retirement protection scheme, improved employment protection provisions . . . criminal sanctions for non-payment of Labour Tribunal awards, extension of the coverage . . . in the compensation scheme for victims of occupational deafness, and in the biggest encroachment yet on Hong Kong's free-market philosophy . . . a general minimum wage law."

[2] See Legislative Council website at <http://legco.gov.hk/database_leg_pro/english/bills/bills.htm> accessed 19 January 2013. For a complete list of subsidiary legislation passed during the same period, much of which is employment law-related, see <http://legco.gov.hk/database_leg_pro/english/sub/subleg.htm> accessed 19 January 2013. Of 36 Bills not on the preceding list because they are currently under consideration, one of them, the Protection of Wages on Insolvency (Amendment) Bill 2011, is concerned with employment law: <http://legco.gov.hk/general/english/bills/bill1112.htm> accessed 19 January 2013.

[3] Construction Workers' Registration Ordinance (Cap 583), Race Discrimination Ordinance (Cap 602) and Minimum Wage Ordinance (Cap 608).

like the Employees' Compensation Ordinance (Cap 282)[4] and Employment Ordinance (Cap 57), were chronically in need of reform, if not overhaul or repeal. Most amendments involved the routine raising of compensation payments or fines to keep abreast of inflation. Leaving aside the Minimum Wage Ordinance and the Race Discrimination Ordinance (Cap 602),[5] enacted in 2008, Hong Kong's labour law has not been the subject of any substantive reform or even review in the past 15 years.[6] There continue to be major gaps in the statutory framework, among them working hours and overtime pay laws; rest break laws; age and sexual orientation discrimination laws; a pay equity law; employment protections for part-time workers;[7] family friendly laws such as those for paternity and parental leave; laws for the recognition of trade unions for collective bargaining purposes; and the recognition of collective bargains for legal enforcement purposes.[8] Moreover, many of the reform initiatives from earlier years have fallen rather short of their objectives, for instance in the areas of job security,[9] and protection against trade

---

[4] This Ordinance, enacted in 1953, was based on turn of the century English legislation repealed long ago in the UK, and despite much academic and judicial criticism, has never been the subject of review or substantial reform.

[5] The Ordinance is a human rights law of general application but its greatest impact is arguably in the employment setting.

[6] In fact, the period of inactivity arguably goes back further, but it was approximately 15 years ago that the Sex Discrimination Ordinance (Cap 480), Family Status Discrimination Ordinance (Cap 527), and Disability Discrimination Ordinance (Cap 487) were enacted, each of which has a significant impact in the workplace. There were also a number of initiatives of lesser impact in 1997, the year of the transfer of sovereignty see n 25 and accompanying text.

[7] In the UK, employment protections and benefits are extended to part-time workers on a pro-rata basis through the Part-time Workers (Prevention of Less Favourable Treatment) Regulations 2000 (SI 2000/1551).

[8] The pre-handover passage of such laws, sponsored by private members, was retracted immediately after the handover by the Provisional Legislative Council: see Glofcheski and Aslam (n 1) [16.046]. For a fuller account of the 1997 laws passed and repealed, see W S Chow and P Fosh, "Political and Legal Parameters for the Representation of Labour in Hong Kong" in P Fosh et al (eds), *Hong Kong Management and Labour: Change and Continuity* (Routledge, 1999) 36–38.

[9] Part VIA of the Employment Ordinance, introduced in 1997, provides very little protection and pales in comparison with the UK model which inspired it: see R Glofcheski, "Job Security Issues in a Laissez-faire Economy" in R Blanpain,

union discrimination.[10] Of the many gaps, perhaps none compares to the virtually untrammeled freedom enjoyed by employers to arrange employment so as to avoid the application of all but the basic provisions of the Employment Ordinance,[11] Hong Kong's key employment protection law.[12] On this analysis, there is a very full labour law reform agenda for any administration prepared to take it seriously.

Hong Kong Government and Economy

Labour law reform in Hong Kong cannot be understood or explained without a basic understanding of Hong Kong's economy and polity. Leaving aside the question of appropriate law reform mechanisms and processes, for law reform there must be political will, and in Hong Kong, the prevailing laissez-faire, non-interventionist and employer-friendly economic philosophy long cultivated by successive Governors and Chief Executives creates institutional resistance to any labour law reforms,[13] especially those that might be perceived

---

W Bromwich, O Rymkevich (eds) *The Modernization of Labour Law and Industrial Relations in a Comparative Perspective* (Kluwer Law International, 2009) 441–458.

[10] See generally Glofcheski (n 9).

[11] Basic entitlements include payment of wages, restrictions on deductions from wages, granting of statutory holidays, protection against anti-union discrimination, and employment protection in respect of unreasonable and unlawful dismissal. Those working under a continuous contract of employment are entitled to more extensive benefits such as rest days, paid statutory holidays, annual leave, sickness allowance, severance payment, long service payment and the like, subject to the specific longevity requirements of each.

[12] The more extensive provisions of the Employment Ordinance apply only to a continuous contract of employment, which requires that the worker must have worked for the same employer during each of the previous four weeks for at least 18 hours in each of those four weeks (known in Hong Kong as the "4–18" requirement). The Hong Kong Court of Appeal has determined, somewhat reluctantly, that the correct interpretation of the Employment Ordinance does not prohibit employers from manipulating workers' schedules in order to break the continuity or avoid the triggering of continuous employment: *Wong Man Sum v Wonderland Seafood*, [2006] HKEC 1930; *Lui Lin Kam v Nice Creation Development Ltd* [2006] 3 HKLRD 655. See further text to n 82.

[13] The *Hong Kong Government Yearbook 2010*, ch 5 (Commerce and Industry) puts it thus: "Hong Kong's continuing economic success owes much to . . . the free flow of capital . . . and the Government's firm commitment to free trade . . . the Government

as increasing operating costs and reducing Hong Kong's competitiveness.[14] The predominance of small-medium sized enterprises (SMEs) in the economy is also routinely used as justification for delaying or withholding substantial reforms on the basis of cost and competitiveness.[15] Thus, the economic and political environment is simply not conducive to major changes in labour law.[16] The recently enacted Minimum Wage Ordinance may appear to contradict this view, but that reform was an exception to, rather than an example of, the rule. A minimum wage law was resisted by the government through various tactics, including a stopgap measure under which property developers were invited to pay higher wages to cleaners and security guards.[17] And it was resisted by business, right to the bitter end.[18] The unchallenged fact remains that the

---

facilitates commerce and industry within the framework of a free market": see <http://www.yearbook.gov.hk/2010/en/pdf/E05.pdf> accessed 19 January 2013. The US-based Heritage Foundation's 2012 Index of Economic Freedom ranked Hong Kong as the world's freest economy for the 19th consecutive year: see <http://www.heritage.org/index/country/HongKong> accessed 19 January 2013.

[14] The ideological stance can be discerned from this reply by the Secretary for Education and Manpower in the 23 September 1998 Legislative Council Proceedings to a question about the introduction of a minimum wage law: "The Government has no intention of establishing a minimum wage system. This is because in a free market like Hong Kong, wage levels vary from trade to trade and from time to time depending primarily on the demand and supply of labour and the prevailing business environment. We do not consider it appropriate for the Government to interfere with the free market by setting a minimum wage for any particular trade": <http://www.legco.gov.hk/yr98–99/english/counmtg/hansard/980923fe.htm> accessed 19 January 2013.

[15] As an example see the reply of the Secretary for Labour and Welfare to a question from Legislative Council member Emily Lau about a paternity leave law: <http://www.info.gov.hk/gia/general/200810/29/ P200810290119.htm> accessed 6 March 2012.

[16] Even where enabling legislation has been put in place, there is official resistance to act: see eg *Leung Kwok Hung v The Chief Executive in Council* CACV 197/2007, where the attempt through judicial review to force the Government to enact a minimum wage under the Trade Boards Ordinance (Cap 63) (in force since 1940 and itself introduced to fulfill obligations under the Minimum Wage-Fixing Machinery Convention ILC 26 (http://www.ilo.org/ilolex/cgi-lex/convde.pl?C026)) was successfully opposed.

[17] The so-called Wage Protection Movement. For a description see 2006–07 Policy Address: <http://www.policyaddress.gov.hk/06–07/eng/p34.html> accessed 19 January 2013.

[18] See R Glofcheski, "A Minimum Wage Law for Hong Kong" (2010) 40 *Hong Kong Law Journal* 531.

government has been able to resist most calls for labour law reform in recent decades, even when it has been publicly castigated for its labour law shortcomings by the International Labour Organization (ILO).[19] Any labour law reform that might take place will be carefully vetted by the Administration and laws will only be enacted if it is politically necessary and has the approval of a sizeable portion of the business community, however reluctant that approval may be.[20] Thus, serious labour law reform in Hong Kong is infrequent, unsystematic and, as will be seen, when it occurs, it is often a response to a social crisis of one sort or another.

A related issue is the absence of universal suffrage. This may seem an obvious point, applicable to most areas of law reform in Hong Kong, but its effects are particularly felt in labour law. The absence of democratic elections means that the government is not directly accountable to the rank and file population for its policies. Moreover, the current configuration of the functional constituency seats in the Legislative Council means that most reform proposals, however generated, can easily be blocked by the business lobby.[21] What new substantive laws are enacted are often introduced only after a long period of pressure from public interest and trade union groups to which the Administration will occasionally succumb if the pressure is sufficiently persistent and publicized.[22]

The absence of universal suffrage and democratic institutions also accounts for the frequent and massive public demonstrations that take place on various

---

[19] As, for instance, in ILO CFA Case 1942 heard in 1998, concerning the repeal by the Provisional Legislative Council of pre-handover collective bargaining legislation (see n 47); and ILO CFA Case 2186 heard in 2003, concerning mass dismissal of Cathay Pacific pilots (see n 48).

[20] As for instance in the case of an old-age pension, resisted by the business community for two decades until 1995 when the government could no longer ignore the calls for its introduction, in the form of the Mandatory Provident Fund Schemes Ordinance (Cap 485); and as in the case of the Minimum Wage Ordinance: see Glofcheski (n 18).

[21] Only three of 35 functional seats are allocated to labour: see <http://legco.gov.hk/general/english/intro/about_lc.htm> accessed 19 January 2013. Another 35, a few of whom have labour affiliations, are directly elected according to geographically determined constituencies.

[22] Typically, the government then takes credit for having introduced the reform, as was the case with the Race Discrimination Ordinance in 2008 and the Minimum Wage Ordinance in 2010.

scales almost every weekend, when one labour group or another has a complaint to air or a demand to make. This is not entirely a recent trend. A review of the last 50 years reveals a pattern whereby large-scale expressions of social discontent are required before the government is prepared to introduce significant labour law reforms. The Employment Ordinance, which contains the bulk of Hong Kong's employment protections, is itself a prime example. Introduced in 1968 to replace the then dated Employment and Servants Ordinance,[23] it was a response to wide-scale, at times violent social unrest in 1966–67 triggered as much by dismal social and economic conditions in Hong Kong as by political hysteria spilling over the border from China during the period of the so-called "cultural revolution".[24] The 1997 handover also provided such an opportunity: 21 items of labour-related legislation were passed that year,[25] at a time of great social anxiety. Another example is the 1989 crisis of confidence triggered by the Tiananmen Square violence, which in turn triggered the enactment of the Hong Kong Bill of Rights Ordinance, entrenching basic human rights including equality provisions applicable to employment.[26] Yet another example, not in relation to labour law, was the government's withdrawal, in the face of a half million-strong public demonstration of protest, of its anti-sedition law proposed in 2003 pursuant to Hong Kong's obligations under Article 23 of the Basic Law. All this leads to the impression that the government will act, and the business community will withdraw its resistance, only when political stability and industrial peace are threatened.[27] This is not a situation that is conducive to long-term law reform planning or to social stability.

---

[23] Ordinance No 45 of 1902.

[24] The Employment Ordinance was merely the centrepiece of a larger body of social legislation: see J England, *Industrial Relations and Law in Hong Kong* (Oxford University Press, 1989) 13–14.

[25] Including the extension of the Occupational Safety and Health Ordinance (Cap 509) to the non-industrial sector: see *Hong Kong Government Yearbook 1997* ch 8: <http://www.yearbook.gov.hk/1997/eindex.htm> accessed 19 January 2013.

[26] Hong Kong Bill of Rights Ordinance (Cap 383). This in turn evolved into the anti-discrimination legislation of the 1990s: C Petersen, "Equality as a Human Right: The Development of Anti-Discrimination Law in Hong Kong" (1996) 34 *Columbia Journal of Transnational Law* 335, 337.

[27] See England (n 24) 196. For a summary of other key pieces of legislation enacted in the twentieth century and some of the events that triggered them, see ibid 161–164.

The Basic Law, the International Labour Organization, and International Human Rights Conventions

Labour law is a somewhat distinct form of domestic law because, its development, indeed its content, is influenced by international standards, through Hong Kong's obligations under international law, in particular, those originating in the International Labour Organization (ILO). The Basic Law recognizes the right of the Hong Kong Special Administrative Region to continue its participation in international organizations and to maintain and implement international legal obligations whether or not the People's Republic of China (PRC) participates in those organizations or comes under the same international legal obligations.[28] Article 39 of the Basic Law specifically continues in force the International Covenant on Civil and Political Rights (ICCPR), the International Covenant on Economic, Social and Cultural Rights (ICESCR), and the ILO conventions as previously applied to Hong Kong.[29]

In the past decade and a half, laws have been passed to protect against various forms of discrimination and these laws have their greatest impact in the workplace.[30] However, their genesis cannot be accounted for simply as an expression of political will, but as much, or more, on the basis of fierce lobbying from women's groups, disability groups and non-governmental organizations (NGOs) representing ethnic minorities, and from Hong Kong's obligations under international conventions. Hong Kong's obligations under the ICCPR, ICESCR, the Convention on the Elimination of Discrimination against Women (CEDAW),[31] the International Convention on the Elimination

---

[28] Basic Law Articles 152 and 153.

[29] In Hong Kong conventions are generally incorporated as law, and enforceable in the courts, only if embodied in legislation (the doctrine of transformation). However, even in the absence of legislation, where domestic law is ambiguous, there is a rebuttable presumption that the Legislative Council did not intend to legislate in breach of Hong Kong's international obligations, which arise on ratification of the convention: eg *Mok Chi Hung v Director of Immigration* [2001] 2 HKLRD 125, [11].

[30] Sex Discrimination Ordinance (Cap 480), Family Status Discrimination Ordinance (Cap 527), Disability Discrimination Ordinance (Cap 487), and Race Discrimination Ordinance (Cap 602).

[31] Once the decision was taken to ratify CEDAW, legislation in the form of the Sex Discrimination Ordinance was soon passed in order to accommodate the actual extension of CEDAW to Hong Kong in 1996. For a discussion see C Petersen and H Samuels, "The International Convention on the Elimination of All Forms of

of Racial Discrimination (ICERD)[32] and most recently the Convention on the Rights of Persons with Disabilities[33] have influenced, indeed required, the introduction of legislation that protects basic human rights such as the right to equal treatment and freedom from discrimination on the basis of sex, race, disability and family status. International obligations force a degree of labour law reform on Hong Kong whether or not it is welcomed by the stakeholders in the business lobby, or those holding political office.[34] For this reason, Hong Kong's continued participation in these and other (future) conventions is vital to the labour law reform process.[35]

ILO Conventions

The ILO is a treaty-making body concerned with the setting of labour standards throughout the world. It sets minimum labour standards that, once adopted in convention form, create obligations for its members to implement.[36] For this reason, the ILO is a potentially vital source of law reform.

Because it is not a state, Hong Kong is not a member of the ILO. However, Hong Kong is able to participate in the activities of the ILO by analogy to

---

Discrimination Against Women: A Comparison of Its Implementation and the Role of Non-Governmental Organizations in the United Kingdom and Hong Kong" (2002) 26 *Hastings International and Comparative Law Review* 1, 42.

[32] Under Article 2.1(d) each state party is obliged to pass legislation to bring racial discrimination to an end. For a discussion of how ICERD influenced the introduction of race discrimination legislation, see C Petersen, "International Norms and Domestic Law Reform: The Difficult Birth of Hong Kong's Racial Discrimination Law" (2011) 6(2) *Directions* 13. See also Chapter 10 (Petersen and Loper).

[33] For a discussion of the effects of the extension of this convention to Hong Kong, see C Petersen, "China's Ratification of the Disabilities Convention and the Implications for Hong Kong" (2008) 38 *Hong Kong Law Journal* 611.

[34] Of course, the government can take some credit for having agreed to accede to the conventions in the first place, but, as mentioned, some of these obligations were undertaken in the colonial era. Nowadays any such obligation can only be undertaken through the PRC as sovereign. This is not to say that Hong Kong has an exemplary record in following its international convention obligations. There is a lot of window-dressing and image saving at play, and some obligations are plainly ignored: see Petersen (n 33) pt IV.

[35] See further Chapter 10 (Petersen and Loper).

[36] ILO Convention adoption also creates expectations for reform: eg J Carney, "Maids Groups Cheer Global Treaty", *South China Morning Post* (18 June 2011) 1.

its former status as a Non-Metropolitan Territory.[37] By virtue of its participation, Hong Kong comes under legal obligations in regard to the standards contained in conventions ratified and extended to Hong Kong[38] and even some not ratified.[39]

Once an ILO convention is adopted by a state, the state comes under an obligation to submit the convention to the competent domestic authorities within 18 months of its adoption, for consideration for ratification. And once a convention is ratified,[40] a duty arises to implement the convention through the state's domestic legislation. So for example, provisions in the Employment Ordinance protecting against pregnancy discrimination and providing for protection against heavy or unsafe work were introduced, at least in part, in order to fulfil Hong Kong's obligations under the ILO Maternity Conventions to which it is bound. The practice of the Hong Kong government is to agree to ratification of any convention only after it has put into place the necessary compliance legislation.

The ILO also makes and publishes recommendations, greater in number than the conventions. A recommendation is often described as aspirational, designed to promote higher standards at a time when it is thought not yet ripe for adoption as a convention. A recommendation is not binding, and states can choose which recommendations to apply as being suitable for its national conditions.

---

[37] Article 35 of the ILO Constitution. ILO conventions in force in Hong Kong prior to the 1997 handover continue in force after the handover by virtue of Basic Law Article 39, and Hong Kong may continue to participate in the activities of the ILO by virtue of Basic Law Article 152.

[38] Before 1 July 1997, the government of the United Kingdom as sovereign ratified conventions on behalf of Hong Kong, while after that date, the PRC does so, after consulting the government of the HKSAR pursuant to Article 153 of the Basic Law. Currently there are 41 ILO conventions applicable in Hong Kong. For the list see Labour Department, *Annual Report 2011* <http://www.labour.gov.hk/eng/public/iprd/2011/ldtannualreport2011.html> accessed 19 January 2013.

[39] The ILO *Declaration of Fundamental Principles and Rights at Work* (1998) requires all ILO members to report on progress made in implementing the standards in eight key conventions whether or not ratified. The conventions address labour rights in four areas deemed as universal and requiring regular action by all members: freedom of association and the right to collective bargaining; forced or compulsory labour; child labour; and discrimination.

[40] Or in the case of Hong Kong, once it is extended to Hong Kong.

A state must supply reports on the progress made in the implementation of standards set by the ILO, not only on conventions that it has ratified, but also, when requested by the Governing Body, on unratified conventions and on recommendations. Reports on ratified conventions are required periodically. They are required every two years for a group of twelve key conventions concerning fundamental rights, and for others, every five years.

Ratification is not necessary in order for a convention's provisions to be adopted and followed by a state. The ILO's conventions and recommendations are influential on their own terms, and many states follow the ILO standards (or even exceed them), without ratification.[41] For instance, the introduction of Part VIA (Employment Protection) into the Employment Ordinance in 1997 appears to have been brought about as a means of complying, at least in part, with ILC 158 (Convention Concerning Termination of Employment at the Initiative of the Employer), despite the fact that the Convention has not been ratified to apply in Hong Kong. Another example is the creation of the Protection of Wages on Insolvency Fund, an insurance fund out of which unpaid workers are entitled to payment of up to four months' wages (and other termination payments, subject to a cap), which appears to have been intended to comply with ILC 173 (Protection of Workers' Claims (Employer's Insolvency) Convention). Moreover, in *Julita F Raza & Others v Chief Executive in Council & Others*[42] the Court of Appeal held that, even in the absence of local legislation of a ratified ILO convention (in that case, ILC 97 on migrant labour), "it is accepted that its application to Hong Kong as a matter of international law gives rise to legitimate expectation that might avail those in the position of the appellants who seek to pray it in aid".[43] Thus,

---

[41] "Legislators base their texts, the government its social policy, employers' organizations and trade unions their collective bargaining positions, companies their codes of conduct, and the judiciary its rulings, on the international labour organization conventions and recommendations. The intrinsic legal influence of conventions and recommendations far exceeds their actual legal force": M. Brassey, "Something New, Something Borrowed . . . Comparative Labour Law in South Africa" in C W Summers, R Blanpain and M Weiss (eds), *The Changing Face of Labour Law and Industrial Relations* (Nomos Verlagsgeschaft, 1993) 139–140.

[42] (2006) CACV 218/2005.

[43] Stock JA appeared to be prepared to go even further, saying that "it is arguable that the Convention has domestic effect to this extent, that if there is a provision in law in Hong Kong that does restrict labour rights in a manner prohibited by the Convention as applied to Hong Kong, that restriction would contravene Article 39 through that

mere participation in the ILO can produce a degree of labour law reform in Hong Kong.

This is not to suggest that incorporation of ILO standards is without controversy. For example, ILCs 87[44] and 98,[45] concerned with freedom of association, the right to organize and collective bargaining, ratified on behalf of Hong Kong during the colonial era, and continuing in force by virtue of Article 39 of the Basic Law, have not been implemented through legislation, at least not fully.[46] In particular, the Hong Kong government continues to resist the introduction of measures to encourage and promote the full development and utilization of machinery for collective bargaining, despite its having been criticized by the ILO Committee on Freedom of Association in Cases 1942[47] and 2186[48] for its failure to do so. The government takes the position that it satisfies its obligations by virtue of its educational and publicity programmes that encourage collective bargaining between employers and employees.[49]

Article's requirement that the restrictions on rights enjoyed by Hong Kong residents shall not contravene the provisions of Article 39; but it is not necessary to decide the point . . .".

[44] Freedom of Association and Protection of the Right to Organize Convention, 1948 <http://www.ilo.org/dyn/normlex/en/f?p=NORMLEXPUB:12100:0::NO:12100:P12100_INSTRUMENT_ID:312 232:NO> accessed 19 January 2013.

[45] Right to Organize and Collective Bargaining Convention, 1949 <http://www.ilo.org/dyn/normlex/en/f?p=NORMLEXPUB:12100:0::NO:12100:P12100_INSTRUMENT_ID:312 243:NO> accessed 19 January 2013.

[46] Section 21B of the Employment Ordinance represents partial compliance with ILCs 87 and 98, recognizing the right to join trade unions and participate in their activities free of the threat of dismissal. See *Campbell Richard Blakeney Williams v Cathay Pacific Airways Ltd* (2012) FACV 13/2011) for a liberal interpretation and application of s 21 (discussed at n 80).

[47] See ILO CFA Report <http://www.ilo.org/dyn/normlex/en/f?p=1000:50002:3200970768663525::NO:50002:P50002_COMPLAINT_TEXT_ID:2904422> accessed 19 January 2013.

[48] See ILO CFA Report <http://www.ilo.org/dyn/normlex/en/f?p=1000:50002:3200970768663525::NO:50002:P50002_COMPLAINT_TEXT_ID:2906947> accessed 19 January 2013.

[49] See the Hong Kong government's reply to ILO CFA Complaint 2186 brought by the International Federation of Airline Pilots' Associations in relation to the 2001 Cathay Pacific sacking of 51 airline pilots: <http://www.ilo.org/dyn/normlex/en/f?p=1000:50002:1359041365320538::NO:50002:P50002_COMPLAINT_TEXT_ID:2906958> accessed 19 January 2013.

Labour Department

The Labour Department, under the Labour and Welfare Bureau, and headed by the Commissioner for Labour, is the branch of government responsible for labour matters including the implementation of labour laws. Among its many functions it initiates and helps formulate proposals for legislative reform. The Policy Support and Strategic Planning Division under the Assistant Commissioner for Labour (Policy Support and Strategic Planning), is tasked with formulating policy and labour legislation, but its exact role and its methodology are unclear.

From various press releases and replies from the Secretary for Labour and Welfare to questions in the Legislative Council, it is evident that the Labour Department carries considerable responsibility in the law reform process: in particular, the consultation process; decisions on whom to consult and how in the study of, and comparison with, overseas laws; and in the formulation of the legislative proposal itself.[50] The government is free to consult as it likes, formally and informally, through surveys or town hall meetings, with labour groups and business forums.[51] There are limits to what a government consultation can achieve, and there is always the danger of managed consultations

---

[50] This 30 November 2011 reply by the Secretary for Labour and Welfare in response to a question in the Legislative Council about a working hours' law is typical and may provide some insight into the process: "As regards standard working hours, this is a highly complex issue. We would not underestimate its implications on employers and employees, as well as society and economy at large. Because of this, the Government will need to adopt an independent, objective and unbiased approach and conduct the policy study in a serious manner. We will conduct detailed analysis and assessment of relevant data, including the collection of statistics on the current working hours situation of our labour force in general and of various sectors of Hong Kong, so as to facilitate in-depth analysis. The findings of the study would deepen society's understanding of the topic, promote deliberation and discussion in this respect, and facilitate the building of consensus.": <http://www.lwb.gov.hk/eng/legco/30112011_2.htm> accessed 24 February 2012. For another example, this one concerning a paternity leave law, see <http://www.info.gov.hk/gia/general/200810/29/P200810290119.htm> accessed 19 January 2013.

[51] For a summary of the consultation process leading up to the introduction of the Minimum Wage Bill, see Legislative Council Brief (File Ref.: LD SMW 1–55/1/4(C)): <http://www.legco.gov.hk/yr10–11/english/subleg/ brief/145–148_brf.pdf> accessed 12 March 2012).

reaching a preferred outcome. There appears to be no interest in utilizing the services of the Law Reform Commission of Hong Kong, probably because labour law reform is considered to be too political, too sensitive for the sort of open and objective inquiry that the Law Reform Commission might undertake.[52]

Regarding international standards and Hong Kong's compliance obligations, the International Liaison Division of the Labour Department is specifically assigned to conduct research, ensure compliance with ILO standards, and to attend to reporting matters.[53] The International Liaison Division studies newly adopted conventions and recommendations, with a view to considering their implementation. This is an important organ for labour law reform purposes because, as has been seen, there is potential for labour law reform here. Hong Kong's labour law is informed by ILO standards and in some instances dictated by such standards.

Once a labour law proposal is settled within the Labour Department, the non-statutory Labour Advisory Board will be consulted for its views. Drafting instructions are eventually issued to the Department of Justice, which is responsible for technical authorship. The debate over the exact form and content of the law continues in the Legislative Council.

Labour Advisory Board

The Labour Advisory Board (LAB) is a non-statutory tri-partite body that advises the Commissioner for Labour on labour matters.[54] It consists of 12 members, six representing employers and six representing employees, with the Commissioner for Labour as chair. Of the six employee representatives, five are elected by registered employee trade unions and one is appointed. Of the six employer representatives, five are nominated by major employer associations and one is appointed. According to its terms of reference, the function of the LAB is to "advise the Commissioner for Labour on matters affecting labour, including legislation and Conventions and Recommendations of

---

[52] See further text to nn 96–98.
[53] See Labour Department *Annual Report 2011*, ch 2.9, <http://www.labour.gov.hk/eng/public/iprd/2011/ldtannualreport2011.html> accessed 19 January 2013.
[54] See generally *LAB Annual Report 2009–10* <http://www.labour.gov.hk/eng/public/dd/lab/report/2010/home/index.htm> accessed 19 January 2013.

the International Labour Organization".[55] Five committees on special subject areas have been set up under the auspices of LAB.[56] Membership on these committees is not restricted to LAB members, allowing for a wider spectrum of opinion. Noteworthy among them is the Committee on Implementation of International Labour Standards, which advises on such matters as: the declarations to be made in respect of the application of ILO conventions in Hong Kong; measures to promote the implementation of conventions or to improve the declarations in respect of conventions applied with modification in Hong Kong; and to advise on questions relating to submission of reports to the ILO.[57]

Over its history the LAB has not enjoyed the unqualified support of employees, making consultation more patchy, if not biased. Until 1980, the China-affiliated Federation of Trade Unions (FTU) refused to participate in LAB elections because of the FTU's then Communist Party sympathies and its ingrained opposition to the colonial government.[58] More recently the independent and democratically inclined Confederation of Trade Unions has expressed criticisms of, and even boycotted, LAB elections because of the potentially skewed election results produced by the electoral system of one vote per registered trade union, no matter how few members in the trade union. It is a fair criticism of the voting system, in which a seven-member trade union has the same vote as an 80,000 member trade union, running an obvious risk

---

[55] See Labour Department website, "About Us" <http://www.labour.gov.hk/eng/rbo/content1_1.htm> accessed 19 January 2013.

[56] They are: Committee on Employees' Compensation, Committee on Employment Services, Committee on Labour Relations, Committee on the Implementation of International Labour Standards, and Committee on Occupational Safety and Health: see *Annual Report 2011* (n 53).

[57] The Committee on the Implementation of International Labour Standards was set up pursuant to Hong Kong's obligations under the Tripartite Consultation (International Labour Standards) Convention (No 144), adopted by the International Labour Conference in 1976 and applied to Hong Kong with modifications in 1978. For some of its activities see ch 6 of the *Labour Advisory Report 2009–10* (the most recent published report) <http://www.labour.gov.hk/eng/public/dd/lab/report/2010/home/chapter6.htm> accessed 19 January 2013.

[58] See England (n 24) 10. In the years leading up to and since the 1997 handover the FTU has become decidedly pro-government, consistent with its Beijing-sympathetic ideology.

of manipulation, and according to its logic, discouraging the growth of large unions.[59]

The LAB *Annual Report 2011* states that the LAB "plays an important part in the formulation of labour policies and gives advice on labour legislation".[60] There can be no doubt that today it is more active than in the decades following its re-configuration in its tri-partite form in 1946, but it is doubtful that its work extends beyond its formal role as a consultative body. In summarizing its major achievements for the period 2009–10, the *Annual Report* describes the LAB as "endorsing" certain proposals, and "giving views"[61] on proposals, suggesting that it is far from being a source for law reform proposals.

Until the 1985 introduction of labour seats in the Legislative Council, the LAB was the only formal means by which labour's views would be received by the government. Today, its role is arguably overtaken to a large degree not only by the three labour functional representatives in the Legislative Council but also by the presence of a number of directly elected members who serve on, or are affiliated with, trade unions in Hong Kong. As representatives with a true electoral mandate their voices and opinions garner more attention in the media, resonate more with the public, and hence are more likely to put pressure on the government.

This is not to say that there is no role for the LAB in law reform. With fairer elections, for instance through weighted trade union voting, and more representative membership, the role of the LAB could be enhanced, its mandate could be strengthened and it could be an important source of policy and laws, taking full advantage of its expertise and specialization. As it is, new ideas come only from political thinkers and policy makers within the Administration, many of whom are likely to be more closely aligned with business than labour.

---

[59] The ILO sympathizes with this criticism, as potentially putting Hong Kong in violation of the Tripartite Consultation (International Labour Standards) Convention 1976 (ILC 144) to which it is bound: see *Comments Made by the Committee of Experts on the Application of Conventions and Recommendations 2009* <http://www.ilo.org/dyn/normlex/en/f?p=1000:13100:2865535430682342::NO:13100:P13100_COMMENT_ID:2318398> accessed 19 January 2013.

[60] *Annual Report 2011* (n 53), ch 2.1.

[61] *Annual Report 2011* (n 53), ch 3.

Trade Union Lobby

The usual function of trade unions is to bargain with employers for employment rights and protections, resorting to collective industrial action as a means of last resort to enforce the collective will at the workplace. However, a strong trade union lobby can be a major influence on law reform, and even more so in a political system in which universal suffrage is absent and democratic institutions weak. Equally, a weak trade union movement means that labour's voice will be drowned out by those with a stronger voice and with greater means and better organizational skills to lobby for their interests, in this case the industrial and business groups. In Hong Kong, the trade union movement has only recently been able to have an impact on labour law reform, and has yet to reach its potential. It has been weak throughout the post-war period, for a variety of historical, cultural and political reasons, ensuring that employers' groups have had the most influence in labour law reform.[62]

First, the trade union law, principally the Trade Union Ordinance (Cap 332), is an inherently restrictive law through which the power, growth and influence of trade unions have been, and are being, contained.[63] It requires trade unions and their union rules to be registered in order to be lawful,[64] and contains provisions that restrict the use of trade union funds[65] and the growth of larger trade union groupings.[66] It accords no recognition to trade unions for collective bargaining purposes, and does not even provide for legal recognition of collective bargains.[67] In this environment, the government and its business allies have been able to sideline labour, while maintaining general peace among the rank

---

[62] The best account is provided in England (n 24) ch 8.

[63] Described by one long-term academic commentator as "a peculiar amalgamation of nineteenth century British law and colonial paternalism with few rights for trade unions and many elements of regulation and supervision": P Fosh et al, "Government Supervision of Trade Unions" in Fosh et al (n 8) 239.

[64] Trade Union Ordinance s 5(1) and s 18(1).

[65] Trade Union Ordinance s 34.

[66] Trade Union Ordinance s 24 and ss 55–57.

[67] The Trade Union Ordinance is silent on the issue, but the courts have been clear on this point: see *Hong Kong Aircrew Officers Association v Cathay Pacific Airways Ltd* [1994] 2 HKLR 367; *Cable & Wireless (Hong Kong) Ltd Staff Association v Hong Kong Telecom International Ltd* [2001] 2 HKLRD 809. The unsatisfactory state of the law was laid bare by the ILO Committee on Freedom of Association in Case 1942 (1998) (n 47), castigating the Hong Kong government for the sorry

and file workforce through periodic offerings of minor labour law improvements in the form of regular but incremental individual entitlements in the Employment Ordinance. Despite periodic pressure as well as criticisms from ILO bodies, the government has been adamant in opposing collective rights that might strengthen the growth and influence of trade unions.[68] It is not surprising then that trade unions have difficulty in recruiting members.

Of possibly equal or greater significance is the trade union fragmentation that has persisted throughout the post-war period. This fragmentation among trade union groupings is traceable to their origins as supporters of either the Chinese Communist Party or the Kuomintang. Because of their refusal to cooperate and join forces to pursue common labour interests, the labour lobby has never been able to speak with one voice.[69] In such an environment, and given the absence of collective bargaining rights, legal enactment is all the more vital for employment protections. Moreover, given trade union fragmentation, initiatives for labour law reform come largely from within the government.[70]

There are, however, some signs to suggest that the influence of the trade union lobby is in the ascendancy. The rise of an independent trade union movement, dating from the late 1980s, in the form of the democratically inclined Hong Kong Confederation of Trade Unions, has energized the trade union lobby and has produced a number of campaigns for reform, most notably that for a minimum wage law, for the success of which that lobby can take much of the credit. Its voice is being heard regarding other issues, with efforts now being directed to a working hours and overtime law. Trade union membership

---

state of its laws following the repeal of collective bargaining laws by the Provisional Legislative Council.

[68] The pre-handover success of labour-friendly legislative councilors in strengthening collective rights through the enactment of laws recognizing trade unions and entitling them to bargain collectively was transient. The reforms were rolled back by the post-handover Provisional Legislative Council and the status quo was restored. For an account of these events, see Chow and Fosh (n 8).

[69] For most of the post-War period, the schism was between the China-sympathetic Federation of Trade Unions (FTU), and the Kuomintang-sympathetic Trade Union Council. With the emergence in the 1990s of the democratically inclined Confederation of Trade Unions, and the conversion of the FTU from its anti-colonial government stance to one of government ally, the reasons for the schism and the lack of inter-confederation cooperation have changed but the position remains the same. For the early history of this ideological schism, see England (n 24) 128–130.

[70] The same point was made by England (n 24) 163.

is again on the rise, increasing by more than 100,000 in the past five years,[71] and the ability to mobilize tens of thousands of members to weekend rallies is ensuring that an independent trade union voice is being heard. The direct election to the Legislative Council of high profile trade unionists such as Lee Cheuk Yan and Leung Yiu Chung, and labour sympathizers such as Leung Kwok Hung, in addition to the three functional constituency-elected labour members, ensures that labour-related issues are the subject of regular questioning and debate in the Council. Although it is far too early to tell, the election of C Y Leung as Chief Executive for the 2012–2017 term may have a positive impact on the promotion of law reform, given his good relations with trade unionists, at least those who are China-sympathetic.[72]

Private Members Bills

Initiation of law reform through the introduction of private members' bills was a strategy used in the pre-handover era with mixed success. A common tactic was to introduce a bill with the intention of forcing a compromise from the Administration in the form of its own, albeit somewhat watered down, version.[73] An early success of sorts was Legislative Council member Anna Wu's Equality Bill in 1993, a comprehensive anti-discrimination law that proved too ambitious for the colonial government.[74] It nonetheless won widespread attention and support and triggered the government's own package of equality laws (1995–97) covering sex, disability and family status discrimination, together with the creation of the Equal Opportunities Commission.[75] These laws have their greatest impact in employment.

In another example, labour-friendly private members introduced three important bills regarding trade union rights, mandatory collective bargaining,

---

[71] See Labour Department website Table 1 <http://www.labour.gov.hk/tc/public/pdf/rtu/ASR2011.pdf> accessed 9 March 2012.

[72] The Hong Kong Federation of Trade Unions, the largest trade union grouping, was among the first to endorse Leung's candidacy in the recent elections: see <http://www.chinadaily.com.cn/hkedition/2012-02/24/content_14680754.htm> accessed 19 January 2013.

[73] In a recent interview Lee Cheuk Yan explained the strategy and some of the successes: see <http://worldlabour.org/eng/node/292> accessed 19 January 2013.

[74] For an account of the background to the Equality Bill, see Petersen (n 26).

[75] See Petersen (n 26) 376–77.

and dismissal, all of which were passed in the weeks before the 1997 handover, only to be largely rolled back by the Provisional Legislative Council in the weeks following the handover. Some remnants of the laws were, however, retained, making this a victory of sorts for labour.[76]

Today, the achievement of labour law reform through the private members' bill process, although possible, is much less likely. Under Legislative Council procedures, "members may not either individually or jointly introduce a bill which, in the opinion of the President, relates to public expenditure or political structure or the operation of the Government";[77] and "in the case of a bill which, in the opinion of the President, relates to Government policies, the notice [of intention to present a bill] shall be accompanied by the written consent of the Chief Executive in respect of the bill".[78] Any bill intending to achieve labour law reform would inevitably be characterized as relating to government policies, and thus come within the rule. The requirement of the Chief Executive's consent effectively closes off this avenue of labour law reform. Of course, any such bill would still have to get by a vote in the business-friendly Legislative Council, all the more difficult given that the Council's voting rules require majority support of both geographical constituency members and functional constituency members for the passage of a private members' bill.[79]

The Courts and Law Reform

Leaving aside the obvious role of the courts in achieving law reform through incremental development of the common law, or progressive interpretation of statutory provisions,[80] judicial decision-making can influence statutory law

---

[76] For a summary and discussion of these, see Fosh (n 8) 36–38.
[77] Rule 51 (3) of the *Rules of Procedure of the Legislative Council of the Hong Kong Special Administrative Region* <http://legco.gov.hk/general/english/procedur/content/partk.htm#51> accessed 19 January 2013. Prior to 1997, such a bill could be introduced with the Governor's permission: see Petersen (n 26) 373–74.
[78] Article 74 of the Basic Law and Rule 51 (4) of the *Rules of Procedure of the Legislative Council of the Hong Kong Special Administrative Region* (n 77).
[79] *Rules of Procedure of the Legislative Council* (n 77) Part J, Rule 46(2).
[80] A recent noteworthy example is *Campbell Richard Blakeney Williams v Cathay Pacific Airways Ltd* (n 46) in which the Court of Final Appeal ruled that a "work-to-rule" or "contract compliance" strategy conducted by Cathay Pacific pilots fell

reform, however indirectly. For instance, this can happen where the judiciary makes a ruling that hints at the need for statutory reform. It is not uncommon to read a judicial decision in which the court reluctantly rules against the plaintiff and in doing so expresses criticism of the law, either because there is no appropriate statute, or because application of the current law leads to an unjust result. The case of *Wong Man Sum v Wonderland Seafood Restaurant*[81] provides such an example. Section 31 of the Employment Ordinance requires a continuous contract of employment for 24 months as a condition of entitlement to severance pay. It was apparent that the employer had manipulated the work schedule, using successive 18-month contracts of employment with breaks in between in order to ensure that 24 months of continuous employment was not achieved. In finding that the employer was not in breach of the Ordinance, Cheung JA said:[82]

> I for one, would very much like to see changes being introduced along the lines of the Fixed-term Employees (Prevention of Less Favourable Treatment) Regulations 2002 of the United Kingdom which implemented the European Union Directive on Fixed Term Work (1999/70/EC). The Regulations provide for, among other things, a maximum limit of four years for fixed term contracts so as to prevent the abuse of the use of successive fixed term contracts. Obviously any change in Hong Kong must cater for local conditions.

It is difficult to assess what impact such expressions of concern have in terms of law reform.[83] No examples come to mind where a judicial criticism was followed by statutory reform, but in the aggregate, such criticism is bound to have some effect on the Administration in the long term.

On yet other occasions the expression of judicial sympathy is not aimed at a particular provision but at the state of employment law generally, given its inherent skew in favour of employers and their superior bargaining power. Judges often express dissatisfaction with the statutory law, as being outdated

---

within the protection of s 21B of the Employment Ordinance as being "activities of the trade union" conducted at an "appropriate time" The pilots were found to have been dismissed for reason of their participation in trade union activities and were awarded compensation under the Employment Ordinance.

[81] [2006] HKEL 1930.

[82] Ibid [9].

[83] The Employment Ordinance provision under consideration in *Wong Man Sum v Wonderland Seafood Restaurant* remains unchanged at the time of writing.

or simply unfair. Cheung JA provides an example of this, also from the case of *Wong Man Sum v Wonderland Seafood Restaurant*:[84]

> The Employment Ordinance is clearly in the nature of social legislation. Its aim is to provide some minimum benefits to workers who, more often than not, do not have equal bargaining powers as their employers. This disparity is even more intense in Hong Kong when there is no system of collective bargaining between employers and workers' unions ... The situation is clearly unsatisfactory when employers are able to adopt devices which relieve them of their obligation towards their employees. The consequence is that a large sector of the labour force is being deprived of the entitlement intended by the legislature for their benefit. This is not conducive towards social harmony ...

A classic example in relation to the Employees' Compensation Ordinance is provided by Yuen JA in *Lau Suet Fung v Future Engineering Co*:[85]

> Regrettably, the ECO which had its origins in English statutes drafted nearly a century ago but which has since incorporated both English and local amendments, is by no means easy to follow. This is particularly regrettable when the purpose of the legislation is to provide for payment of compensation to injured employees, a class covering a wide spectrum of the community with various educational backgrounds. Their interests would be better served by a statute which is more "layman-friendly".

Another judge has spoken of the "changing social matrix" of the employment relationship,[86] and yet another that a purposive interpretation of legislation is called for in "this new social dimension, which takes into account of a modern employment relationship".[87] More recently, Stone J in the Court of Appeal disagreed with an approach that sees the Employment Ordinance as "the current high water mark of employment protection, beyond which courts should not venture."[88] Rather, in his view, the Ordinance "represents that which, for want of a better term, constitutes an 'irreducible minimum' ... I fail

---

[84] Note 81, [5]–[6].
[85] (2004) CACV 110/2003, [32].
[86] *Cheung Shuk Wah v Wong Kang Hung* [2009] 6 HKC 182, [5] (Judge Leong).
[87] *Hsu Shu Chiao v Lung Cheong Toys Ltd* [2002] 1 HKC 479 (Cheung JA).
[88] *Tadjudin v Bank of America National Association* [2010] 3 HKLRD 414, [11].

to see why its terms necessarily preclude development of the common law, if ultimately thought appropriate".[89]

In a system of government in which law reform is slow and riddled with obstacles, as Hong Kong's can be described to be, judicial pressure, and general expressions of dissatisfaction with the law, if persistent, may serve as an encouragement, if not a catalyst for law reform.

On the other hand, when judicial sympathy becomes judicial activism, it is arguable that the need for statutory labour law reform may be viewed as unnecessary, or at least less urgent. The Employees' Compensation Ordinance (ECO) may be a case in point. The ECO is an outdated system that, even when introduced in 1946, was based on the system already discarded in the UK. Its critics are legion and the criticisms diverse, focusing on the costliness of the system, and the advantages of a centrally administered system with its fewer technical hurdles, at less cost, that can deliver increased awards.[90] But reforms have never been taken up by the government. In interpreting some of its key provisions, and in particular those in section 5 which speak to the basic qualifications for entitlement to compensation, the courts have strained to ensure ample coverage through creative interpretations of what constitutes an "accident arising out of and in the course of employment", and, even more so, what constitutes a contract of service as opposed to self-employment or independent contracting.[91] In doing so, the courts have become a guardian of labour rights, tipping the balance in favour of workers in a statutory framework that otherwise favours employers, but, in the process, making the need for reform from the Administration's perspective less urgent.[92]

---

[89] Ibid [12]. See also *Chung Yuen Yee v Sam Woo Bore Pile Foundation Ltd* (2010) HCPI 1053/2006: "The wages of a worker are often calculated from his toil but the risk he suffers is seldom taken into consideration" (Yam J).

[90] See, for instance, the observations of in *Lau Suet Fung v Future Engineering Co* (text to n 85) (Yuen JA). For academic criticism see A Chen and S H Ng, *The Workers' Compensation System in Hong Kong* (Centre of Asian Studies, University of Hong Kong, 1987).

[91] See generally Glofcheski and Aslam (n 1) ch 2.

[92] Other Employment Ordinance examples from the Court of Final Appeal include *Leung Ka Lau v Hospital Authority* (unrep., FACV 22, 23/2008, [2009] HKEC 1707) (interpreting "rest day" and "public holiday"); *Kao Lee & Yip v Lau Wing* (2008) 11 HKCFAR 576 (interpreting "agreeing to pay"); and *Hong Kong Ming Wah Shipping v Sun Min* [2006] 1 HKLRD 75 (interpreting "notice of pregnancy" under

Judicial decision-making can have an effect on labour law in yet another way, where the court interprets a statutory provision in such a way that the need for statutory amendment is triggered. This can happen for instance where a court interprets a statutory provision in a way that exposes a loophole in the law or that runs against the intention of the legislature in passing the law in the first place.[93] In *Lisbeth Enterprises Ltd v Mandy Luk*,[94] the respondent was a beauty consultant employed by the defendant and was paid a basic monthly salary plus commissions based on sales. She sought to have her commission income included as wages in the calculation of her holiday and annual leave pay under the Employment Ordinance. Section 41(1) provided that "Holiday pay shall be a sum equivalent to the wages which the employee would have earned on a full working day". Section 41C(1), concerning annual leave pay, similarly refers to wages which the employee "would have earned" if she had worked every day during the period of annual leave. The Employment Ordinance, section 2(1), provided "unless the context otherwise requires . . . 'wages' . . . means all remuneration, earnings, allowances including travelling allowances and attendance allowances, attendance bonus, commission . . . capable of being expressed in terms of money, payable to an employee in respect of work done or to be done under his contract of employment . . . ". Gratuitous and discretionary commissions were excluded by section 2(2) and (3), but it was agreed that the respondent's commission was contractual. Despite the plain meaning of section 2(1), the Court of Final Appeal decided that for the purposes of calculating holiday and annual leave pay, wages would not include commissions. In other words, holiday and annual leave pay would be calculated on the basis of basic salary exclusive of commissions. The decision was made on principles of statutory interpretation, the court holding that the "context" required commissions not be included in wages for the purposes of holiday and annual leave pay entitlement because the Ordinance did not provide a formula for calculating wages that "the employee *would*

---

s 15 (1)(a). See R Glofcheski and H Y Leung, "Job Security and Entitlements within Hong Kong's Maternity Protection Legislation" (2009) 25 *International Journal of Comparative Labour Law and Industrial Relations* 327, 333.

[93] A notorious example from the House of Lords is *Barker v Corus UK Ltd* [2006] 2 AC 572. The decision to impose proportionate rather than joint and several liability on the defendants who employed the plaintiff at different times was reversed within months by the Compensation Act 2006.

[94] [2006] 1 HKLRD 1005.

have earned on a full working day" in section 41. The decision took almost everyone by surprise, including the government, and within months it enacted the Employment (Amendment) Ordinance 2007 to unambiguously include commission as wages for the purposes of holiday and annual leave pay.[95] The amendments included a mechanism, however cumbersome, to calculate wages in circumstances of variable monthly commissions.

An Environment for Law Reform?

It is evident that there is much work to be done in labour law reform in Hong Kong. Large gaps exist, and much of the statutory law in place is in need of overhaul, if not outright repeal and replacement. The current practice of tweaking through minor amendments is cumbersome, piecemeal, and fails to address basic shortcomings in the core legislation, discussed earlier in this chapter. There is an almost institutional resistance to change.

Lost in the debate is the body that is specifically tasked with the job of law reform. The Hong Kong Law Reform Commission, like its counterparts overseas, was established to provide a reform mechanism that would satisfy the requirements described in the first paragraph of this chapter.[96] However, it has never been asked to undertake a study of any area of labour law in the 32 years since its establishment.[97] Of the reports produced by the Law Reform Commission since its establishment in 1980, none pertain to labour

---

[95] The explanatory memorandum reads in part: "The main objective of the Amendment Ordinance is to ensure that all components of wages as defined under the EO (including commission and allowance . . .) are included in the calculation of relevant statutory entitlements." For a detailed explanation of the amendments triggered by *Lisbeth*, see <http://www.labour.gov.hk/eng/public/wcp/GuideEAO2007.pdf> accessed 19 January 2013.

[96] From its own website the HKLRC mission is: "to present proposals for reform which make the law in Hong Kong more effective, more accessible, and more in tune with the community's needs . . . and to engage the public in the law reform process, and to arouse public interest in that process by the dissemination of law reform material and by effective communication with the community". See further Chapter 4 (Stoker).

[97] Of the many subject areas listed on the HKLRC website, labour/employment law is not even included: see <http://www.hkreform.gov.hk/en/publications/subject.htm> accessed 19 January 2013. The *Report on the Winding Up Provisions of the Companies Ordinance* (1999), the Consultation Paper on *Interim Proposals for a Sex Offender Registry* (2008), and the *Report on Young Persons — Effects of Age in*

law. The government appears to have consciously excluded the Law Reform Commission from this process, thereby passing up the opportunity for the kind of open and objective debate about labour law that only a law reform commission can produce.[98]

In the absence of objective studies and recommendations, NGOs, trade unions, legislative councilors and other stakeholders are left to their own resources to study and argue for labour law reform, and to their own strategies, in the Legislative Council, in the courts and, increasingly, in the streets, to push for reform. The system appears to be configured to resist labour law reform, and that resistance is not easily overcome. History shows that substantial law reform will take place only if triggered by a social crisis of one sort or another,[99] or after persistent campaigning and the exertion of pressure in all forms, and then only when the need for law reform can be shown to be desperate, embarrassing for the government if it does not act.[100]

Is it possible to read the recent enactment of a minimum wage law as indicating a changed dynamic? As I have written elsewhere,[101] the enactment of the Minimum Wage Ordinance would not have occurred but for the persistence of trade unionists, NGOs and labour representatives in the Legislative Council, whose campaign dates back almost 15 years, at least to the so-called

---

Civil Law (1986) have tangential provisions concerning employment law, but the focus of the studies is elsewhere.

[98] The situation is not unique to Hong Kong. In the UK as in Hong Kong, neither employment nor labour law are included on the list of subjects for investigation, and as in Hong Kong, labour law issues are only tangentially investigated in studies that are focused on other subject areas — see <http://www.justice.gov.uk/lawcommission/a-to-z-projects.htm> accessed 19 January 2013. In Australia, the Australian Law Reform Commission lists Employment Law as one of the topics for investigation, and there is at least one employment law-related inquiry currently underway entitled Barriers to Mature-Aged Workplace Participation Inquiry: see <http://www.alrc.gov.au/news-media/media-release/age-discrimination-commissioner-susan-ryan-appointed-part-time-commissioner> accessed 19 January 2013. Similarly, in Ontario, there is a background paper (<http://www.lco-cdo.org/en/vulnerable-workers-background-paper>) and a consultation paper <http://www.lco-cdo.org/en/vulnerable-workers-consultation-paper> (both dated December 2010) on "Vulnerable Workers" (both sites accessed 19 January 2013).

[99] See text to nn 24–27.

[100] See text to nn 30–35.

[101] Glofcheski (n 18).

Asian financial crisis of the late 1990s.[102] Nonetheless, with the coming of direct elections for the Chief Executive in 2017, and for the Legislative Council in 2020, there is reason for optimism. Accountability, having to answer to an electorate, is bound to have an effect on the making of policy and on the Administration's attitude towards labour law reform. The recent Chief Executive election has already provided a glimpse of the future, with the candidates explicitly seeking popular support despite the disenfranchised status of the citizenry, an acknowledgment of the general expectation that popular support is vital to the legitimacy of the new Chief Executive despite the small-circle nature of the election. It is too early to speculate how much or how quickly official attitudes will change, or how that will impact on the progress and content of law reforms, but change there will be, in particular with an incoming Chief Executive known to have close contacts with trade unions.[103] In such an environment it is even possible to envisage an enlarged role for the Law Reform Commission, and a possibly more meaningful law reform role for the Labour Advisory Board, once the law reform agenda begins to expand and all hands are put to work. The Minimum Wage Ordinance may be the beginning of this new process, anticipating a changed political environment, in which the government can no longer afford to distance itself from the reasonable expectations of the work force.

---

[102] For a useful resource mapping the history of the struggle for a minimum wage law and some of the main players involved, see the Manpower Panel Database on Particular Policy Issues <http://www.legco.gov.hkdatabase/ english/data_mp/mp-min-wage.htm> accessed 19 January 2013.

[103] See n 72.

Chapter 10
Equal Opportunities Law Reform in Hong Kong: The Impact of International Norms and Civil Society Advocacy

Carole J Petersen and Kelley Loper[1]

Introduction

This chapter considers the enactment of the Race Discrimination Ordinance (Cap 602) (RDO) in Hong Kong in 2008, as well as prospects for further equal opportunities law reform. It reflects on factors that influenced the government's initial decision to legislate to prohibit racial discrimination, the nature of the process, and the substance of the law as it was eventually enacted. In particular, the chapter examines the impact of Hong Kong's commitments under international human rights law, especially the International Convention on the Elimination of all Forms of Racial Discrimination (ICERD), and the interaction among the United Nations (UN) human rights treaty monitoring bodies, the government, non-governmental organizations (NGOs) and civil society advocacy at the local level. This study of a particular law reform effort in Hong Kong illustrates the role of international human rights treaty bodies, transnational legal processes,[2] and civil society in achieving domestic implementation of human rights norms.

The chapter concludes that the international human rights norms that apply to Hong Kong require a more extensive reform of equal opportunities law to address weaknesses and gaps in the current legislative framework. Human

---

[1] Portions of this chapter were originally published in Carole J Petersen, "International Norms and Domestic Law Reform: The Difficult Birth of Hong Kong's Racial Discrimination Law" 6(2) *Directions* 13–21 (Canadian Race Relations Foundation, 2011). Kelley Loper would like to thank Paula Lam for her helpful research assistance.

[2] Harold Hongju Koh, "How Is International Human Rights Law Enforced?" (1999) 74 *Indiana Law Journal* 1397.

rights treaty bodies and Hong Kong activists have called for new anti-discrimination legislation covering additional grounds, such as age and sexual orientation, and amendments to the existing ordinances in order to more effectively address discrimination in the Hong Kong context. To achieve full compliance with its human rights obligations, however, the authorities must conduct a comprehensive review and pursue a more holistic strategy that ensures substantive equality for members of all out-groups, including those who experience multiple forms of discrimination.

The development of a right to equality in Hong Kong began in the early 1990s, while Hong Kong was still a British colony and has continued since the territory became a Special Administrative Region (SAR) of the People's Republic of China in 1997. Hong Kong provides a compelling example of the potential power of international human rights norms and transnational legal processes. The RDO probably would not have been enacted in 2008 had it not been for Hong Kong's obligation to comply with the ICERD and the persistent recommendations of the United Nations Committee on the Elimination of Racial Discrimination (the CERD Committee) and other treaty-monitoring bodies.

The Hong Kong government is sensitive to international opinion and has an interest in demonstrating that human rights are protected in the territory, particularly since reunification with China in 1997.[3] Recognizing this, activists from Hong Kong have made good use of the reporting processes for international human rights treaties, by drafting alternative reports (known as "shadow reports") to the treaty-monitoring bodies and by using the concluding observations in their local advocacy. The Hong Kong courts have also assisted the process by relying upon international law when interpreting and applying domestic law, thus updating local law with international jurisprudence.[4]

Yet the process of enacting a law prohibiting race discrimination in Hong Kong also illustrates the inherent limits of international human rights

---

[3] Carole J Petersen, "From British Colony to Special Administrative Region of China: Embracing Human Rights in Hong Kong" in Randall Peerenboom, Carole J Petersen, and Albert H Y Chen (eds), *Human Rights in Asia: A Comparative Legal Study of Twelve Asian Jurisdictions, France and the USA* (Routledge, 2006).

[4] Carole J Petersen, "Embracing Universal Standards? The Role of International Human Rights Treaties in Hong Kong's Constitutional Jurisprudence" in Fu Hualing, Lison Harris, and Simon N M Young (eds), *Interpreting Hong Kong's Basic Law: The Struggle for Coherence* (Palgrave Macmillan, 2007).

law in domestic politics. The RDO that was enacted in 2008 embraces certain principles of the ICERD but does not fully comply with it. Indeed, the RDO was a huge disappointment to many advocates, as it is substantially weaker than the Sex Discrimination Ordinance (Cap 480) (SDO) and the Disability Discrimination Ordinance (Cap 487) (DDO), which were enacted in 1995.[5] This is almost certainly because ethnic minorities enjoy less political support in Hong Kong than women and persons with disabilities. Although liberal legislators succeeded in securing a few amendments to the government's bill, the RDO is still riddled with exemptions and narrow definitions, which the government has defended when criticized by the CERD Committee.[6]

The next section of this chapter briefly reviews the history of discrimination law in Hong Kong, the gradual development of a right to equality, and the reasons why ethnic minorities have had to wait longer than women and persons with disabilities for legislation protecting their rights. The ensuing part of the chapter then analyses the role that the CERD Committee and other treaty-monitoring bodies played in persuading the Hong Kong government to promise, in 2004, that it would introduce a bill specifically addressing racial discrimination. The chapter then moves on to analyse the legislative process and the weaknesses in the law that was finally enacted in 2008, before considering prospects for further reform and the potential of international human rights standards and processes to contribute to these efforts in the future. The chapter concludes by proposing that Hong Kong move beyond its current piecemeal approach and embrace a more holistic and comprehensive law that promotes substantive equality and addresses all forms of invidious discrimination, including multiple or intersectional discrimination.

---

[5] For the history of the enactment of the Sex Discrimination Ordinance, see Carole J Petersen, "Equality as a Human Right: The Development of Anti-Discrimination Law in Hong Kong" (1996) 34 *Columbia Journal of Transnational Law* 335.

[6] *The Concluding Observations of the Committee on the Elimination of Racial Discrimination: China (including Hong Kong and Macau Special Administrative Regions)*, UN Doc CERD/C/CHN/CO/10–13 (September 15, 2009) [27]–[28]. As discussed later in this chapter, during the legislative process the CERD Committee also wrote to the Chinese government and utilized the "early warning" mechanism to try to persuade the Hong Kong government to enact a stronger law.

Decolonization and the Right to Equality

The United Kingdom (UK) was often described as a relatively "benign" colonial ruler in Hong Kong. It is true that the British allowed the people of Hong Kong a good deal of freedom, particularly economic freedom. However, the colonial system was inherently undemocratic and institutionalized racial inequality. Hong Kong's history books are full of examples of official discrimination against the local Chinese population[7] and also against women.[8] The British government appointed the Governor of Hong Kong (invariably a white male) as well as the legislature, a body dominated by expatriate businessmen. In the years following World War II, there were calls for greater democracy but these demands were rejected, initially because of political developments in Mainland China and the fear of communism, and later on the assumption that China would not tolerate increased democracy in Hong Kong because it would make it harder for China eventually to regain control of the territory.

In the 1960s and 1970s, the colonial government became bound by a number of international treaties that included a right to equality and non-discrimination. The British government ratified, on behalf of Hong Kong, the International Covenant on Civil and Political Rights (the ICCPR), the International Covenant on Economic, Social, and Cultural Rights (the ICESCR), and the ICERD. However, in practice, these treaties did not give the people of Hong Kong a right to equal treatment because they were not directly enforceable and there was no local legislation implementing them.[9] Prior to June 1989, the Hong Kong colonial government successfully opposed

---

[7] Richard Klein, "Law and Racism in an Asian Setting: An Analysis of the British Rule of Hong Kong" (1995) 18 *Hastings International and Comparative Law Review* 223, which provides a detailed account of laws and government policies (dating back to the start of British rule) that sought to segregate the expatriate and Chinese populations.

[8] For examples of sex discrimination in laws and government policies, see Petersen (n 5) esp 339–46; Harriet Samuels, "Women and the Law in Hong Kong: A Feminist Analysis" in Raymond Wacks (ed), *Hong Kong. China and 1997: Essays in Legal Theory* (Hong Kong University Press, 1993); Carol Jones, "Women and the Law in Colonial Hong Kong" in Benjamin K P Leung and Teresa Y C Wong (eds), *25 Years of Social and Economic Development in Hong Kong* (Centre of Asian Studies, University of Hong Kong, 1994).

[9] Andrew Byrnes, "Equality and Non-Discrimination" in Raymond Wacks (ed), *Human Rights in Hong Kong* (Oxford University Press, 1992) ch 6. The Convention on the Elimination of All Forms of Discrimination Against Women (CEDAW) was not

any sort of domestic human rights law, taking the position that the Sino-British Joint Declaration[10] and the Hong Kong Basic Law[11] would adequately protect human rights after 1997. It was particularly opposed to anti-discrimination laws, arguing that as a colonial government it had an obligation to respect traditional Chinese customs, including those that discriminated against women. The government also maintained that anti-discrimination legislation that applied to the private sector would conflict with the government's laissez-faire economic policies, which it considered essential to Hong Kong's economic development.

The enactment of the Bill of Rights Ordinance in 1991 was a significant first step in the campaign for equality rights. The Bill of Rights was a direct result of the Beijing massacre on June 4, 1989.[12] In Hong Kong, one million people took to the streets to protest against the Chinese government. With reunification only eight years away, the Hong Kong government needed to reassure the public that their rights would be protected after 1997. The colonial government thus announced, in October 1989, that it would draft a bill for public consultation. The first draft was released in March 1990 and the bill was formally introduced into the Legislative Council in July 1990. After further consultation and debate, the Hong Kong Bill of Rights Ordinance was enacted in July 1991.

In drafting the proposed Bill of Rights, the Hong Kong government used the ICCPR as its model. The main reason for choosing the ICCPR was the fact that the Chinese government had already agreed, in the Sino-British Joint Declaration, that the provisions of the ICCPR "shall remain in force" after

---

applied to Hong Kong until 1996 (although the UK ratified it in 1986) because of resistance by the local colonial government.

[10] Joint Declaration of the Government of the United Kingdom of Great Britain and Northern Ireland and the Government of the People's Republic of China on the Question of Hong Kong 1984 ("Joint Declaration"), which sets forth rights and freedoms to be enjoyed by the people after reunification <http://www.cmab.gov.hk/en/issues/joint3.htm> accessed 30 November 2012.

[11] Basic Law of the Hong Kong Special Administrative Region of the People's Republic of China ("Basic Law") enacted in 1990 by the National People's Congress and brought into force on 1 July 1997 <http://www.cmab.gov.hk/en/issues/basic.htm> accessed 30 November 2012.

[12] Academics and activists had proposed a domestic bill of rights for Hong Kong prior to 1989, but the government did not endorse the idea until after 4 June 1989: see Nihal Jayawickrama, "The Bill of Rights" in Wacks (n 9) 63–76.

1997.[13] The two drafts of the Basic Law that had been published at that time (as well as the final version of the Basic Law) further stated that "the provisions of the ICCPR shall remain in force and shall be implemented by the laws of the Hong Kong Special Administrative Region."[14] The Hong Kong government thus hoped that China would find it more difficult to repeal a Bill of Rights that essentially repeated the rights already guaranteed in the Basic Law by its reference to the ICCPR.[15]

Most of the rights articulated in the ICCPR address issues directly related to freedoms — freedom of speech, of association, of movement, etc. However, the ICCPR also contains several articles relating to equality. Article 2 requires state parties to ensure equal enjoyment of the rights recognized in the Covenant itself and article 3 specifically prohibits gender discrimination in the enjoyment of rights provided in the Covenant. These two articles were replicated in both the draft and the final versions of the Hong Kong Bill of Rights Ordinance. More importantly, however, the ICCPR proclaims a right to equality in areas beyond the specific rights recognized elsewhere in the Covenant. Article 26 states:

> All persons are equal before the law and are entitled without any discrimination to the equal protection of the law. In this regard, the law shall prohibit any discrimination and guarantee to all persons equal and effective protection against discrimination on any ground such as race, colour, sex, language, religion, political or other opinion, national or social origin, property, birth or other status.

This language was copied in Part II, article 22, of the Hong Kong Bill of Rights Ordinance.[16]

---

[13] Joint Declaration (n 10) Annexe I, Section XIII.

[14] Basic Law (n 11) article 39. This language appeared in article 39 of the February 1989 draft and in article 38 of the April 1988 draft.

[15] Although the Chinese government threatened to repeal the Bill of Rights Ordinance, it ultimately deleted only sections 2(3), 3, and 4, which simply state common law rules of interpretation. See Yash Ghai, "The Continuity of Laws and Legal Rights and Obligations in the SAR" (1997) 27 *Hong Kong Law Journal* 136.

[16] For a discussion of a constitutional right to equality in Hong Kong as currently expressed in the Bill of Rights and the Basic Law and interpreted by Hong Kong courts, see Kelley Loper, "Right to Equality and Non-discrimination" in Johannes Chan and C L Lim (eds), *Law of the Hong Kong Constitution* (Sweet and Maxwell, 2011) 828–848.

The Hong Kong women's movement and other victims of discrimination viewed the Bill of Rights, throughout the consultation process, as a potentially powerful weapon against discrimination. They were encouraged by the fact that the initial draft of the Bill of Rights applied not only to government but also to private persons. However, the business community argued strongly against private application, claiming that article 22 was too vague to be enforced against private entities. Although the women's movement lobbied to preserve private application, the business community was ultimately successful. When the Bill of Rights was enacted, in July 1991, it was amended to state that the Ordinance would bind only the government and public authorities. However, several legislators simultaneously called for the enactment of detailed anti-discrimination legislation.[17]

The debate on the Bill of Rights had raised expectations and women were not prepared to let the issue die. Meanwhile, the Legislative Council was becoming more democratic. In 1991, the first direct elections were finally held for 18 of the 60 seats in the Legislative Council. This limited increase in democracy dramatically changed the role of the Legislative Council and its relationship with both the community and the executive branch. Prior to the introduction of the elected seats, new legislation was proposed and drafted by the government. With the introduction of the elected seats, the Legislative Council became more accountable to the people and more willing to challenge government policies.[18] For example, in December 1992, the Legislative Council adopted a motion calling for the extension of the Convention on the Elimination of all Forms of Discrimination against Women (CEDAW) to Hong Kong, directly contradicting the government's opposition to the treaty.

The most dramatic legislative move occurred in September 1993 when legislator Anna Wu decided to draft her own package of anti-discrimination legislation. Wu introduced the Equal Opportunities Bill (EOB)[19] which sought to prohibit discrimination on a wide range of grounds (including race, sex, marital status, pregnancy, family responsibility, disability, sexuality, age, political and religious conviction) in the fields of employment, education, housing,

---

[17] See the Legislative Council's Debate on the Bill of Rights Bill, *Official Report of the Proceedings of the Legislative Council*, 5 June 1991, 2307–2339.

[18] Kathleen Cheek-Milby, *A Legislature Comes of Age: Hong Kong's Search for Influence and Identity* (Oxford University Press, 1995) 7.

[19] Equal Opportunities Bill 1994, *Hong Kong Government Gazette Legal Supplement* (July 1994) 3, 991–1275.

and the administration of laws and government programmes. This was the first time in Hong Kong's history that an individual legislator sought to create a new field of law through a private member's bill.

The government initially dismissed Wu's EOB as radical and far-fetched. However, officials became concerned when Wu began to attract pledges of support from other legislators. In October 1994, the government suddenly announced that it would introduce its own competing bills: a Sex Discrimination Bill and a Disability Discrimination Bill. The government argued that Hong Kong should gain experience with two areas of discrimination before adopting broader legislation. The government's insistence on drafting its own sex and disability bills (rather than simply supporting those provisions in Wu's EOB) was part of a strategy to regain control over the legislative process. The strategy worked. The Sex Discrimination Ordinance and the Disability Discrimination Ordinance were enacted and the Hong Kong Equal Opportunities Commission (EOC) was established to assist with enforcement.[20] However, Wu's proposals to prohibit discrimination on additional grounds, including race, were defeated. Although the Democratic Party and a majority of the members of the Bills Committee supported Wu's broader proposals, the pro-business Liberal Party voted against them, echoing the government's arguments.

After the 1995 elections a group of legislators re-introduced major portions of Wu's EOB. The government countered by offering to conduct public consultation on selected grounds of discrimination: family status, race, age, and sexuality.[21] At the end of these consultation exercises, the government

---

[20] Carole J Petersen, Janice Fong and Gabrielle Rush, *Enforcing Equal Opportunities: Investigation and Conciliation of Discrimination Complaints in Hong Kong* (Centre for Comparative and Public Law, Faculty of Law, the University of Hong Kong, 2003).

[21] See *Equal Opportunities: A Study on Discrimination in Employment on the Ground of Age: A Consultation Paper* (1996); *Equal Opportunities: A Study on Discrimination on the Ground of Family Status: A Consultation Paper* (1996); *Equal Opportunities: A Study on Discrimination on the Ground of Race: A Consultation Paper* (1997); and *Equal Opportunities: A Study on Discrimination on the Ground of Sexual Orientation: A Consultation Paper* (1996). For a critique of the sexuality consultation exercise and its significance to the gay and lesbian rights movement in Hong Kong, see Carole J Petersen, "Values in Transition: The Development of the Gay and Lesbian Rights Movement in Hong Kong" (1997) 19 *Loyola of Los Angeles International and Comparative Law Journal* 337, 358–362.

concluded that only family status discrimination legislation enjoyed sufficient public support (and was sufficiently non-controversial) to justify legislation.[22] On the basis of these results, the government strongly opposed the private members' bills that sought to prohibit age, sexuality, and race discrimination. These bills were defeated in the final legislative session before Hong Kong ceased to be a British colony and became a Special Administrative Region of China.[23]

ICERD and the Promise to Legislate against Racial Discrimination

After reunification with China, in July 1997, the Hong Kong government continued to oppose broader anti-discrimination legislation. Under the new constitutional order, it was almost impossible for progressive legislators to pressure the government (in the way that Anna Wu had done with her EOB) because the Hong Kong Basic Law restricts the types of private members' bills that can be introduced. Article 74 provides that individual legislators must obtain the written consent of the Chief Executive before introducing a bill relating to government policies. The Hong Kong government used this clause to prevent legislator Christine Loh from introducing a bill to prohibit race discrimination (taking the position that it contradicted government policy on the issue, which was not to legislate). Thus, after July 1997, government support was essential if one hoped to expand the scope of Hong Kong's anti-discrimination law. Given the Administration's historic opposition to race discrimination legislation, this did not bode well for a domestic law that would comply with the ICERD.

In response to pressure from civil society and comments by UN human rights treaty bodies, the Hong Kong government issued a consultation paper in 1996 seeking public views on whether race discrimination legislation was

---

[22] Home Affairs Branch, *Equal Opportunities: Family Status and Sexual Orientation* (Hong Kong: Legislative Council Brief, 1996). The government duly drafted a Family Status Discrimination Bill, which was enacted in June 1997.

[23] The one private member's bill that was enacted over the government's objections, introduced by Christine Loh, improved the remedies for discrimination and sexual harassment. See Sex and Disability Discrimination (Miscellaneous Amendments) Ordinance 1997, *Hong Kong Government Gazette, Legal Supplement* (27 June 1997) 1, Part I of II.

desirable. According to the resulting report, 83% of the respondents opposed legislation and the government concluded that reports of racial discrimination were often simply examples of "rudeness" or "misunderstandings".[24] In fact, a number of the respondents who opposed legislation expressed racist or xenophobic views.[25] Nevertheless the government relied upon those views to argue that public support for legislation was insufficient and a new equal opportunities ordinance was undesirable.

Public opinion, as well as the level of political will, began to change a few years after the 1997 consultation exercise. In 2002 the government undertook a survey of selected business associations and non-governmental organizations asking whether these groups supported legislation to prohibit racial discrimination. This time, a majority of the respondents — 25 of the 35 business groups and all 44 of the NGOs that were contacted — indicated they would not oppose such legislation.[26]

In September 2004, the Hong Kong government changed its position and issued another document entitled *Legislating Against Racial Discrimination: A Consultation Paper*.[27] Unlike the prior consultation exercises, which had asked whether legislation was necessary (and downplayed the extent of discrimination in the community), the 2004 Consultation Paper primarily sought views on the content of a bill and assumed that race discrimination legislation that applied to the private sector would be enacted.

---

[24] Home Affairs Bureau, Hong Kong Government, "Equal Opportunities: A Study on Discrimination on the Ground of Race" (February 1997).

[25] For example, one respondent commented: "Mainland Chinese complain about 'racial discrimination' probably because many of them behave in an anti-social manner, they should learn how to mingle and blend into the local community . . . ". Another stated: "How can anyone think about anti-racial legislation to restrict people's treatment of others on ground of race when they have not looked into whether the way these groups are being treated is because of their own unacceptable behaviour. I think to introduce laws on racial discrimination based on the complaints from these so-called minority groups is utterly ridiculous.": see Home Affairs Bureau, Hong Kong Government, *Consultative Document on Equal Opportunities: A Study of Discrimination on the Ground of Race, Compendium of Submissions*, June 1997 (on file with the first author).

[26] Home Affairs Bureau, Government of the Hong Kong Special Administrative Region, *Legislating Against Racial Discrimination: A Consultation Paper*, September 2004 ("Consultation Paper") [11].

[27] Ibid.

What accounted for the change? International criticism and the duty to comply with the ICERD certainly played an important role. Although Hong Kong is now a part of China, it continues to submit separate reports to the committees that monitor compliance with the core United Nations human rights treaties. Hong Kong's reports are formally submitted by the Chinese government but the treaty monitoring committees review Hong Kong separately and produce distinct concluding comments for the territory (as well as for Macau, which was a Portuguese colony until 1999). Hong Kong also sends its own delegation to answer questions from the committees. In general, this is good for Hong Kong's international reputation because the concluding comments on the territory are generally more positive than the comments related to Mainland China's human rights record. However, by 2003, the absence of specific legislation on racial discrimination had become a serious liability for Hong Kong — a lightning rod for criticism, not only by the CERD Committee but also by other treaty monitoring bodies. Non-governmental organizations consistently raised the issue in their shadow reports and the committees repeatedly asked the official delegation to explain why Hong Kong had not prohibited racial discrimination in the private sector.

For many years, the government attempted to defend itself with a fairly creative interpretation of Article 2(d) of the ICERD, which provides that state parties have an obligation to "prohibit and bring to an end, by all appropriate means, including legislation as required by circumstances, racial discrimination by any persons, group, or organizations." The government argued that this provision only mandated legislation where the "circumstances" required it and that Hong Kong's circumstances did not justify legislation because racial discrimination simply was not a serious problem in the private sector. The CERD Committee rejected this line of reasoning when it reviewed Hong Kong in 2001, as it interprets the ICERD to obligate state parties to legislate. Moreover, the notion that Hong Kong simply had no problem with racial discrimination was difficult to accept, particularly in light of its colonial past.

Other international bodies, such as the Human Rights Committee (in 1999 and 2001) and the Committee on Economic Social and Cultural Rights (in 1996 and 2001), were equally critical of the government's position. Although the Hong Kong government disputed the negative comments for many years, it was also keeping track of them and it provided a succinct summary of the criticism in the 2004 Consultation Paper.[28] It also noted that the United

---

[28] Ibid [2] and [6].

Nations High Commissioner on Human Rights had called for legislation when she visited Hong Kong in 2000.

This is not to suggest that the Hong Kong government accepts all international recommendations, as it has frequently disregarded them for many years. However, the Administration attempts to show some improvement when it is time to submit the next periodic report. This was particularly true in the early years after reunification with China, when the world was closely watching human rights in the territory. The period 2003–2004 was particularly trying for the Hong Kong government due to the disagreements over the slow pace of democratic reforms and the Article 23 saga (the failed attempt to introduce national security legislation, which was requested by Beijing but had to be withdrawn after more than 500,000 people marched in protest).[29] Thus, the decision to promise, in 2004, to introduce a bill to prohibit race discrimination may have been motivated by a desire to obtain at least some positive comments from the human rights treaty-monitoring bodies in the coming years.

Hong Kong's NGOs have also been active in the reporting process and lobbied strongly for race discrimination legislation, both at the international and the local levels. One of these groups, Hong Kong Against Racial Discrimination (HARD), was particularly successful in persuading victims of racial discrimination to come forward and tell their stories. Interestingly, in the mid-1990s (when Wu's EOB was being studied in the Legislative Council), ethnic minorities who suffered discrimination rarely complained. There was some doubt during the transition period regarding the right of abode of non-Chinese in Hong Kong after 1997 and this may have inhibited minorities from participating in calls for law reform. However, after reunification, the position of these groups became more certain and some members of ethnic minorities felt confident enough to come forward. Their stories were shocking for a city that liked to portray itself as modern and cosmopolitan. For example, these included employers who openly paid Nepalese employees lower salaries than Chinese employees; landlords who refused to rent apartments to South Asians; schools that only wanted to hire Caucasians to teach English; nightclubs that charged different entrance fees depending upon the customer's race;

---

[29] Carole J Petersen, "Hong Kong's Spring of Discontent: The Rise and Fall of the National Security Bill in 2003" in Fu Hualing, Carole J Petersen and Simon Young (eds), *National Security and Fundamental Freedoms: Hong Kong's Article 23 Under Scrutiny* (Hong Kong University Press, 2005), 13–62.

and security guards who would try to dissuade Indonesian guests from visiting an apartment building.[30]

To the government's credit, it included these and other examples in the 2004 Consultation Paper, acknowledging that they constituted violations of basic rights and should be addressed. The stories were also publicized in the press, which increased public support for legislation.[31] By this time the government's Home Affairs Bureau had also established a Race Relations Unit, which received and recorded complaints of race discrimination. The government acknowledged that the Race Relations Unit had collected "well-founded" examples of racial discrimination in the private sector,[32] and while the Race Relations Unit could attempt to conciliate these complaints, it had to inform complainants that it had no real enforcement powers.

The other important development was that the business community became more supportive of legislation, particularly when it became apparent that Hong Kong's international reputation was at stake.[33] Apparently even wealthy professionals were not immune to racial discrimination. South Asians who tried to rent luxury flats reported that landlords routinely rejected their applications when they discovered the prospective tenant's ethnicity. An Indian businessman had to pretend to be Italian in order to secure a lease.[34] One Indian woman was rejected by landlords so many times that her Caucasian rental agent concocted the following scheme: when they looked at flats the Indian woman posed as the agent while the Caucasian woman pretended to be the prospective tenant. Hearing these stories, international companies and chambers of commerce gradually realized that the absence of legislation prohibiting racial discrimination was bad for business. If Hong Kong developed a reputation for tolerating racial discrimination then some tourists and international conventions might avoid the territory. International staff might also resist living in Hong Kong, which could lead multinational companies to locate elsewhere in the region. This recognition of the cost of discrimination was an important development because the government had traditionally cited the business community's views as a primary reason for not enacting a law.

---

[30] See Consultation Paper (n 26) Annex B at 42–44.

[31] Ibid [13]–[16] and Annex C (noting evidence of increased public support).

[32] Ibid [16].

[33] Ibid [20]. See also Ravina Shamdasani and Quinton Chan, "Strong Backing for Race Bias Law" *South China Morning Post* (5 November 2001).

[34] Consultation Paper (n 26) Annex B, 43.

Thus, by the end of 2004, it appeared that Hong Kong would finally legislate against racial discrimination. However, this was only the beginning of what eventually would be an extremely long and contentious debate on the content of the bill. As the next section demonstrates, there are limits to the influence of international law as well as its usefulness to local advocacy efforts. At some point, domestic politics — and political will — become more important.

The Disappointing Race Discrimination Ordinance

Academics and civil society organizations advocating for the rights of ethnic minorities in Hong Kong initially hoped that the Race Discrimination Bill would incorporate recent reforms to the race discrimination laws in the UK and Australia, which have often served as models for Hong Kong. Commentators published articles suggesting that Hong Kong incorporate updated definitions of indirect discrimination and include grounds of discrimination beyond the strict definition of "racial discrimination", such as discrimination on the grounds of religious affiliation and immigrant status.[35] However, at a minimum, the expectation was that the government would introduce a bill that was as strong as Hong Kong's SDO and the DDO, which had been enacted in 1995. The government had stated that the Race Discrimination Bill would be "modelled on the structure and format" of the existing anti-discrimination ordinances[36] and that it would use the existing definitions of direct and indirect discrimination.[37] It further stated that the bill "should make it unlawful for the government to discriminate against a person or group of persons on the ground of race in the performance of its functions or the exercise of its powers."[38] Nowhere in the Consultation Paper did the government reveal any intention to narrow the definition of unlawful discrimination or to insert any general exemption for governmental acts and policies.

Yet when the bill was finally introduced into the Legislative Council, in December 2006, the government appeared to have changed its approach

---

[35] See Carole J Petersen, "Racial Equality and the Law: Creating an Effective Statute and Enforcement Model for Hong Kong" (2004) 34 *Hong Kong Law Journal* 459; Kelley Loper, "One Step Forward, Two Steps Back? The Dilemma of Hong Kong's Draft Race Discrimination Legislation" (2008) 38 *Hong Kong Law Journal* 15.
[36] Consultation Paper (n 26) [26].
[37] Ibid [34]–[35].
[38] Ibid [56].

without any explicit explanation as to why it had done so. The Race Discrimination Bill was much weaker than the existing SDO and DDO. This was largely because the bill limited the extent to which it could be applied to governmental functions and added lengthy clauses qualifying (and narrowing) the definition of unlawful discrimination, thus excluding acts that many people would consider to be classic examples of racial discrimination. For the most part, these clauses were not contained in the 2004 Consultation Paper and they were highly complex, making it difficult for a layperson to understand the bill. It was clear, however, that ethnic minorities were about to receive less favourable treatment than victims of gender and disability discrimination — arguably making the Race Discrimination Bill itself an example of official discrimination and a violation of the government's obligations under the ICERD.

The government also declined to address the well-documented discrimination suffered by new immigrants from Mainland China, arguing that the discrimination they suffered was a form of "social" discrimination, although it is probably more analogous to discrimination on the ground of national origin, which is covered by article 1 of the ICERD.[39] The decision to leave new immigrants from the Mainland out of the bill was disappointing to community organizations that serve immigrant families, partly because the Hong Kong government had previously included information on new arrivals from China in its 2000 report to the CERD Committee.[40]

A few months after the Race Discrimination Bill was introduced, the Centre for Comparative and Public Law at the University of Hong Kong organized a conference to study the bill. Carole Petersen presented a paper that focused on the differences between the Race Discrimination Bill and the existing SDO and DDO,[41] criticized the unduly complex, overly narrow definition of discrimination, and argued that the bill would likely exclude from coverage many

---

[39] There is a strictly controlled border between Hong Kong and China, which makes the analysis of national origin somewhat different than it would be in countries without internal immigration controls.

[40] Consultation Paper (n 26) [56].

[41] Carole J Petersen, "How Many Clauses Does it Take to Define Discrimination? A Comparison of the Racial Discrimination Bill with Existing Legislation", paper presented at the Conference on Hong Kong's Race Discrimination Bill, Centre for Comparative and Public Law, The University of Hong Kong (31 March 2007) (copy on file with the first author).

important governmental functions. Many other academics and NGOs also presented papers that challenged the government's drafting approach. However, the official who attended the conference was unsympathetic to these views and left participants with the distinct impression that the government might withdraw the bill if legislators tried to amend it in any significant manner. Of course, this would intimidate organizations that had been lobbying for years for race discrimination legislation that applies to the private sector.

Carole Petersen later submitted her views to the Legislative Council's Bills Committee and presented examples of situations that would likely be excluded from legislative protection if the Bill were not amended.[42] The government did not dispute the basic premise that the Race Discrimination Bill would provide narrower coverage than the SDO and DDO, particularly with respect to governmental acts and functions. The government's chief response was that people could still sue the government under the Bill of Rights Ordinance (which applies to the government and public authorities). But the Equal Opportunities Commission (EOC) has no jurisdiction to enforce the Bill of Rights Ordinance and most of the successful litigation against governmental discrimination has been supported by the EOC. For example, the EOC successfully sued the government in two major cases, one under the SDO and one under the DDO.[43] Indeed, these two cases may be what motivated the government to depart from the model of the SDO and the DDO; it is possible that nervous officials deliberately drafted the Race Discrimination Bill in narrow terms, in order to minimize the opportunities for EOC-supported litigation against government departments.

Human rights organizations were convinced that the Race Discrimination Bill would not comply with ICERD and thus brought the matter to the attention of the CERD Committee, which responded quickly. In August 2007,

---

[42] Carole J Petersen, *Hong Kong's Race Discrimination Bill: A Critique and Comparison with the Sex Discrimination and Disability Discrimination Ordinances* (June 2007), published on the Hong Kong Legislative Council's website: <http://www.legco.gov.hk/yr06-07/english/bc/bc52/papers/bc52cb2-2232-1-e.pdf> accessed 30 November 2012. For the government's response, see <http://www.legco.gov.hk/yr06–07/english/bc/bc52/papers/bc521029cb2–173-1-e.pdf> accessed 30 November 2012.

[43] For analysis of these two cases, which revealed how unprepared the government was to comply with the SDO and DDO, see Carole J Petersen, "The Right to Equality in the Public Sector: An Assessment of Post-Colonial Hong Kong" (2002) 32 *Hong Kong Law Journal* 103.

the CERD Committee used its "follow-up procedure" and "early warning mechanism" and wrote to the Chinese government. Noting that it had already expressed its concern (in 2001) regarding the absence of race discrimination legislation in Hong Kong, the Committee stated that:[44]

> According to information made available to the Committee, a Race Discrimination Bill has been introduced into [the] Hong Kong Special Administrative Region Legislative Council in December 2006, which does not appear to be in conformity with the Committee's recommendation. In particular, it has been brought to the attention of the Committee that the Bill provides for a narrow definition of direct and indirect discrimination differing from the Sex Discrimination and Disability Discrimination Ordinances. Furthermore, Clause 3 of the Bill as presently drafted appears to exclude a substantial portion of Government action from the legislation and thus from the statutory right to seek redress against racial discrimination perpetrated by State authorities.

When the government did not amend its bill, the CERD Committee again wrote to the Chinese government in March 2008, reiterating the concerns it expressed in 2007 asking that the Hong Kong government amend any provisions in the Race Discrimination Bill that did not comply with ICERD.[45]

The critique from the CERD Committee and from local commentators did help to bring about some limited amendments to the Race Discrimination Bill. However, most of the amendments introduced by legislators were defeated due to the undemocratic voting procedures in post-1997 Hong Kong. Any bill or amendment introduced by an individual legislator (as opposed to the government) will pass only if it receives a majority of the votes of *both* groups of legislators: the representatives of the functional constituencies and the representatives returned by other methods (direct elections and the Election Committee).[46] This means that the legislators chosen by the functional

---

[44] See Letter, dated 24 August 2007, from Regis de Gouttes, Chairman of the Committee on the Elimination of Racial Discrimination, to the Permanent Representative of the Permanent Mission of China to the United Nations: <http://www2.ohchr.org/english/bodies/cerd/followup-procedure.htm> accessed 30 November 2012.

[45] See Letter, dated 7 March 2008, from Fatimata-Binta Victoire Dah, Chairperson of the Committee on the Elimination of Racial Discrimination, to the Permanent Representative of the Permanent Mission of China to the United Nations: <http://www2.ohchr.org/english/bodies/cerd/early-warning.htm> accessed 30 November 2012.

[46] Basic Law (n 11) Annex II, Part I.

constituencies (who tend to be more conservative and pro-government than the directly elected legislators) can effectively veto bills and amendments proposed by directly elected legislators. As a result, the RDO that finally came into force in July 2009 (a full five years after the 2004 Consultation Paper) retains many of the flaws that the CERD Committee and other commentators had identified.

These weaknesses have already undermined the RDO's ability to protect people from racial discrimination in practice and have caused frustrations for some individuals attempting to access a remedy. For example, some banks in Hong Kong have allegedly refused to allow people of certain nationalities to open ordinary savings accounts. In one such instance, the EOC told the claimant that they were not able to provide further assistance after an attempt to conciliate with the banks broke down.[47] The Commission's hands were apparently tied by the broad exceptions in the RDO in the definition of "race" which explicitly excludes "nationality", "residency status" and other similar categories. Although a bank's failure to provide services on the basis of nationality could be a form of indirect racial discrimination — if it has a disproportionate, negative effect on people of certain national origins — the wording of the exceptions in the RDO seems to preclude claims of indirect, as well as direct, discrimination in these cases.[48]

When the CERD Committee last reviewed Hong Kong in August 2009, numerous non-governmental and professional organizations criticized the Race Discrimination Ordinance.[49] Although the Hong Kong delegation duly defended the legislation, the Committee concluded that it did not comply with the ICERD and urged the government to amend it. The Committee expressed its concern regarding the definition of racial discrimination in Hong Kong's RDO (noting that it "was not completely consistent with article 1" of the ICERD) and also regarding the limited coverage of government activities and

---

[47] Personal email and documents from the claimant provided to Kelley Loper (on file with the second author).

[48] RDO ss 4 and 8(2)–(3).

[49] For example, the submissions by the Hong Kong Bar Association and the Centre for Comparative and Public Law at the University of Hong Kong to the UN Committee on the Elimination of Racial Discrimination 75th Session, August 2009, for the review of China (including Hong Kong and Macau): <http://www2.ohchr.org/english/bodies/cerd/cerds75.html> accessed 30 November 2012.

powers.⁵⁰ Indeed the RDO seems to have had little impact so far and the types of discrimination reported during the earlier campaign for legislation have apparently continued without significant challenge.⁵¹

This is not to suggest that Hong Kong's RDO was not an achievement. It is the first time that race discrimination has been prohibited in the private sector and this is where many of the complaints of discrimination have arisen. To that extent, Hong Kong is still a useful case study of the influence of the ICERD and the value of the obligation of the government to report periodically to the CERD Committee. However, by going out of its way to protect government departments from potential litigation, the Hong Kong government has done little to enhance the territory's reputation as a jurisdiction that respects and implements international human rights law. Ironically, that was supposed to be one of the motivating forces for enacting the new law. It is unfortunate that Anna Wu's comprehensive EOB was not enacted in 1995. She viewed anti-discrimination legislation as a kind of social contract: in exchange for protection from discrimination that might affect us, we agree to give similar protection to other groups, including those who may fall outside our normal range of empathy. This view was discarded when the government insisted on dealing with discrimination as slowly as possible and then only on a piecemeal basis.

For now, ethnic minorities have achieved a limited victory, one that might not have been achieved without assistance from the United Nations human rights system and the ability of local NGOs to leverage the process to advocate locally. Granted, racial discrimination is addressed by a far less comprehensive law than discrimination on the grounds of gender and disability. However, additional law reform is possible, particularly if Hong Kong continues to report separately to the CERD Committee and other treaty-monitoring bodies and non-governmental organizations continue to actively contribute to that process. The next section considers on-going efforts to achieve further reform, including the continuing engagement with the UN human rights system and the role of civil society.

---

⁵⁰ *Concluding Observations of the Committee on the Elimination of Racial Discrimination: China (including Hong Kong and Macau Special Administrative Regions)*, UN Doc CERD/C/CHN/CO/10–13 (15 September 2009) [27].

⁵¹ Jennifer Ngo, "Race bias a hurdle for South Asians" *South China Morning Post* (23 March 2012).

Lessons from the RDO and Prospects for Further Reform

As discussed above, despite its international obligations to prohibit discrimination on a range of grounds, the Hong Kong government has rejected a comprehensive approach to law reform in this area. Instead, it has introduced — over a period of nearly twenty years — four single pieces of legislation, each addressing discrimination on only one, or a limited number, of protected characteristics. In the case of the RDO the decision to legislate occurred only after a decade-long campaign, and the substance of the legislation remains weak and incomplete. In the face of continuing intransigence, lack of political will, and even outright opposition by certain interests, further reform of existing equal opportunities laws or the introduction of new laws appears unlikely in the short or medium term. Nevertheless the RDO case study — despite the limitations of the enacted ordinance — suggests the potential value and contribution of international human rights mechanisms to law reform efforts in the future. Indeed, civil society organizations have continued to advocate for protections that address the remaining gaps. Their strategy includes leveraging the treaty monitoring bodies' reporting procedures, an exercise that has contributed to further developing and promoting the positions of these groups.

For example, activists have been stepping up their campaign for an ordinance prohibiting discrimination on the grounds of sexual orientation and gender identity (a SOGIO) despite opposition from within the legislative and executive branches of government and some vocal religious organizations.[52] In November 2012, Legislator Cyd Ho proposed a motion in the Legislative Council urging the government "to expeditiously launch [a] public consultation on enacting legislation to safeguard equal opportunities for and the basic rights of people of different sexual orientations".[53] Although the motion merely called for consultation — rather than legislation — it was ultimately defeated.

---

[52] Jennifer Cheng, "Hong Kong's LGBT Community Seeks Ban on Discrimination", *South China Morning Post* (15 November 2012). For an introduction to discrimination against gay men and the transgender community in Hong Kong and the extent to which the ICCPR has been used to challenge such discrimination, see Carole J Petersen, "Sexual Orientation and Gender Identity in Hong Kong: A Case for the Strategic Use of Human Rights Treaties and the International Reporting Process" (2013) 14(2) *Asian-Pacific Law and Policy Journal* 28.

[53] See "Motion on 'Equal rights for people of different sexual orientations' to be moved by Hon Cyd Ho at the Council meeting of 7 November 2012": <http://www.legco.

Legislators expressed a range of views during the course of the debate. While many supported the initiation of a consultation exercise and even the eventual enactment of a SOGIO, others did not want to begin the process and worried that anti-discrimination legislation would have a negative impact on traditional Chinese values, freedom of religion, and the interests of employers.[54]

Interestingly, a majority of members from the geographical constituencies in the Legislative Council voted in favour of the motion while the majority of legislators representing functional constituencies voted against it.[55] Although the motion received majority support overall, it was defeated because of the rule that a motion introduced by a private member (rather than the government) must pass by a majority of both constituencies rather than a simple majority of all legislators.[56] This is reminiscent of the failure in 2008 of the Bills Committee to secure amendments that would have improved the Race Discrimination Bill despite majority support among democratically elected legislators. This democratic deficit in the legislative branch tends to favour government interests and has an impact on the outcome of debates on human rights issues.

There were initial indications that the government would proceed with a public consultation exercise anyway, and the Secretary for Constitutional and Mainland Affairs, Raymond Tam Chi-yuen, told the press on 14 January 2013 that "[w]e are ready [for a public consultation] once the chief executive finds it is the appropriate time . . . Once there are further communications and public discussions [in the community], I believe there will be an opportunity to conduct a public consultation, details of which will be addressed in the policy address."[57] The Chief Executive, C Y Leung, however, announced in his policy address a few days later that the government had no plans to conduct a

---

gov.hk/yr12–13/english/counmtg/motion/m_papers/cm1107cb3–73-e.pdf> accessed 16 February 2013.

[54] Hong Kong Legislative Council, *Official Record of Proceedings (Hansard)*, 7 November 2012, 1566–1567, 1577.

[55] Voting Results on the Motion on "Equal Rights for People of Different Sexual Orientations" 7 November 2012: http://www.legco.gov.hk/yr12–13/chinese/counmtg/voting/v20121107.pdf> accessed 18 February 2013.

[56] *Rules of Procedure of the Legislative Council of the Hong Kong Special Administrative Region* Rule 46(2) <http://www.legco.gov.hk/general/english/procedur/content/rop.pdf> accessed 18 February 2013.

[57] See Johnny Tam, "Christians in Prayer Rally to Fight Gay Law Proposal", *South China Morning Post* (14 January 2013).

consultation. In explaining this position, he noted that deep divisions existed in society on the issue:[58]

> Some are in support from the perspective of equal opportunity. Others are concerned that launching a consultation exercise may deal a blow to family, religion and education. The Government understands that this is a highly controversial issue which must be tackled cautiously. We will continue to listen to different views from various sectors . . .

The resistance to the introduction of a SOGIO, or even conducting public consultation on the issue, has had decidedly religious overtones and often focuses on potential conflicts between freedom of religion and expression and a right to equality and non-discrimination.[59] While religious concerns may be especially salient when considering approaches to addressing this particular form of discrimination, many of the sentiments expressed by opponents are reminiscent of earlier debates about the RDO, SDO and other equal opportunities laws. For example, prior to the enactment of the RDO, some queried whether the prohibition of racial discrimination, including the proposed vilification, or "hate speech", provisions would stifle people's freedom to use common, possibly offensive, Cantonese expressions for certain racial and ethnic groups. Others were concerned that the SDO, and addressing discrimination against women in particular, would undermine traditional Chinese values. Some representatives of the business community also raised issues of cost and inconvenience to employers during the legislative debates on all four of the existing anti-discrimination ordinances. The government's cautious attitude and unwillingness to challenge these views is strikingly similar to the approach it took during consultations on the RDO and even during the legislative process after it had made the commitment to legislate.

Reference to Hong Kong's human rights obligations can help clarify these issues and resolve apparent tensions between freedom of religion/expression, cultural values and a right to non-discrimination, which must be guaranteed through the implementation of equal opportunities laws. In this sense, the treaty monitoring bodies have provided important guidance that can contribute to local discussions about the type of law reform necessary for Hong Kong to

---

[58] *The 2013 Policy Address: Seek Change, Maintain Stability, Serve the People with Pragmatism* [131]: <http://www.policyaddress.gov.hk/2013/eng/pdf/PA2013.pdf> accessed 16 February 2013.

[59] Tam (n 57).

fully comply with its duties under international human rights law. Civil society groups continue to rely on this guidance and engage with the international human rights system as they continue their push for reform.

First, the treaty-monitoring bodies, including the CERD Committee as discussed above, have explained that the equality and non-discrimination provisions in core international human rights instruments require states to enact legislation that prohibits discrimination on a range of grounds and to ensure an appropriate remedy for those affected. For example, in its General Comment on Non-discrimination, the Committee on Economic, Social and Cultural Rights notes that, since discrimination is frequently encountered in many sectors of society, such as in families and workplaces, "States parties must . . . adopt measures, which should include legislation, to ensure that individuals and entities in the private sphere do not discriminate on prohibited grounds."[60] The Committee adds:[61]

> Adoption of legislation to address discrimination is indispensable . . . States parties are therefore encouraged to adopt specific legislation that prohibits discrimination in the field of economic, social and cultural rights. Such laws should aim at eliminating formal and substantive discrimination, attribute obligations to *public and private actors* and cover the prohibited grounds discussed above [including sexual orientation, gender identity, age, religion, language, etc.].

As noted above, the Committee has emphasized Hong Kong's obligations in this regard in its concluding observations on three occasions. In 2001, it urged the Hong Kong government to enact legislation prohibiting discrimination on the grounds of sexual orientation and age.[62] In 2005 it reiterated these concerns, explaining that the current discrimination legislation did not cover all of the necessary protected characteristics.[63] The Human Rights Committee

---

[60] Committee on Economic Social and Cultural Rights, *General Comment No 20, Non-discrimination in Economic, Social and Cultural Rights (art 2, para 2, of the International Covenant on Economic, Social and Cultural Rights)* UN Doc E/C 12/GC/20 (2 July 2009) [11].

[61] Ibid [37].

[62] Committee on Economic, Social and Cultural Rights, *Concluding Observations, People's Republic of China (including Hong Kong and Macao)*, UN Doc E/C 12/1/Add 58 (21 May 2001) [31].

[63] Committee on Economic, Social and Cultural Rights, *Concluding Observations, People's Republic of China (including Hong Kong and Macao)*, UN Doc E/C 12/1/Add 107 (13 May 2005) [78](a).

considered Hong Kong's third periodic report under the ICCPR in March 2013 and asked the government in its "List of Issues" arising from the report to provide information about legislative or administrative measures "relating to the protection against discrimination on the grounds of language, religion, political or other opinion, sexual orientation or age".[64] The Committee also asked for more information about the RDO, including the measures "taken to ensure that all government functions and powers are brought within the scope of the [RDO]".[65]

In addition to emphasizing the requirement to legislate, the UN human rights treaty bodies have also elaborated on other aspects of relevant rights and duties that apply to Hong Kong providing direction for navigating the boundaries of conflicting rights. For example, the treaty bodies have provided clarification that the principle of non-discrimination does not imply that every "distinction" amounts to discriminatory treatment. The Human Rights Committee observed in its General Comment on Non-discrimination "that not every differentiation of treatment will constitute discrimination".[66] However, "the criteria for such differentiation" must be "reasonable and objective" and the aim of the treatment "is to achieve a purpose which is legitimate under the Covenant". The Committee on Economic, Social and Cultural Rights has similarly stated that:[67]

> Differential treatment based on prohibited grounds will be viewed as discriminatory unless the justification for differentiation is reasonable

---

[64] Human Rights Committee, *List of Issues to be taken up in connection with the consideration of the third periodic report of Hong Kong, China*, adopted by the Committee at its 106th session (15 October-2 November 2012), UN Doc CCPR/C/CHN-HKG/Q/3 (16 November 2012) [5].

[65] Ibid [4]. See also Human Rights Committee, *Concluding Observations on the Third Periodic Report of Hong Kong, China*, UN Doc CCPR/C/CHN-HKG/CO/3 (29 April 2013) [19].

[66] Human Rights Committee, *General Comment No 18: Non-discrimination*, 10 November 1989, [13]: <http://www.unhchr.ch/tbs/doc.nsf/(Symbol)/3888b0541f8501c9c12563ed004b8d0e?Opendocument> accessed 17 February 2013. For discussion of how Hong Kong courts have applied this test in constitutional cases, see Kelley Loper (n 16).

[67] Committee on Economic Social and Cultural Rights, *General Comment No 20, Non-discrimination in Economic, Social and Cultural Rights (art 2 para 2 of the International Covenant on Economic, Social and Cultural Rights*, UN Doc E/C 12/GC/20 (2 July 2009) [13].

and objective. This will include an assessment as to whether the aim and effects of the measures or omissions are legitimate, compatible with the nature of the Covenant rights and solely for the purpose of promoting the general welfare in a democratic society. In addition, there must be a clear and reasonable relationship of proportionality between the aim sought to be realized and the measures or omissions and their effects.

Hong Kong policymakers must apply these tests and principles when determining whether to exempt certain types of differential treatment from future legislation or when reviewing the legitimacy of exceptions in the current laws.

For example, some may argue that a SOGIO should include an exemption allowing religious institutions, including schools, to distinguish on the ground of sexual orientation when deciding whether to hire someone for a job. Lawmakers should apply the equality and non-discrimination principles in the ICCPR and ICESCR and consider whether the aims of such an exception are reasonable. They must also determine whether allowing discrimination against sexual minorities is a proportionate, or necessary, means of achieving those aims. While the ICCPR protects the freedom to manifest one's religious beliefs, this right may also be limited if "necessary to protect public safety, order, health or morals, or the fundamental rights and freedoms of others".[68] Arguably, the fundamental rights and freedoms of lesbian, gay, bisexual and transgender (LGBT) people to be free from discrimination could justify limiting the freedom of religious institutions to discriminate in their hiring practices. In the case of religious schools, the content of the right to education elaborated by the Committee on Economic, Social and Cultural Rights and the Committee on the Rights of the Child[69] may also influence these deliberations. For example, a school's policy not to hire LGBT teachers could contribute to a homophobic atmosphere that leads to intolerance and even bullying of LGBT students.[70] While certain exceptions to anti-discrimination laws may be legitimate, international human rights law provides a framework to guide debates

---

[68] Human Rights Committee, *General Comment 22 The Right to Freedom of Thought, Conscience and Religion (Art 18)*, UN Doc CCPR/C/21/Rev1/Add4 (30 July 1993).

[69] Committee on Economic, Social and Cultural Rights, *General Comment No 13, The Right to Education*, E/C 12/1999/10 (8 December 1999); Committee on the Rights of the Child, *General Comment No. 1, The Aims of Education*, UN Doc CRC/GC/2001/1 (17 April 2001).

[70] The Committee on the Rights of the Child has listed gay, lesbian, and transgender or transsexual children among those children in many societies who are particularly vulnerable and likely to be exposed to violence. See Committee on the Rights of the

about how best to balance various issues and interests and reach principled solutions to conflicting rights.

Indeed the Hong Kong government's failure to engage in these types of discussions when drafting the RDO partly explains the existence of the weaknesses and gaps described above, including the law's broad exceptions for certain government functions and some types of indirect discrimination. Policymakers apparently did not consider whether these exceptions pursued a legitimate aim or, if they did, whether there was a reasonable relationship of proportionality between the aims and the discriminatory effects of the exclusions. As discussed above, the treaty-monitoring bodies' consideration of Hong Kong's reports and the concluding comments urging Hong Kong to prohibit racial discrimination in the private sector probably contributed to the commitment to legislate in the first place. It also provided the government with a convenient justification for this decision when addressing local opposition. However, the authorities have thus far ignored the CERD Committee's subsequent comments on problems with the law's substance. It remains to be seen whether the human rights monitoring processes will ultimately have some effect.

In the meantime, civil society organizations continue to refer to human rights standards and the comments of the treaty monitoring bodies when advocating for reform of Hong Kong's equal opportunities framework. They have also remained actively engaged with the international mechanisms. For example, several organizations prepared reports setting out their concerns about Hong Kong's lack of compliance with the ICCPR, including the failure to enact a SOGIO and the need to amend the RDO. They submitted these documents to the Human Rights Committee prior to its adoption of a list of issues related to Hong Kong's report in November 2012.[71] The Hong Kong Human Rights

---

Child, *General Comment No 13, The Right of the Child to Freedom from all Forms of Violence*, UN Doc CRC/C/GC/13 (18 April 2011) [72](g).

[71] See, for example, the submissions to the Human Rights Committee at its 106th session, 15 October–16 November from (1) the Equal Opportunities Commission, Hong Kong <http://www2.ohchr.org/english/bodies/hrc/docs/ngos/EOC_HongKong_HRC106.pdf> accessed 17 February 2013; (2) Hong Kong Human Rights Monitor, [33]–[34] <http://www2.ohchr.org/english/bodies/hrc/docs/ngos/HKHRM_China HongKong106.pdf> accessed 17 February 2013, and (3) Hong Kong Unison <http://www2.ohchr.org/english/bodies/hrc/docs/ngos/HongKongUnison106.doc> accessed 17 February 2013.

Monitor also organized an informal Skype briefing for Committee members with a broad range of Hong Kong based NGOs in October 2012. A number of groups also submitted alternative, "shadow" reports to the Committee in advance of its session in March 2013 when it considered Hong Kong's report and issued its concluding comments.[72]

The Need for a Holistic Approach to Law Reform

The Hong Kong government's intransigence and general unwillingness to enact strong equal opportunities legislation has no doubt influenced advocates' current strategy to campaign for one anti-discrimination law at a time covering particular grounds. There have been no further attempts to push for comprehensive legislation since Anna Wu proposed her EOB in 1993. However, developments in international human rights law and significant reform in other jurisdictions suggest that a multi-faceted, all-inclusive approach to addressing discrimination may be more effective.

In recent years, the treaty bodies have clarified that the right to equality and non-discrimination in international human rights law includes protection from discrimination on more than one ground at a time. The Committee on Economic, Social and Cultural Rights has noted that the reference to "other status" in the list of protected characteristics in Article 2(2) of the ICESCR includes "multiple" or "intersectional" discrimination:[73]

> Some individuals or groups of individuals face discrimination on more than one of the prohibited grounds, for example women belonging to an ethnic or religious minority. Such cumulative discrimination has a unique and specific impact on individuals and merits particular consideration and remedying.

---

[72] See, for example, submissions from the Hong Kong Bar Association <http://www2.ohchr.org/english/bodies/hrc/docs/ngos/HongKongBarAssociation_HongKong_HRC107.pdf> accessed 17 February 2013; Hong Kong Unison <http://www2.ohchr.org/English/bodies/hrc/docs/NGOs/HongKongUnisonLimited_HongKong_HRC107.pdf> accessed 17 February 2013, and LGBT Joint Submission <http://www2.ohchr.org/english/bodies/hrc/docs/ngos/LGBTJointSubmission_China HongKong107.pdf> accessed 17 February 2013.

[73] Committee on Economic Social and Cultural Rights, *General Comment No 20, Non-discrimination in Economic, Social and Cultural Rights (art 2 para 2 of the International Covenant on Economic, Social and Cultural Rights)*, UN Doc E/C 12/GC/20 (2 July 2009) [17] and [27].

Intersectional discrimination often manifests differently than discrimination that occurs on the basis of a single ground and does not generally fit neatly into the particular categories of protected characteristics typically included in anti-discrimination laws.[74] As a result, members of the groups affected — who often face the most severe forms of discrimination — are unable to access legal remedies.

For example, in Hong Kong migrant domestic workers (MDWs), mainly women from Southeast Asian countries such as the Philippines and Indonesia, often face discrimination based on a combination of three aspects of their identity: their gender, national origin, and low social status. However, it would be difficult to make out a coherent discrimination claim under the RDO or the SDO on the basis of these characteristics either in combination or in isolation. In other words, the discrimination experienced by a MDW because of her national origin is inextricably linked to, and cannot be separated from, her identity as a woman of low social status in Hong Kong society. Hong Kong's anti-discrimination laws require that a claimant show that she has been treated less favourably than a similarly situated comparator who does not have the protected characteristic in order to demonstrate direct discrimination. If the discrimination stems from a combination of characteristics, however, finding an appropriate comparator is almost impossible.[75]

The Committee on the Elimination of Discrimination against Women, the body that monitors the implementation of CEDAW, has recognized this problem, noting that:[76]

> Intersectionality is a basic concept for understanding the scope of the general obligations of States parties contained in article 2 [of CEDAW]. The discrimination of women based on sex and gender is inextricably linked with other factors that affect women, such as race, ethnicity,

---

[74] For discussion of the limitations of discrimination law when addressing multiple or intersectional discrimination, see Aileen McColgan, "Reconfiguring Discrimination Law" [2007] *Public Law* 74; Joanne Conaghan, "Intersectionality and UK Initiatives" (2007) 23 *South African Journal on Human Rights* 317; Judith Squires, "Intersecting Inequalities" (2009) 11 *International Feminist Journal of Politics* 496.

[75] McColgan (n 74).

[76] Committee on the Elimination of Discrimination against Women, *General Recommendation No 28 on the Core Obligations of States Parties under article 2 of the Convention on the Elimination of All Forms of Discrimination against Women*, UN Doc CEDAW/C/GC/28 (16 December 2010) [18].

religion or belief, health, status, age, class, caste and sexual orientation and gender identity. Discrimination on the basis of sex or gender may affect women belonging to such groups to a different degree or in different ways to men. States parties must legally recognize such intersecting forms of discrimination and their compounded negative impact on the women concerned and prohibit them.

It observes in another General Recommendation that:[77]

> [W]omen migrant workers often experience intersecting forms of discrimination, suffering not only sex-and gender-based discrimination, but also xenophobia and racism. Discrimination based on race, ethnicity, cultural particularities, nationality, language, religion or other status may be expressed in sex-and gender-specific ways.

The treaty bodies have also underscored states' duties to ensure substantive, rather than merely formal, equality. For example, the Committee on Economic, Social and Cultural Rights points out that:[78]

> The effective enjoyment of Covenant rights is often influenced by whether a person is a member of a group characterized by the prohibited grounds of discrimination. Eliminating discrimination in practice requires paying sufficient attention to groups of individuals which suffer historical or persistent prejudice instead of merely comparing the formal treatment of individuals in similar situations . . . In order to eliminate substantive discrimination, States parties may be, and in some cases are, under an obligation to adopt special measures to attenuate or suppress conditions that perpetuate discrimination.

In other words, depending on the context, special measures might be necessary to address past or current inequalities that hold members of certain groups back from accessing equal opportunities. In addition, as part of this duty to pay attention to the relative disadvantage of some groups in society, the ICESCR requires that states prohibit indirect, de facto discrimination that may arise

---

[77] Committee on the Elimination of Discrimination against Women, *General Recommendation No 26 on Women Migrant Workers*, UN Doc CEDAW/C/2009/WP.1/R (5 December 2008) [14].

[78] Committee on Economic Social and Cultural Rights, *General Comment No 20, Non-discrimination in Economic, Social and Cultural Rights (art 2 para 2 of the International Covenant on Economic, Social and Cultural Rights)*, UN Doc E/C 12/GC/20 (2 July 2009) [8](b) and [9].

from apparently neutral measures that have a disproportionate and negative impact on particular groups and individual members of those groups.[79]

A clear and effective legal definition of indirect discrimination is an important step in this direction. While Hong Kong's four anti-discrimination laws currently prohibit indirect discrimination, the definition is narrow and makes it difficult for individuals to substantiate a claim and relatively easy for an alleged discriminator to justify the impugned restrictions.[80] As discussed above, the RDO also exempts indirect discrimination that might occur when measures that limit access to rights and benefits on the basis of nationality or immigration status have discriminatory effects on particular racial or ethnic groups.

As the treaty bodies' comments indicate, international human rights law demands a more holistic approach to addressing systemic and intersectional discrimination and ensuring substantive equality than the current Hong Kong model requires. Reform in the area of equal opportunities law should proceed accordingly and provide comprehensive legal protection from discrimination on all grounds required by international law and in all areas of life.

In contrast to Hong Kong's piecemeal and protracted approach to developing equal opportunities legislation, the UK has moved in the opposite direction, having successfully consolidated its laws into one, streamlined Equality Act in 2010. Broad recognition of the limits of its previous anti-discrimination regime, including the failure of the law to tackle entrenched, systemic discrimination and the absence of certain groups and areas of activity from the scope of protection, led to extensive review and comprehensive reform.[81] The Equality Act 2010 expanded the range of protected characteristics and scope of activities covered by the law and created positive duties on public bodies to promote equality. The Act consolidated more than one hundred pieces of legislation, and another Act merged various separate equal opportunities bodies into one Equality and Human Rights Commission. Despite some remaining problems — for example, the equality duties are relatively weak, merely requiring public bodies to "have due regard to the need to" eliminate discrimination[82] — the Act is a significant achievement.

---

[79] Ibid [10] and [12].
[80] Petersen (n 42).
[81] Sandra Fredman, *Discrimination Law* (Oxford University Press, 2011) 6–7.
[82] Ibid 8.

Because Hong Kong's current anti-discrimination laws replicate certain aspects of older UK legislation, including outdated definitions of discrimination, the Equality Act 2010 may serve as an appropriate model if Hong Kong initiates its own law reform process. In fact, during deliberations over the RDO, activists and legislators campaigned for adoption of a more inclusive definition of indirect discrimination based on newer UK provisions reflecting developments in European Union law.[83] The Bills Committee for the Race Discrimination Bill also attempted to introduce a duty on "Government and specified public authorities to draw up a Race Equality Scheme for the purpose of eliminating racial discrimination and promoting racial harmony".[84] This was originally proposed by the EOC and inspired by the UK equality duties that were already in force before the introduction of the Equality Act 2010. While the Administration rejected both of these proposals, these debates during the legislative process could set the stage for further discussion. Hong Kong may also usefully observe the UK's experience with its new Equality Act in the future.

Conclusions

While it seems unlikely that Hong Kong will pursue substantial, or even moderate, reform of equal opportunities law in the short term, lessons from the campaign for an RDO and the subsequent legislative process can help inform on-going advocacy strategies. In particular, it is clear that government and civil society engagement with the treaty monitoring bodies can influence and promote the domestic implementation of human rights norms. International human rights standards and the treaty monitoring bodies' interpretations of those standards, are important starting points when considering the need to legislate to prohibit discrimination and promote equality as well as the substance of the law itself.

These standards demand a holistic approach and any new legal provisions should take into account the cross-cutting nature of identity, the reality

---

[83] See Legislative Council, Report of the Bills Committee on Race Discrimination Bill, 9 July 2008, LC Paper No CB(2)2478/07–08, 9–12: <http://www.legco.gov.hk/yr06-07/english/bc/bc52/reports/bc520709cb2-2478-e.pdf> accessed 18 February 2013.
[84] Ibid 18–19.

of intersectional discrimination, the need to consider relative disadvantage of certain groups, and the existence of de facto as well as de jure discrimination. In other words, reform of equal opportunities law in Hong Kong should aim to ensure comprehensive protection from discrimination on all relevant grounds required by international law and in all areas of life.

Part D

Law Reform and Privacy

Chapter 11
Reviewing the Personal Data (Privacy) Ordinance through Standstill and Crisis[1]

Allan Chiang

Protection of Privacy Interests

Privacy is an all-embracing concept, which covers the following interests:[2]

- That of the person in controlling the information held by others about him, or "information privacy" (or "informational self-determination" as it is referred to in Europe);
- That of controlling entry to "personal place", or "territorial privacy";
- That of freedom from interference with one's physical person, or "personal privacy"; and
- That of freedom from surveillance and from interception of one's communications, or "communications and surveillance privacy".

Various sources of privacy law afford protection to these interests. First, articles 28, 29 and 30 of the Basic Law provide constitutional protection to personal privacy, territorial privacy and communications privacy, respectively. In addition, article 17 of the International Covenant of Civil and Political Rights (ICCPR) (incorporated in article 14 of the Hong Kong Bill of Rights Ordinance (Cap 383)) provides for a guarantee against arbitrary or unlawful interference with privacy. The ICCPR also imposes on the government an obligation to adopt legislative and other measures to give effect to the prohibition against interference with the right to privacy. In this regard, a series of reports was issued by the Law Reform Commission of Hong Kong (HKLRC)

---

[1] This chapter depicted the state of affairs as at 13 July 2011 when the Personal Data (Privacy) (Amendment) Bill 2011 was introduced into the Legislative Council. The bill was passed, with amendments, on 27 June 2012.

[2] Australia Law Reform Commission, *Privacy* (Report 22, 1983) 21.

recommending that legislation be introduced to better protect these privacy interests. The reports are:

- *Reform of the Law Relating to the Protection of Personal Data* (August 1994),
- *Privacy: Regulating the Interception of Communications* (December 1996),
- *Stalking* (October 2000),
- *Civil Liability for Invasion of Privacy* (December 2004),
- *Privacy and Media Intrusion* (December 2004), and
- *Privacy: The Regulation of Covert Surveillance* (March 2006).

Only the recommendations of the first two and the last reports were duly taken up by the government and implemented.[3] In particular, the Personal Data (Privacy) Ordinance (PDPO) came into effect in December 1996. Why and how did legislation on personal data protection receive priority treatment?

Personal Data (Privacy) Bill: Getting Off the Ground

The first clue can be found in the statement of purpose put forward by the government when it introduced the Personal Data (Privacy) Bill into the Legislative Council (LegCo) on 19 April 1995, namely:[4]

(i) to protect the privacy interests of individuals in relation to personal data, and

(ii) to safeguard the free flow of personal data to Hong Kong from the imposition of restrictions by the increasing number of countries that already have data protection laws.

Clearly, the first point provides a generic reason, while the second points to the real driver for change. As Berthold and Wacks suggest, the government at that time perceived a risk that Hong Kong's trade position could be jeopardized if

---

[3] The Interception of Communications and Surveillance Bill (subsequently Ordinance 20 of 2006) was introduced prior to publication of the HKLRC report on *Privacy: The Regulation of Covert Surveillance*, but mirrors some of the HKLRC's recommendations.

[4] Legislative Council Secretariat, Legislative Council Meeting, 19 April 1995, 3159 <http://www.legco.gov.hk/yr94-95/english/lc_sitg/hansard/h950419.pdf> accessed 4 July 2012.

legislation on data privacy was not in place[5] — specifically, concerns relating to the adoption of the EU Directive on Privacy by the European Parliament in 1995,[6] the year that the Hong Kong Bill was introduced. Article 25(1) of the EU Directive provides that member states shall provide that the transfer to a third country of personal data that are undergoing or are intended for processing after transfer may take place *only* if the third country in question ensures an adequate level of protection. The colonial administration moved swiftly to introduce relevant data protection legislation in Hong Kong for the purpose of safeguarding the continued free flow of cross-border data. There was urgency in the process as the sovereignty of Hong Kong was to be returned to China in two years' time.

The government's concerns were vehemently supported by members of LegCo in the course of the second reading of the bill on 27 July 1995:

> Advanced countries of the world have already legislated to protect personal data. To ensure that Hong Kong can continue to exchange information, especially electronic data, with these countries, including Hong Kong's most important trading partners, Hong Kong must have in place corresponding legislations, which are of utmost important in maintaining and developing Hong Kong as the international centre for communication of the Asia-Pacific region. The community has already come to a very clear political and policy understanding in this regard.[7]
>
> . . . I could say that the Administration would like to (have) this Bill passed into law as soon as possible because the Administration knows clearly that if by 1996 we still do not have such legal protection in place, the exchange of trade and commercial information would be greatly affected, especially when the European Union has already passed a resolution in this regard.[8]

---

[5] Mark Berthold and Raymond Wacks, *Hong Kong Data Privacy Law: Territorial Regulation in a Borderless World* (2nd ed, Sweet & Maxwell Asia, 2003) 31.

[6] Directive 95/46/EC of the European Parliament and of the Council of 24 October 1995 on the Protection of Individuals with regard to the Processing of Personal Data and on the Free Movement of Such Data <http://eur-lex.europa.eu/smartapi/cgi/sga_doc?smartapi!celexapi!prod!CELEXnumdoc&lg=EN&numdoc=31995L0046&model=guichett> accessed 4 July 2012.

[7] R Luk, Legislative Council Meeting, 27 July 1995, 6192 <http://www.legco.gov.hk/yr94–95/english/lc_sitg/hansard/h950727.pdf> accessed 4 July 2012.

[8] Ibid, 6194 (J To).

On the same day, the bill was read a third time and passed with amendments. Looking back, the Bills Committee, set up only on 16 May 1995 to study the bill, completed its mission in about two months. This was a miraculous achievement. It led to the enactment of the PDPO on 3 August 1995. The core provisions of the Ordinance came into effect on 20 December 1996, shortly before the handover of the sovereignty of Hong Kong from Britain to China.

Legislative Proposals to Protect Other Privacy Interests in Limbo

On the other hand, the other three HKLRC reports on privacy interests are still in limbo. In reply to a question raised in the Legislative Council on 10 November 2010, the government responded as follows:[9]

> As regards the LRC's Report on Civil Liability for Invasion of Privacy and Report on Privacy and Media Intrusion, there were mixed responses and divergent views in the community. The proposed recommendations of the two reports were highly contentious and involved a number of complicated legal concepts (for example, the definitions of "reasonable expectation of privacy" and "unwarranted publicity given to the private life of another person"). When deciding the way forward, we need to reach a *consensus* in the community and strike a *balance between different rights* such as rights to personal privacy and freedom of the press.
>
> Among the LRC reports on privacy, the report on "stalking" is comparatively less *controversial*. Hence, we will first deal with that report. The report proposed the introduction of legislation in order to render the pursuit of a course of conduct causing another person alarm or distress a criminal offence and a civil wrong. We are examining the report and will cautiously consider those proposals which may impact on press freedom. We are also examining latest developments on overseas legislation such as how they regulate collective harassment. As an important step to follow up on the LRC report, we will make practical preparation for conducting public consultation in the coming few months. We plan to launch a consultation exercise in mid-2011.

---

[9] Legislative Council, Legislative Council Meeting 10 November 2010, 1765–1766 <http://www.legco.gov.hk/yr10–11/english/counmtg/hansard/cm1110-translate-e.pdf> accessed 4 July 2012 (emphasis added).

The Hypothesis

While the government's intention to protect privacy interests generally is not disputed, the history outlined above seems to indicate that the real impetuses for introducing new legislation are events or even crises outside its control, rather than a proactive lead from the government.

Judging from the government's response or non-response to the proposed legislation for personal and territorial privacy, it would appear that its priorities in law reform are very much influenced by how controversial the subject matter is. Priorities would be devoted to less controversial subjects because, in these cases, it would be easier to reach a consensus in the community and strike a balance between privacy rights and other conflicting rights.

This hypothesis can be further tested in tracing the developments in the review of the PDPO leading to the introduction of the Personal Data (Privacy) (Amendment) Bill in July 2011.

Review of the PDPO

The PDPO is a robust piece of legislation on personal data protection.[10] It covers any data relating directly or indirectly to a living individual ("data subject") from which it is practicable to ascertain directly or indirectly the identity of the individual and which are in a form in which access or processing is practicable. It applies to any person ("data user") who controls the collection, holding, processing or use of personal data. Data users must follow the six Data Protection Principles (DPPs) in Schedule 1 to the PDPO in relation to the purpose and manner of data collection; accuracy and duration of data retention; use of personal data; security of personal data; transparency of data protection policies and practices; and access to and correction of personal data.

The PDPO is in line with international privacy standards as the six DPPs are broadly consistent with the 1980 OECD Guidelines.[11] It is even stronger in some important aspects, having incorporated some of the requirements of the

---

[10] For an overview of the PDPO, see HKSAR Government, *Consultation Document on Review of the Personal Data (Privacy) Ordinance* (Aug 2009) <http://www.cmab.gov.hk/doc/issues/PDPO_Consultation_Document_en.pdf> ch 2, 5–9, accessed 4 July 2012.

[11] The Organization for Economic Co-operation and Development, *OECD Guidelines on the Protection of Privacy and Transborder Flows of Personal Data* (1980) <http://

1995 EU Directive. However, in light of operating experience in an evolving privacy landscape, the need for amendments to the PDPO was quickly felt soon after it became effective.

Since 1998, the Office of the Privacy Commissioner for Personal Data (PCPD) had submitted proposals for piecemeal legislative amendments to the Home Affairs Bureau (the Hong Kong SAR government's policy bureau responsible for human rights and access to information at that time) for the government's consideration. The proposals were largely technical in nature aimed at addressing practical issues identified in relation to the implementation of the PDPO. The bureau had given the green light to some of the proposals and had in fact given draft drafting instructions to the Law Drafting Division of the Department of Justice in preparing an Amendment Bill. The first draft of the Amendment Bill was prepared in 2002 but was subsequently stalled.

A renewed strength in pushing for legislative changes emerged in recent years when Hong Kong witnessed a series of privacy catastrophes gaining widespread media attention. In March 2006, a serious data leakage occurred involving disclosure on the internet of the personal data of some 20,000 people who had lodged complaints against the police with the Independent Police Complaints Council (IPCC). The data included names, addresses, Hong Kong ID card numbers and in some cases details of criminal convictions. Their leakage, caused by IPCC's contractor for computing services, immediately posed an alarming threat to the persons affected. PCPD conducted an investigation and found that IPCC had contravened DPP 4 of Schedule 1 to the PDPO by failing to take all reasonably practicable steps to ensure that personal data held by it are protected against unauthorized or accidental access, processing, erasure or other use.[12] An enforcement notice was issued to the IPCC directing it to take various remedial measures, including the formulation and implementation of policy, guidelines and measures to protect the complaint data when dealing with an outsourced contractor. As the PCPD found that the IPCC had complied fully with the enforcement notice, no prosecution was initiated.

---

www.oecd.org/document/18/0,3746,en_2649_34255_1815186_1_1_1_1,00.html> accessed 4 July 2012.

[12] Office of the Privacy Commissioner for Personal Data, Hong Kong, "Must Take Security Measures to Protect Personal Data when Engaging Outsourced Contractor" (October 2006) <http://www.pcpd.org.hk/english/publications/files/IPCC_e.pdf> accessed 4 July 2012.

In the subsequent two to three years, more incidents of data leakage or loss occurred, involving large quantities of personal data held by major data users.[13] These included:

(a) Loss of portable storage devices containing patient records by a number of public hospitals, exemplified by the loss reported by the Prince of Wales Hospital on 6 May 2008 of a USB flash drive containing 10,000 patients' personal data;

(b) The recording of the personal particulars of 13,400 taxpayers in July 2007 by an officer of the Inland Revenue Department for his future personal use;

(c) The leakage of classified and sensitive documents containing personal data held by the Immigration, Police and Fire Services Departments on the Internet through the file-sharing software called "Foxy" from May 2008 to February 2009;

(d) Incidents that took place in the commercial sector, including the leakage from the recruitment website Recruit.net of the personal data of 40,000 on line job seekers in June 2007, and the loss by the Hongkong and Shanghai Banking Corporation of a computer server containing 159,000 customer records in April 2008.

This spate of data breaches attracted a lot of media attention and created much public debate about the role of the PCPD and the adequacy of the PDPO in protecting personal data.

Against this background, it was no coincidence that the PCPD took the initiative in June 2006 to form an internal working group to conduct a comprehensive review of the PDPO with a view to identifying necessary amendments to ensure its continued relevance in safeguarding personal data. These proactive efforts culminated in a formal submission in December 2007 of various amendment proposals to the government's Constitutional and Mainland Affairs Bureau (CMAB), the policy bureau which took over responsibility for human rights from the Home Affairs Bureau in July 2007. The subject was discussed at the meeting of LegCo's Panel on Home Affairs on 4 July

---

[13] Legislative Council Secretariat, Information Note: Implementation problems of the Personal Data (Privacy) Ordinance (2008) <http://www.legco.gov.hk/yr07–08/english/sec/library/0708in21-e.pdf> Appendix II–III, accessed 4 July 2012.

2008.[14] Members of the panel expressed overwhelming support for enhanced protection of personal data privacy. The panel also thought that the government should study the amendment proposals seriously. Upon request for a timetable for the government to complete an evaluation of the amendment proposals, the CMAB responded that ". . . it aimed at coming up with concrete proposals to amend the PDPO for consultation with the Fourth Term LegCo as early as possible".

Areas of Concern in Implementing the PDPO

The major data breach incidents that took place following implementation of the PDPO highlighted a number of areas of concern.

It was generally felt that the existing provisions of the PDPO are inadequate in safeguarding personal data protection. In the event of data leakage, data users are not mandated to notify the affected persons. Further, the PCPD does not have adequate sanctioning power to ensure compliance with the PDPO. It has no specific function to mediate between the parties concerned to reach a mutually satisfactory settlement. It has no authority to award compensation to aggrieved data subjects or to impose monetary penalties on data users for contraventions of the DPPs. The aggrieved data subject is left on his own to institute legal proceedings against the data user concerned to seek compensation under the PDPO. Such civil action claims have rarely been brought before the court by the aggrieved data subject. This is understandable due to high litigation costs relative to the amount of damages to be awarded in normal circumstances, and that there is no guarantee that the claimant may remain anonymous throughout the legal proceedings.

In fact, contravention of the DPPs is not an offence per se. The most forceful action the PCPD may take is to issue an enforcement notice to direct the data user to take specified remedial steps within a specified period. Only if the data user contravenes the enforcement notice will he commit an offence. The punitive effect of this arrangement is weak. The PCPD may serve an enforcement notice only when a contravention is likely to continue or be repeated. Further, in the event that a data user resumes the same contravening act shortly after compliance with the enforcement notice, the PCPD can only

---

[14] Panel on Home Affairs, Meeting of the Legislative Council, 4 July 2008 <http://www.legco.gov.hk/yr07–08/english/panels/ha/minutes/ha080704.pdf> accessed 4 July 2012.

issue another enforcement notice. This represents a loophole for data users to circumvent PCPD's escalation of regulation from the issue of an enforcement notice to prosecution of an offence.

Where prosecution of an offence is contemplated for contravention of the requirements under the PDPO, including breach of an enforcement notice, the PCPD is not empowered to institute prosecutions directly against the data users concerned. Instead, it has to refer suspected offences to the police for criminal investigation and, where deemed necessary, to the Department of Justice for prosecution.

The Amendment Proposals and Public Consultation

One year after its formal pledge to LegCo, the CMAB completed a review of the PDPO in conjunction with the PCPD and published, on 28 August 2009, a consultation document inviting views from the public, on or before 30 November 2009, on a series of proposed amendments to the PDPO.[15] By way of background introduction, it recognized the following developments that had prompted the need to review whether the existing provisions of the PDPO were still adequate for protecting personal data:

- Challenges posed by the rapid advancement in information technology, prevalence of the Internet and exponential growth of e-commerce;
- Operational and technical issues identified since the implementation of the PDPO; and
- The community's increasing concern about personal data privacy protection.

The CMAB made it clear in the document that the review was guided by the following factors.[16]

(a) The right of individuals to privacy is not absolute. It must be balanced against other rights and public and social interests;

(b) Balance is needed between safeguarding personal data privacy and facilitating continued development of information and communications technology;

---

[15] HKSAR Government, *Consultation Document on Review of the Personal Data (Privacy) Ordinance* (Aug 2009) <http://www.cmab.gov.hk/doc/issues/PDPO_Consultation_Document_en.pdf> accessed 4 July 2012.

[16] Ibid [4].

(c) Any changes to the privacy law should not undermine Hong Kong's competitiveness and economic efficiency as an international city;
(d) The need to avoid putting an onerous burden on business operations and individual data users;
(e) Due account should be given to local situations;
(f) The PDPO should remain flexible and relevant in spite of technological change;
(g) Legislative intervention may not always be the most effective way. In certain circumstances, personal data privacy protection may be achieved by administrative measures; and
(h) Consensus in the community about privacy issues is important.

While the starting point is the protection of personal data privacy, the emphasis on protecting business interests and arriving at a community consensus is very strong and it will be apparent in the analysis below that these are the main factors determining whether a proposal will be followed up by the government.

In the consultation document, the CMAB put forward 12 "key proposals". These are discussed in the following paragraphs.

Sensitive personal data

Personal data commonly regarded as sensitive by overseas jurisdictions include racial or ethnic origin, political opinion, religious or philosophical beliefs, membership of trade union, health status, sexual life, criminal record and biometric information. At present, the PDPO does not differentiate personal data that are sensitive from those that are not. Given the grave harm that may be inflicted upon the data subject in the event of leakage or accidental disclosure to third parties of sensitive personal data, the issue is whether the processing of sensitive personal data should be subject to more stringent data protection requirements to better protect the personal data privacy of individuals. A more stringent regulatory regime, such as prohibiting the collection, holding, processing and use of such data, is in line with international practices and standards.

Regulation of data processors and sub-contracting activities

The rising trend of data users sub-contracting and entrusting data processing work to third parties has increased the risk to which personal data may be exposed. At present, the PDPO regulates data users but not their agents. In the event of a data breach committed by the agent, the protection afforded to the data subjects is for the data user to assume liability as the principal. The issue is whether to regulate the data processors directly, or to regulate them indirectly by requiring the data user to use contractual or other means to ensure its agents observe the requirements under the PDPO as regards use, security and safekeeping of the personal data entrusted to them, or a combination of these two options.

Personal data security breach notification

At present, there is no requirement under the PDPO for a data user to notify a personal data breach to the PCPD or to individuals affected by the breach. The issue is whether such a notification system should be instituted, on a mandatory or voluntary basis, so that the affected data subjects may take steps to protect themselves or to mitigate the harm that could be done to them.

Granting criminal investigation and prosecution power to PCPD

At present, the PDPO confers powers on the PCPD to investigate suspected breaches of the PDPO's requirements and to inspect personal data systems for promoting compliance with the PDPO. These powers include entry into premises, summoning witnesses and requiring such persons to furnish relevant information, but exclude search for or seizure of evidence. Criminal investigations are conducted by the police and prosecutions, where necessary, are initiated by the Department of Justice. The issue is whether the PCPD should be given the criminal investigation and prosecution power, as well as the incidental powers to search and seize evidence with a view to achieving more effective enforcement of the PDPO.

Legal assistance to data subjects

At present, a data subject who suffers damage by reason of a contravention of a requirement under the PDPO by a data user is entitled to compensation from the data user for that damage. However, as the aggrieved party has to bear the legal costs, recourse to civil remedy under the PDPO is rarely invoked.

The issue is whether the PCPD should be empowered to offer legal assistance to the data subject to seek redress with a view to achieving greater deterrent effect to acts or practices which intrude into personal data privacy.

Award compensation to aggrieved data subjects

As noted above, an aggrieved data subject may under the PDPO seek compensation from the data user for the damage he has suffered by reason of the data user's contravention of a requirement under the PDPO. However, the court proceedings involved could be lengthy and costly, and the outcome is unpredictable. The issue is whether, as a quick and additional means of redress, the PCPD should be empowered to determine and award compensation to the aggrieved data subject.

Making contravention of a DPP an offence

The PCPD is empowered to remedy a contravention of a DPP by issuing an enforcement notice to the data user concerned. Contravention of the enforcement notice is an offence but contravention of the DPPs per se is not. The issue is whether to make the contravention of a DPP an offence in order to achieve a greater deterrent effect.

Unauthorized obtaining, disclosure and sale of personal data

Unauthorized use of personal data may intrude into personal data privacy and cause serious harm to data subjects. These may include intentional or wilful acts such as unauthorized access and collection of customers' personal data by the staff of a company for sale to third parties for profit, and malicious disclosure of a patient's sensitive health records by hospital staff to third parties. The issue is whether to make these blatant acts an offence.

Repeated contravention of a DPP on same facts

At present, a data user may, shortly after compliance with an enforcement notice issued against him within a specified period, resume the same contravening act without fear of a criminal sanction. This is because the PCPD, in the circumstances, can only issue yet another enforcement notice. The issue is whether to make such a repeated contravention an offence in order to forestall possible circumvention of the regulatory regime.

Imposing monetary penalty on serious contravention of DPPs

The issue is whether to empower the PCPD to require data users to pay a monetary penalty for serious contravention of DPPs, in order to produce a greater deterrent effect.

Repeated non-compliance with enforcement notice

At present, the PDPO does not differentiate, in terms of severity of sanctions, between the first contravention of an enforcement notice and repeated contraventions. The issue is whether to subject a repeated offender to a heavier penalty in order to achieve a greater deterrent effect.

Raising penalty for misuse of personal data in direct marketing

Under section 34 of the PDPO, a data user shall not use any personal data for direct marketing activities if the data subject has made an opt-out request, otherwise he commits an offence and is liable to a fine at Level 3 (up to $10,000). In view of the prevalence of direct marketing activities in Hong Kong and that many unsolicited telemarketing calls are causing a nuisance to many people, the PCPD is of the view that the existing level of penalty may be too low to serve as an effective deterrent. The issue is whether the penalty level for a section 34 offence should be raised.

In addition, the consultation document includes 31 proposals on which public comments were also invited. They cover the following areas:

- Rights of data subjects under the PDPO;
- Rights and obligations of data users under the PDPO;
- Enforcement powers of the PCPD;
- Exemptions from the requirements of the PDPO; and
- Streamlining the operation of the PDPO and addressing the technical and operational problems encountered in the implementation of the PDPO.

Under the third point, one proposal is to provide the PCPD with wider discretion to serve an enforcement notice. At present, it may serve an enforcement notice on a data user if the latter is contravening a requirement under the PDPO or has contravened such a requirement in circumstances that make it likely that the contravention will continue or be repeated. To enhance the effectiveness of the PDPO, it was proposed to allow the PCPD to serve an enforcement notice even if the contravening act has ceased and there is no likelihood of repetition, provided that the act involved has caused or is likely to cause damage or distress to the data subject.

Furthermore, the consultation document includes a number of proposals made by the PCPD but not favoured by the government. Of these, two proposals on revamping the regulatory regime of direct marketing are worth noting here: the opt-in recommendation in respect of direct marketing; and the recommendation for a do-not-call register.

Opt-in

Apart from raising the penalty level for a section 34 offence, the proposal requires the data user to obtain the explicit consent of the data subject (that is, "opt-in") before using the latter's personal data from any source for direct marketing purposes. This recognizes the data subject's right of self-determination in respect of his personal data, as opposed to the alternative of "opt-out" which places the burden on the data subject to indicate his wish not to be approached by direct marketers.

Central do-not-call register

The PCPD recognizes that under the Unsolicited Electronic Messages Ordinance (Cap 593) (UEMO), the Office of the Telecommunications Authority (OFTA) is already operating a "do-not-call" register prohibiting the sending of commercial electronic messages to any telephone or fax number registered. The PCPD proposes, therefore, that OFTA's "do-not-call" register should be expanded to include person-to-person telemarketing calls. Under this proposal, consumers may "opt-out" by registering their personal data (i.e. names and telephone numbers) in a central "do-not-call" register operated by the government. Telemarketers making calls to selected consumers would need to check this register beforehand and it would be an offence for them to make unsolicited calls to registered consumers against their opt-out wish.

As noted in the consultation document, the CMAB planned to set the general directions on the way forward based on the views gathered from the consultation exercise, and "arrange for further public discussions on *possible legislative proposals*".[17] There was no promise that the exercise would definitely lead to legislative amendments. However, when the CMAB released its report on the public consultation on 18 October 2010, the prospects for legislative amendments were brighter.[18] As noted in the report, the government has formulated general directions on the way forward and agreed to further collect public views and meet with relevant organizations or stakeholders for "in-depth discussions on the details of the proposals planned to be taken forward, including the *contents of the legislative amendments*, so as to ensure smooth operation of the amended PDPO".[19] The process of "further public discussions" ended on 31 December 2010 and a report was released on 18 April 2011 in which it is noted that "in the light of the views received, [the Administration] has revised and refined the details of some of the proposals and will implement the proposals . . . [The Administration is] *preparing a bill to amend the PDPO* to implement these proposals. [Its] aim is to introduce it into the LegCo in July 2011".[20] As it turned out, the Personal Data (Privacy) (Amendment) Bill 2011 was introduced into the LegCo on 13 July 2011.

Looking back, it took less than two years for the government to prepare the bill, counting from the release of the first public consultation document. By any yardstick, this is an impressive record. It is suggested that the main driver for this accelerated pace of change was a major privacy intrusion incident that took place in 2010 committed by the Octopus group of companies.

The Octopus Incident

The Octopus incident was a landmark privacy intrusion event that concerned the misuse of customer data held by a group of companies which operate a

---

[17] Ibid [5] (emphasis added).
[18] HKSAR Government, *Report on Public Consultation on Review of the Personal Data (Privacy) Ordinance* (Oct 2010) <http://www.cmab.gov.hk/doc/issues/PCPO_report_en.pdf> accessed 4 July 2012.
[19] Ibid [1.8] (emphasis added).
[20] HKSAR Government, *Report on Further Public Discussions on Review of the Personal Data (Privacy) Ordinance* (April 2011) <http://www.cmab.gov.hk/doc/issues/Report_on_FPD_en.pdf> [5.2] accessed 4 July 2012 (emphasis added).

smartcard payment system called Octopus. The Octopus card is widely used by the person in the street for day-to-day needs. It almost obviates the need for cash in the daily lives of Hong Kong people.

Octopus's majority shareholder is the Mass Transit Railway Corporation (MTR). In turn, the majority shareholder of MTR is the Hong Kong SAR government.

Capitalizing on its huge customer database, Octopus collaborated with its business partners to deliver direct marketing and customer loyalty programmes. In particular, it operated a customer reward programme whereby registered members could earn reward dollars for making purchases from Octopus's business partners by presenting the Octopus card. The reward dollars earned could be redeemed for goods and services from these business partners.

In March 2010, subscribers to the programme started to complain about Octopus's transfer of their personal data to third parties for direct marketing purposes without their knowledge or consent. The PCPD investigated the complaints and found, among other things, the following contraventions:

- First, the notice informing the customers of the purpose of the use of the personal data collected, and the classes of persons to whom the data would be transferred, was poorly laid out and presented. For example, the font size used for the notice was so small (about 1mm × 1mm for English) that people with normal eyesight would find the words difficult to read unless aided by a magnifying glass.
- Secondly, the purpose of use of personal data and classes of data transferees were couched in liberal and vague terms. It would not be practicable for customers to ascertain with a reasonable degree of certainty how their personal data would be used and who would have the use of them.
- Thirdly, Octopus had, without the customers' explicit consent, transferred their personal data to a number of partner companies for marketing the latter's products and services. Octopus played little or no part in the marketing process. But it received monetary benefits from the partner companies as a reward for the data transfer. The transaction in essence was a sale of personal data.
- Finally, under prior agreement with Octopus, one partner company promoted its products and services by calling Octopus's customers in the name of Octopus. In effect, the customers were deceived as regards the identity of the caller.

The Octopus incident attracted prolonged media attention and strong protests from different interest groups in Hong Kong. It was rated as one of the top ten news stories of 2010 by many newspapers in Hong Kong. It is indeed a major milestone in the history of personal data protection in Hong Kong, characterized by a number of unique features:

- It represented the tip of an iceberg as similar misuse of customers' personal data was not uncommon in business enterprises, such as banks, with a large customer database.[21]
- It involved the handling of the personal data of 2.4 million people, one-third of the entire population of Hong Kong, for substantial monetary gain.
- Octopus is a household name for which all Hong Kong citizens have a high regard. When they found out that their personal data had been traded like a commodity for the private gain of Octopus, it was no surprise that they reacted with a sense of betrayal and fury.

The effects on Octopus for its outright failure to observe privacy and data protection were detrimental. The loss of public trust and damage to its corporate image are probably irreparable. The public outcry did not subside until it had taken a series of drastic remedial actions as follows:

- It accepted all the recommendations of the PCPD and those of other regulators as regards enhancing personal data protection.
- It donated to charity all the revenue generated by its data transfer to third parties, namely HK$57.9 m.
- It pledged that it would focus its core business on providing smart card services to customers and it would no longer participate in activities that require the provision of customer data to merchant partners for marketing purposes.

---

[21] See PCPD's reports on subsequent investigations into four banks: Fubon Bank (Hong Kong) Limited <http://www.pcpd.org.hk/english/publications/files/R11_1696_e.pdf> accessed 4 July 2012; Citibank (Hong Kong) Limited <http://www.pcpd.org.hk/english/publications/files/R11_1982_e.pdf> accessed 4 July 2012; Wing Hang Bank Limited <http://www.pcpd.org.hk/english/publications/files/R11_2853_e.pdf> accessed 4 July 2012; Industrial and Commercial Bank of China (Asia) Limited <http://www.pcpd.org.hk/english/publications/files/R11_7946_e.pdf> accessed 4 July 2012.

- Both its CEO and Board chairman resigned (the latter purportedly as part of a natural succession plan).

It is perhaps no exaggeration to say that the Octopus incident provided a human rights lesson for the Hong Kong community. It raised public awareness and understanding of their privacy rights over personal data to an unprecedentedly high level. Media reports on privacy and data protection issues are more prevalent than ever before. In a subsequent survey conducted by an Internet security company from February to March 2011, it was found that 85% of Hong Kong people surveyed were extremely or very concerned about misuse of their personal data.[22]

The Octopus incident had important implications for corporate data users too. It served as a wake-up call to those who might not have accorded adequate priority to the issue of personal data privacy. Transfer of customers' personal data to third parties for direct marketing purposes is pretty common in Hong Kong. The business sectors involved include banks, telecommunication operators and the insurance industry. The corresponding trade regulators for these sectors came under great pressure to address the issues raised by Octopus's malpractice. For example, the Hong Kong Monetary Authority, which oversees the banks, went so far as to direct the banks to suspend the transfer of personal data to unrelated third parties for marketing purposes unless and until they were able to confirm full compliance with the law and the guidance note issued by the PCPD.

As the ownership of Octopus can be traced to the government, the incident generated immense political interest and fuelled vicious attacks against the government for maladministration. Legislators blamed the Secretary for Transport and the Secretary for Financial Services, who sit on the MTR Board, for dereliction of duty and held them accountable for Octopus's contraventions.[23] Both legislators Wong Kwok-hing and James To had proposed to invoke the Legislative Council (Powers and Privileges) Ordinance to

---

[22] Unisys Security Index Hong Kong, *A Synovate Survey* (May 2011) <http://www.unisyssecurityindex.com/system/reports/uploads/95/original/Unisys%20Security%20Index%20-%20Hong%20Kong%20-%20May%202011.pdf> accessed 4 July 2012.

[23] Legislative Council Secretariat, Legislative Council Meeting 20 Oct 2010, Speech of Wong Kwok-hing <http://legco.gov.hk/yr10–11/english/counmtg/hansard/cm1020-translate-e.pdf> 389, accessed 4 July 2012.

investigate the Octopus incident. The latter went even further to propose the appointment of a select committee under this Ordinance to inquire into issues relating to the transfer and sale of customers' personal data in the banking, the telecommunications, the insurance sectors and large-scale chain stores which had induced members of the public to provide them with personal data through various reward programmes.[24]

Legislator Wong claimed victory for making the MTR accept responsibility for Octopus's misdeeds and for taking drastic remedial action, and withdrew his proposal accordingly.[25] He noted that the Chief Executive had made a special note in his policy address on 13 October 2010 that the government would put forward legislative proposals to enhance personal data protection.[26] He was reported to have said, "as the Administration was expected to complete the review (on the PDPO) by the end of the year, he considered that the way forward should be to press the administration to submit its legislative proposals to LegCo as soon as possible in early 2011."[27]

After an intense debate and voting in LegCo's House Committee on 26 November 2010 legislator To's proposals were not supported.[28] It is worth noting that the debate made a great deal of reference to the CMAB's concurrent effort in reviewing the PDPO. There seemed to be a consensus among the House Committee members that the existing legislation is inadequate in protecting personal data privacy. They noted that, under the PDPO, the PCPD was not even able to serve an enforcement notice on Octopus because the evidence showed the contraventions would not continue or be repeated. Among other things, legislator To stressed that his proposed cross-industry inquiry would compel the organizations concerned to produce all relevant information regarding transfer and sale of customers' personal data and this would serve as a factual basis for LegCo to consider the government's proposals for amending the PDPO. On the other hand, many other House Committee members present shared the views of legislator Wong that, given the government had initiated a

---

[24] Legislative Council, Meeting of House Committee, 26 November 2010 <http://legco.gov.hk/ yr10–11/english/hc/minutes/hc20101126.pdf>, item IX [53]–[54] accessed 4 July 2012.
[25] Ibid [71].
[26] See n 23, 388.
[27] See n 24, [63].
[28] See n 24.

review of the PDPO, it would be more fruitful for them to focus on the review and to be more vigilant in the scrutiny of the legislative proposals in future.

In short, there is no question that the government was put on the spot to expedite the required legislative amendment process to enhance personal data protection. This probably provided the parties concerned with the quickest escape from an embarrassing political turmoil.

Further Legislative Proposals to Regulate Collection and Use of Personal Data for Direct Marketing

In the report on public consultation issued on 18 October 2010,[29] the CMAB specifically introduced further legislative proposals to address the urgent need to strengthen regulation over the collection and use (including sale) of personal data for direct marketing. These included:

- The introduction of additional specific requirements on the collection and use of personal data for direct marketing purposes, and to make it an offence if a data user does not comply with the requirements and subsequently uses the personal data for direct marketing:
    - requiring the data user's notice to the data subject about data collection to be reasonably specific about the intended marketing activities, the classes of persons to whom the data may be transferred and the kinds of data to be transferred;
    - the presentation of the information should be understandable and reasonably readable; and
    - the data subject should be provided with an opportunity to opt out from the intended use of his/her personal data.

  The offence attracts a maximum fine of HK$500,000 and imprisonment for three years.
- Making unauthorized sale of personal data by data user an offence, punishable by a maximum fine of HK$1,000,000 and imprisonment for five years.

---

[29] See n 18.

Screening Out Legislative Proposals

It is interesting to explore how the government decided to take forward a legislative proposal based on the views collected from the consultation exercises. As expected, the amendment proposals attracted diverse views from the public and they were duly recorded in the reports released on 18 October 2010 and 18 April 2011 respectively. The CMAB attempted to adopt a qualitative and analytical approach in examining the public views and coming to a conclusion on the way forward. Reading between the lines, however, one cannot help suggesting that the screening process could well be a simple mathematical game:

(1) Proposals that had the majority support (in terms of percentage of submissions arguing in favour) were taken forward;
(2) Proposals with a majority arguing against were stalled; and
(3) Proposals with no clear support or opposition were stalled as well.

Included in category (1) were the following proposals:

(a) Personal Data Security Breach Notification (on voluntary basis);
(b) Legal assistance to data subjects;
(c) Unauthorized obtaining, disclosure and sale of personal data;
(d) Repeated non-compliance with enforcement notice;
(e) Raising the penalty for misuse of personal data in direct marketing;
(f) Introduction of specific requirements on collection and use of personal; data for direct marketing purpose;
(g) Making unauthorized sale of personal data an offence.

Included in category (2) were the following proposals:

(a) Granting criminal investigation and prosecution power to PCPD;
(b) Award compensation to aggrieved data subjects;
(c) Making contravention of a DPP an offence;
(d) Imposing monetary penalty on serious contravention of DPPs.

Included in category (3) were the following proposals:

(a) Sensitive personal data;
(b) Regulation of data processors and sub-contracting activities;
(c) Central do-not-call register.

There are three notable exceptions to the above simple mathematical approach to the screening of legislative proposals. First, as regards whether to make a repeated contravention of a DPP on the same facts an offence, it was reported that there were mixed views supporting and opposing the proposal, but no indication was mentioned as regards which side was outnumbered. The conclusion was that the government would implement the proposal.[30]

Secondly, as regards whether to allow the PCPD to serve an enforcement notice even if the contravening act had ceased and there was no likelihood of repetition, it was reported that some 40% of the submissions opposed the implementation of the proposal while over 30% indicated their support. Despite the lack of a majority support, the CMAB recommended proceeding with the proposal.[31] It is conceivable that this extraordinary decision was prompted by the inability of the PCPD to issue an enforcement notice in the Octopus case. This impotence was criticized by some media and legislators as setting the culprit free.

Thirdly, as regards the choice between an "opt-in" or an "opt-out" regime for seeking customers' consent to use their personal data for direct marketing, the reports did not mention at all which option had more support from the public. Instead, the Government argued in favour of "opt-out" on grounds that it is less onerous to the operations of enterprises and it is more widely adopted in overseas jurisdictions.[32]

A strict mathematical approach counting the number of submissions for and against a proposal is beset with flaws. To begin with, the system works on the basis of one submission equals one vote, with little or no weighting assigned based on the identity of the person making the submission and the arguments therein. Even the PCPD's submission, which represented the wisdom gained through years of experience of enforcing data protection in Hong Kong and well-grounded research based on worldwide trends and overseas experience, attracted one plain vote.

Further, not to proceed with a proposal due to the lack of a clear majority support may be an overly restrictive approach. The words usually used in this regard in the consultation reports include "views . . . are evenly split", "mixed views", "no consensus could be reached" and "views . . . are diverse". Bearing in mind that human rights issues including personal data protection are by nature controversial, the government does not seem to be prepared to take a

---

[30] *Report on Public Consultation on Review of the Personal Data (Privacy) Ordinance* (n 18), 69–73.
[31] Ibid 52–54.
[32] Ibid 8–13.

proactive lead in promoting further public debate on the controversial issues and resolving them with the stakeholders concerned.

A case in point is the PCPD's proposal to accord greater protection to sensitive personal data by prohibiting the collection, holding, processing and use of such data except under prescribed circumstances. The CMAB came to the following conclusion on this proposal:[33]

> [M]ost of the views support the general direction that a higher degree of protection should be afforded to certain types of personal data which are more sensitive. Nevertheless, views received are diverse with regard to the coverage of sensitive personal data with no mainstream consensus reached ... There are also quite a lot of views considering that the Government should consult the public further before arriving at any conclusion ... We shall keep in view the community's discussion on whether sensitive personal data should be subject to more stringent regulation and the coverage of sensitive personal data, as well as the development and experience of overseas jurisdictions ... before we further consider whether to take forward the proposal.

Conclusion

The experience of the initial enactment of the PDPO and its impending amendment outlined above seems to indicate that the government's approach to legislative reform is reactive rather than proactive. The drive for change can be traced back to a perceived imminent risk to Hong Kong's trade position in 1995 and a public outcry in 2010 underlining the inadequacy of the existing legislation. Without these drivers, one wonders whether real progress would have been made.

This passive approach is explicable in terms of the government's philosophy of pragmatic politics. The former Chief Executive's policy address made at the end of his first term of office reveals the government's reluctance to "engage in ideological debates or utopian social projects". In lieu of a moral pledge to promote human rights and consumer interests, the Chief Executive's priorities are to "build a harmonious society" by "resolving conflicts" and "fostering consensus".[34]

---

[33] Ibid 123–124.
[34] Chief Executive's Policy Address 2006–07, 67–76 <http://www.policyaddress.gov.hk/06–07/eng/p67.html> accessed 4 July 2012.

At this stage of Hong Kong's constitutional development, the government lacks a strong direct mandate acquired through the electoral process, and is therefore prone to be a hostage to public opinion rather than a leader of public opinion. The initiative to amend the PDPO may be merely a passive reaction to the Octopus crisis, as evidenced by the emphasis on regulation of the direct marketing and sale of personal data, and the avoidance of issues where no consensus was reached in the public consultations. We probably need further public outcries to prompt the government to address seriously and expeditiously other and perhaps more controversial aspects of data protection and other privacy areas.

Chapter 12
Privacy and Law Reform: What Can We Learn from the Hong Kong Process?

John Bacon-Shone

Introduction

It is now more than twenty years since the Attorney General and Chief Justice asked the Law Reform Commission of Hong Kong (HKLRC) to examine legislative and other measures to protect privacy, with particular reference to data protection, intrusion into private premises and interception of communications. The privacy subcommittee completed six reports during the period from 1990 up to 2006, only one of which (reform of the law relating to the protection of personal data) has been comprehensively implemented to date.[1] As the current Privacy Commissioner for Personal Data, Mr. Allan Chiang, has reviewed the legislation relating to personal data in Chapter 11 of this volume, I will review the five other reports that have not been comprehensively implemented. The non-implementation of these reports could be viewed as illustrating failures of the law reform process.

The privacy sub-committee was originally chaired by Justice Barry Mortimer and then by Professor Ray Wacks, both eminent and erudite lawyers, so it may seem presumptuous for a non-lawyer such as myself to comment on the process of legal reform, but I did participate and observe the process in this case over a 16 year period as a member of the HKLRC privacy sub-committee (and as its final chairman after outlasting my superiors), including six years

---

[1] The HKLRC reports for Reform of the Law Relating to the Protection of Personal Data (August 1994), Regulating the Interception of Communications (December 1996), Stalking (October 2000), Civil Liability for Invasion of Privacy (December 2004), Privacy and Media Intrusion (December 2004), The Regulation of Covert Surveillance (March 2006) can all be found at: <http://www.hkreform.gov.hk/en/publications/subject.htm#privacy> accessed 7 July 2012.

as a member of the HKLRC and five subsequent years as a citizen. This has left a lasting impact on my attitudes towards, concerns about, and knowledge of privacy and gives me a specific perspective on the law reform process and indeed generally on reform processes in Hong Kong.

The reader might expect some degree of cynicism about the process from me, given that only one report out of six was widely adopted. Indeed, one of my fellow sub-committee members has noted that in the case of interception of communications and covert surveillance "an activist in the Courts achieved what a decade of law reform had not".[2] However, I believe that it is important to note that, in the case of interception and surveillance, the legislation drew extensively on the two HKLRC reports, although it only adopted the elements that addressed actions by law enforcement agencies and failed to adopt any of the proposals that would have regulated private interception and covert surveillance.

Where Are We Now?

For all six reports, the HKLRC adopted the normal process of a subcommittee drafting a consultation paper, which, after review by the HKLRC, was issued to the public for comment. After reviewing the public feedback a final report was issued. The one complication in the case of privacy was that only five consultation papers were issued as covert surveillance and interception of communications were dealt with in a single consultation paper, but the reports were divided up, with the interception report issued in 1996 and covert surveillance issued as the final report in 2006. This was in response to the view that the law governing interception of communications was in much more urgent need of reform before the return of sovereignty to China. However, although the government issued a white paper on interception in February 1997, it was never introduced into the Legislative Council (LegCo). Instead, a private members bill, sponsored by the Hon James To, was passed in June 1997, just before the return of sovereignty, but never brought into operation by the post-handover government.

---

[2] R McLeish and G Greenleaf, "Hong Kong" in J B Rule and G Greenleaf (eds), *Global Privacy Protection: The First Generation* (Edward Elgar Publishing, 2008) ch 8.

All reports were presented to the Home Affairs panel of the legislature, where the proposals on personal data protection, covert surveillance and interception of communications were quite positively received, while the proposals on media intrusion, stalking and privacy torts received a much less positive response due to concerns raised primarily by the Hong Kong Journalists Association (HKJA) which argued that the proposals would threaten press freedom.

In all cases, the Home Affairs Bureau (which was at that time the responsible bureau, even though there were important implications for the Security Bureau) failed to present any proposals in response.

If no specific privacy problems had arisen since then, it is arguable that there would still have been no advances in privacy protections. However, two key events put pressure on the government to reconsider taking action.

In 2005, two separate court decisions involving covert surveillance made clear that the courts did not accept the existing administrative controls as sufficient, both making clear that a legislative framework was needed.[3] Thanks to legal action by activists Leung Kwok-hung and Koo Sze-yiu, an executive order by the Chief Executive, Donald Tsang, was also ruled as insufficient, although the courts did give the Administration six months leeway to put legislation in place.[4] As a consequence, the government adopted key elements of the HKLRC reports on both covert surveillance and interception of communication, although it only addressed the issues of legal authority and control of law enforcement agencies, ignoring the problems and proposed solutions mentioned in the HKLRC reports relating to private actors. This means that, for example, private detectives still operate largely unregulated without legal controls on covert surveillance and inadequate restrictions on interception of communications.

In 2006, *Easy Finder*, a tabloid magazine published by one of the newspaper groups that ignores the voluntary Hong Kong Press Council, printed pictures of "Twins" pop star Gillian Chung partially clothed, apparently taken in her changing room by a reporter.[5]

---

[3] *HKSAR v Li Man-tak* [2005] HKEC 1308 (DC); *HKSAR v Shum Chiu*, unreported, DCCC687/2004, 5 July 2005.

[4] *Leung Kwok Hung v Chief Executive* [2006] HKEC 239, aff'd [2006] HKEC 816.

[5] See <http://www.thestandard.com.hk/news_print.asp?art_id=25834&sid=9581694> accessed 7 July 2012.

Following widespread condemnation, the Chief Executive, Donald Tsang, promised that the government would revisit the HKLRC proposals to address this.[6] However, instead of taking positive action, the government transferred responsibility for privacy from the Home Affairs Bureau to the Constitutional Affairs Bureau. Meanwhile, the Obscene Articles Tribunal classified the published photographs as "indecent". While this might seem like a reasonable stopgap approach to the problem in the absence of proper privacy protections, the pictures could in no rational way be judged as indecent outside the privacy intrusion context as they are indistinguishable from many pictures regularly published in Hong Kong. This case alone may not be persuasive to everyone, given that pop stars often seek publicity to assist their careers and these pictures certainly yielded massive amounts of publicity and sympathy. However, magazines like *Easy Finder* do not limit their practice of publishing privacy intrusive photographs to people already in the public eye. Annex 1 of the HKLRC report on privacy and media intrusion lists about 300 cases of extreme intrusion taken from just three best-selling newspapers in 2000 and 2001.[7] To take just one of these horrific cases as an example: *Apple Daily* reported the story and published a picture of an identifiable German woman lying on a stretcher who had been the victim of an attempted rape that failed, but was so frightened that she became incontinent.[8]

In November 2010, the government finally gave some room for optimism by stating, in response to a LegCo question, that they would move forward first with stalking, although they claimed that, on privacy torts and media intrusion, there were "divergent views" and that "we need to reach a consensus in the community and strike balance between the different rights such as rights to personal privacy and freedom of the press", ignoring the fact that the proposals had already considered an appropriate balance between those rights. It is also noteworthy that the remaining aspects of interception of communications and covert surveillance are not mentioned at all. Since then, the government has presented proposals for consultation on stalking in late 2011 as promised, although the government proposals arguably greatly increased

---

[6] See <http://www.thestandard.com.hk/news_print.asp?art_id=26196&sid=9645338> accessed 7 July 2012.

[7] See <http://www.hkreform.gov.hk/en/publications/rmedia.htm> accessed 7 July 2012.

[8] Ibid, Case A3.

the risk of infringing other human rights by extending the HKLRC proposals to cover harassment by and against groups. However, as the consultation was undertaken so late in the term of the then current government, it was unclear if or when legislative proposals might finally arrive after the new government had taken office in July 2012.

With regard to the proposals on privacy torts and regulation of the media, the government still has not presented any proposals to address the recommendations, and it is unclear whether such proposals will ever arrive.

Assessment

Probably the most positive assessment of the privacy law reform process in Hong Kong would be to highlight the implementation of protections against the three major elements of privacy invasion that involves the State, namely personal data protection, covert surveillance and interception of communications, and arguably the most extensive area of privacy invasion by business, namely personal data protection.

The most negative assessment would be to highlight the failure to address key elements of private invasion of privacy, namely covert surveillance and interception by non-government actors, media intrusion and stalking, and the failure to introduce torts that would protect against unwarranted intrusion on the solitude or seclusion of an individual, or unwarranted publicity concerning private life. Chapter 11 in this volume analyses the reasons for success in the domain of personal data protection. This begs the question why the process apparently worked so well in one domain and not the other, which I will investigate in more detail below in the hope that the comparison will yield deeper insights into the law reform process.

Process Elements

I believe we need first to distinguish the different elements of the law reform process, namely: identification of an area where reform is sorely needed, identification of effective reforms, and effective implementation of the reforms. I would argue that, in the case of privacy, there is no argument that there was a strong need for reform, so the first element is clearly met. For areas other than personal data protection, the key question is whether the reforms identified were ineffective, the implementation process failed, or both.

As noted above, although the pre-and post-handover governments failed to implement reforms for surveillance or interception of communication in a timely manner, when reform was forced on the government by the courts, they made very broad use of the proposals in the HKLRC reports. This suggests that, in this domain at least, the failure was entirely one of implementation, not of the effectiveness of the proposals.

Stakeholder Interests

If we look at the different reports in terms of stakeholders who might support or work against the proposals, we see what I would argue is a clear picture.

In the case of personal data protection, large businesses, who might be expected to resist, were supportive because of their fear of being cut off from all European personal data, while the colonial government could safely support it as one human rights initiative that business would support and hence Beijing would accept.

In the case of surveillance and interception, law enforcement was very reluctant because it would force them to be transparent about the scale of interception that took place pre-and post-handover. Only a threat by the courts to disallow all interception was able to force the government to enact the necessary reforms.

Media Intrusion

In the case of stalking, media intrusion and the privacy torts, the need for reform is felt by private individuals, while the print media, which has made substantial profits from intruding on the privacy rights of individuals in Hong Kong, distorting the public's need to know into the public's desire to know, was able to stand against reform on the basis that it *might* impinge on press freedom. The Hong Kong Press Council (HKPC), which was setup as a private voluntary initiative to address these intrusions is widely seen as irrelevant, given that the worst offenders refuse to join and can simply ignore it.

The Gillian Chung experience mentioned above shows similarity with the experience in the United Kingdom, which has also shown the reluctance of politicians to bite the hand that provides them with the publicity they need to get re-elected. Unfortunately, this suggests that, until Hong Kong experiences an even more extreme case of media privacy intrusion, private individuals, whether they have chosen to be in the public eye or not, will continue to suffer privacy intrusion from the media.

Role and Value of Social Science Research

One other element of the law reform process that I, as a social scientist, would like to comment on is the role of social science research in the law reform process in Hong Kong. So far, the role has been nearly non-existent. During the consultation period for personal data protection, I collaborated with Harold Traver, a sociologist who had conducted the only previous research on privacy in Hong Kong, to undertake a survey of public attitudes to privacy. I believe the survey was useful in that it settled an argument inside the sub-committee about sensitive data, by illustrating the difficulty of identifying what data was sensitive and how sensitivity depended on social context, with religion not being sensitive, while income and address were sensitive. The survey findings were included as an appendix to the HKLRC report.

However, as a survey methodologist, I feel strongly that it is important to be aware of how surveys of public opinion may and may not be useful in the policy reform process. The public cannot usually provide useful feedback on the value of policy proposals in a simple survey because properly evaluating policy proposals requires people to understand the full context. This is especially difficult if the policy involves new concepts. For example, the early surveys I did on personal data protection were hampered by the fact that there was not a simple standard translation of the key terms in Cantonese that the general public recognized.

This does not mean that public opinion is irrelevant, just that it can best inform whether ideas have been communicated well and whether specific problems are common. Understanding social problems in detail and the viability of specific solutions requires much more in-depth social research, which takes time and money. Fortunately, there is now government funding for public policy research in Hong Kong. If that had been the case during the life of the subcommittee, I would certainly have submitted a proposal to look at some of the issues, including stalking, which I still believe to be a very serious problem for a small but significant number of people. Indeed, such a proposal is still timely, so that there would be some hard evidence to combat the shameful resistance to reform from the media.

Conclusions

In conclusion, I believe that the lessons that we can learn about law reform from the case of privacy are as follows:

- It is important to identify areas where law reform is needed.
- It is worthwhile to invest the time and energy to create effective proposals for reform.
- Whether implementation can be achieved in the short term depends much more on the political climate than on the value of the proposals.
- Public policy research should help make the case for reform, especially when the political climate appears initially negative or the people to benefit are a minority.
- When the political climate is right, proposals drafted carefully may be invaluable and may form the basis for reform proposals that are implemented, even years after being drafted, especially if the implementation is seen as urgent.

Chapter 13
Reforming Privacy Law in New South Wales: Lessons for Law Reform Agencies

Michael Tilbury

A Tale of Two Commissions

Once upon a time, there were two law reform agencies, the Australian Law Reform Commission (ALRC) and the New South Wales Law Reform Commission (NSWLRC).[1] The ALRC was the federal law reform agency in Australia, while the NSWLRC was a state law reform agency. Both Commissions were established on a statutory basis to give effect to what Professor Geoffrey Sawer called the "qualitatively new principle" that emerged in the British Commonwealth in the 1960s and 1970s, that "the *whole* body of the law stood potentially in need of reform, and that there should be a *standing* body of appropriate professional experts to consider reforms continuously".[2] For most of the first decade of the twenty-first century, both bodies could be described as permanent, authoritative, full-time, independent, generalist, inter-disciplinary, consultative and implementation-minded.[3] Both Commissions acted in response to references from their respective governments. The ALRC was, however, a much larger body than its counterpart in New South Wales: its budget was approximately three times that of the NSWLRC, supporting many more research and support staff than the NSWLRC. The ALRC also had

---

[1] While the two Commissions continue to exist, times have, in fact, changed. New funding arrangements resulted, in 2010, in a substantial reduction of the ALRC's budget, staff and management: see Parliament of Australia, The Senate, Legal and Constitutional Affairs References Committee, *Inquiry into the Australian Law Reform Commission* (April 2011).

[2] G Sawer, "The Legal Theory of Law Reform" (1970) 20 *University of Toronto Law Journal* 183, 183. The emphasis is in the original.

[3] See D Weisbrot, "The Future of Institutional Law Reform" in B Opeskin and D Weisbrot, *The Promise of Law Reform* (Federation Press, 2005) ch 2.

three full-time Commissioners (including a full-time Chair), while the NSW Commission had a part-time Chair and one full-time Commissioner.

This was the position that obtained in 2006 when both the ALRC and the NSWLRC received terms of reference to review the law of privacy. Although these terms of reference overlapped considerably in practice, this is not apparent from their wording, which reflected different drafting styles and a focus on the different statutory provisions in force in the Commissions' respective jurisdictions. The ALRC's terms reference required it to "identify and consult with relevant stakeholders" including "relevant State and Territory bodies",[4] while those of the NSWLRC expressly required that Commission to "liaise" with the ALRC in its review.[5] In the early stages of their respective reviews, the two Commissions co-operated on one particular aspect of their inquiries — on a point on which the terms of references of the two Commissions did not overlap. The NSWLRC's terms of reference specifically required it to consider the "desirability of introducing a statutory tort of privacy in New South Wales".[6] On the other hand, the ALRC's terms of reference made no mention of any introduction of a general cause of action, however described, that would protect privacy.[7] This difference in their terms of reference provided the ALRC and the NSWLRC with one way of initially allocating their resources in reviewing this very large area of statutory and common law. It was agreed that the NSWLRC would begin its inquiry by examining the merits of introducing a general cause of action for invasion of privacy.

The NSWLRC therefore set about addressing the question of the desirability of introducing a general action to this effect, issuing a consultation paper on the subject in 2007.[8] About a year later, in 2008, the ALRC proposed, in its final report, *For Your Information: Australian Privacy Law and Practice*, that there should be a statutory cause of action for invasion of privacy in

---

[4] The terms of reference are set out in Australian Law Reform Commission, *For Your Information: Australian Privacy Law and Practice* (Report 108, 2008) vol 1, 19–20.

[5] The terms of reference are set out in NSW Law Reform Commission, *Invasion of Privacy* (Consultation Paper 1, 2007), vii.

[6] Ibid.

[7] One reason for this may be because there may be some doubt about the ability of the federal government to legislate generally in the area of privacy: see Report 108 (n 4) vol 1, ch 3.

[8] See Consultation Paper 1 (n 5).

federal legislation, largely along the lines outlined in the NSWLRC's consultation paper.[9] It was to be almost another year before the NSWLRC itself finally reported on this aspect of its privacy reference. By then, the NSW Commission's thinking had developed significantly in the light of: further research; legal developments overseas; further consultation; the results of the deliberations of its International Advisory Panel; and the experience of drafting model legislation to accompany its report. As a result there are some significant divergences in the recommendations of the ALRC and the NSWLRC on the content of the proposed statutory cause of action for invasion of privacy.

The divergences were not the result of disagreement between the two Commissions, but were rather attributable to the way in which the general processes of law reform worked themselves out in the context of the Commissions' respective inquiries, with the result that the two Commissions did not co-operate in developing their final proposals. The next section of this chapter explains how this could come about and considers what it implies about the desirability of co-operation between law reform agencies.

The chapter has a second objective: to investigate the implications for law reform agencies of the very different responses of the federal and NSW governments to the reports of their respective law reform commissions on privacy. On the one hand, the federal government formally launched the ALRC's final report on privacy and undertook to respond to its 295 recommendations in two stages.[10] The first stage considered various recommendations relating to the structure and content of federal privacy legislation, especially to what have become known as the "Australian Privacy Principles", and to the ALRC's recommendations relating to credit reporting and to the protection of credit reporting information. This resulted, at the end of 2012, in the enactment of the Privacy Amendment (Enhancing Privacy Protection) Act 2012 (Cth), which will come into force in 2014.[11] Consideration of a statutory cause of action for invasion of privacy was initially allocated to the second stage of the government's response. However, the News International phone-hacking scandal in 2011 in the United Kingdom brought forward the government's consideration

---

[9] Report 108 (n 4) vol 3, ch 74.

[10] For a convenient summary of the various stages of the federal government's response, see the website of the Office of the Australian Information Commissioner (OAIC) <www.privacy.gov.au/law/reform> accessed 23 January 2013.

[11] See <www.ag.gov.au/RightsAndProtections/Privacy/Pages/Privacyreforms.aspx> accessed 23 January 2013.

of the cause of action issue. Responding to that "crisis", the federal government released, in September 2011, a discussion paper on the desirability of introducing a statutory cause of action for invasion of privacy.[12] Responses to that paper were due by 18 November 2011. At the beginning of 2013, the federal government is still considering the issue.

On the other hand, the NSW government made no response to the release of the NSWLRC's 2009 report on the desirability of introducing a statutory cause of action for invasion of privacy. Moreover, the final report of the NSWLRC on privacy was only released 10 months after its delivery to the government.[13] Indeed, it was then only "deemed tabled in Parliament" following a change of government in NSW.[14]

There was one exception to the lack of response of the NSW government to the privacy inquiry. In 2009, the Attorney General expanded the terms of the NSWLRC's privacy reference to require the Commission to examine how effectively privacy was protected, and would be protected, under existing freedom of information legislation, and proposed new legislation, in so far as that legislation related to the handling of access to personal information.[15] One of the Commission's privacy reports had already examined the interface of privacy legislation and freedom of information legislation. However, proposed legislation in NSW, responding to initiatives in several Australian jurisdictions, created a new freedom of information regime that envisaged greater facilitation of public access to government information. The proposed legislation also created a new office of "Information Commissioner" (which immediately raised questions about the relationship between this new office and that of the Privacy Commissioner). The Attorney General stressed the urgency of responding to these additional terms of reference, and the Commission published two reports in less than a year, one dealing with access to personal information, the other with the Offices of the Information and Privacy

---

[12] See Commonwealth of Australia, Department of Prime Minister and Cabinet, *A Statutory Cause of Action for Serious Invasion of Privacy*, Issues Paper, September 2011 <http://www.ag.gov.au/Consultations/Pages/Righttosueforserious invasionofprivacyissuespaper.aspx> accessed 23 January 2012.

[13] See NSW Law Reform Commission, *Protecting Privacy in New South Wales* (Report 127, 2010).

[14] See <http://www.lawlink.nsw.gov.au/lrc.nsf/pages/digest113> accessed 23 January 2013.

[15] See <http://www.lawlink.nsw.gov.au/lrc/ll_lrc.nsf/pages/digest124> accessed 23 January 2013.

Commissioners.[16] The Commission's reports were swiftly released and implemented in legislation without a great deal of alteration.

This chapter addresses the differing responses of the federal and NSW governments to the privacy inquiries in their respective jurisdictions. These responses engage the important, and broader, topic of the relationship between governments and law reform agencies, which, in turn, may have implications for the reform of law reform machinery and processes.

Before turning to the substance of this chapter, two points should be noted by way of background. First, as in Hong Kong, privacy law in Australia looks fairly well developed in so far as statute regulates the handling of personal information, particularly by government. Again, like Hong Kong (but unlike New Zealand[17] and Ontario),[18] the common law of Australia knows no general common law action that is aimed specifically at enabling an individual to seek redress for an invasion of their privacy.[19]

Secondly, the ALRC and the NSWLRC were not the only Australasian law reform agencies that had the reform of privacy law on their respective agendas in the first decade of the twenty-first century. The Victorian Law Reform Commission, which had begun work on aspects of privacy law in 2002, reported on workplace privacy in 2005 and surveillance in public places in 2010.[20] And the New Zealand Law Commission completed a comprehensive four-stage review of privacy law in 2011.[21]

---

[16] NSW Law Reform Commission, *The Offices of the Information and Privacy Commissioners* (Report 125, 2009); NSW Law Reform Commission, *Access to Personal Information* (Report 126, 2010).

[17] *Hosking v Runting* [2005] 1 NZLR 1 (CA) (tort of wrongful disclosure of personal information).

[18] *Jones v Tsige* [2012] ONCA 32 (January 18, 2012) (tort of intrusion on seclusion).

[19] The closest is the old tort of *Wilkinson v Downton* [1897] 2 QB 57 and the equitable action for breach of confidence, neither of which seem sound vehicles for the more general protection of privacy at general law: see M Tilbury, "Privacy and Private Law: Developing the Common Law of Australia" in E Bant and M Harding (eds), *Exploring Private Law* (Camb UP, 2010) 86, 98–107.

[20] For details, see <http://www.lawreform.vic.gov.au/inquiries/workplace-privacy> accessed 23 January 2013 (workplace privacy); <http://www.lawreform.vic.gov.au/inquiries/surveillance-public-places> accessed 23 January 2013 (surveillance in public places).

[21] For details, see <http://www.lawcom.govt.nz/project/review-privacy> accessed 23 January 2013.

Co-operation Between Law Reform Agencies

Law reform agencies now exist in a globalized world, where the experience of other jurisdictions (particularly other common law jurisdictions) is increasingly a feature of all law reform projects. Knowledge of this experience is generated largely by contact and co-operation among law reform agencies. Co-operation exists not only between law reform agencies within federations, such as Canada or Australia, but also across national borders.[22] It takes many forms: from the provision of information about the state of an agency's current projects or about the current state of the law within the law reform agency's jurisdiction, to providing material assistance in the form of library materials or sending or taking staff on secondment from another agency. None of this is, or ought to be, controversial.[23] From the perspective of any law reform agency (which will typically be under-funded, under-staffed and over-worked), the only issue will be that of setting aside an appropriate amount of time for the co-operative activity. And most law reform agencies will, of course, find the time to liaise with those involved in similar endeavours to their own.

This chapter focuses on "co-operation" of a more formal and structured nature, namely, where law reform agencies act together on a particular project or a review of a particular area of law. There are many instances of this occurring (for example, between law reform agencies in Australia, and between the English and Scottish Commissions), though not generally across international borders.[24] Yet it is co-operation across international boundaries — that is, co-operation with law reform agencies in other common law jurisdictions — that could be of most relevance to Hong Kong in the future. At first glance, it seems obvious that such co-operation, with the potential savings it involves in avoiding duplication, should be encouraged. However, as Michael Sayers, former Chief Executive of the Law Commission for England and Wales and first General Secretary of the Commonwealth Association of Law Reform Agencies, has pointed out, co-operation of this nature is "difficult".[25] There are, I suggest, at least two general reasons why this is so: the first relates to the

---

[22] See generally M Sayers, "Co-operation across Frontiers" in Opeskin and Weisbrot (n 3) ch 17.
[23] Consider HKSAR Government, *The Law Reform Commission of Hong Kong 2011* (Government Logistics Department, 2011) 7–8.
[24] Sayers (n 22) 249–50.
[25] Ibid 249.

very nature of law and to the function of law reform agencies; the second, to considerations of a practical nature focusing on the circumstances and practices of law reform agencies.

The nature of law and the function of law reform agencies

Sir Henry Maine pointed out that, in the seventeenth century, juristic law reform was directed to the reform of law in the books, especially in a search for a satisfying philosophical ordering of law.[26] Whatever view is taken of the nature of law generally, no law reform agency today would seriously regard itself as limited to reforming the law in the books.[27] Such an agency would also have regard to the law in action, at least to the way in which the law operates in practice. It would generally do so through some process of consultation that necessarily exposes the law in its political, social and economic contexts. Where those contexts differ between jurisdictions, legal rules, however stated, are unlikely to operate similarly in practice. Given the necessarily different focus of reform, this may diminish the value of a joint project that is aimed at reform. The difficulty obviously diminishes to the extent to which the political, social and economic conditions between the countries are similar, and to the extent to which the body of law in question has divorced itself from its origins in the customary or local law of the countries involved so that issues do not arise in fitting proposed reforms into existing legal concepts or structures.

This general consideration is important in Hong Kong. The common law system that applies in Hong Kong is a relic of its colonial past.[28] Reform of the law in other common law jurisdictions may provide guidance to reform of the law in Hong Kong, just as developments in other common law jurisdictions

---

[26] H S Maine, *Dissertations on Early Law and Custom* (John Murray, 1914) 392–93.

[27] Though prevailing legal theory may influence what is thought to be appropriate questions for law reform agencies, in particular, whether they ought to focus on "black letter" law topics (though, even if they do, they are likely to discover discrepancies between the law in the books and the law in action): see M Tilbury, "Why Law Reform Commissions?: A Deconstruction and Stakeholder Analysis From An Australian Perspective" (2005) 23 *Windsor Yearbook of Access to Justice* 313, 330–333.

[28] The common law applies in Hong Kong by virtue of the Basic Law, which it must not contravene: see the Basic Law of the Hong Kong Special Administrative Region of the People's Republic of China (Basic Law) art 8. See also art 18.

may guide the courts in the development of the common law of Hong Kong.[29] It will, however, be rare that law reform in other common law countries will be directly relevant to, or capable of direct application in, Hong Kong. Any reform of the law of Hong Kong must not only take account of prevailing social conditions in the territory, but also of its status as a Special Administrative Region of the People's Republic of China,[30] as well as of considerations enshrined in the Basic Law, such as those relating to the fundamental rights and duties of residents[31] and the position of the territory as an international financial centre.[32]

Practical considerations

The value of a joint project may further be reduced in the light of the practical difficulties that attend such projects. These difficulties centre on the time that has to be devoted to the co-operative exercise itself in terms of ongoing issues relating to communication, to research, to consultations, to meetings, and to reaching agreement. This may result not only in delays in the completion of the project, with less than timely outcomes, but may also bring other disadvantages. The following are the principal factors that are likely to lead to less than desirable outcomes.

Different resources

Law reform agencies come in a variety of forms and are resourced at different levels. The inevitable general result of this is that the agency that is better resourced will become the "lead" agency at the expense of the other, simply because the better resourced agency is capable of doing more in terms of driving the project, the consultation processes associated with the project, the production of reports and dealings with the media. This was certainly true of the privacy references of the ALRC and the NSWLRC, where the ALRC, the better resourced agency, was undoubtedly the "lead agency" in privacy reform in Australia, especially in terms of the public's perception of the reference.

---

[29] See Basic Law art 84 (Hong Kong courts "may refer to precedents from other common law jurisdictions"). See also *Solicitor (24/07) v Law Society of Hong Kong* (2008) 11 HKCFAR 117.

[30] Basic Law, Preamble and Chapter I, especially art 11.

[31] Basic Law, Chapter III.

[32] Basic Law art 109.

In the context of a federation, this is not a bad thing: it is, indeed, probably inevitable, if not desirable, that the lead role should fall to the federal body, at least on issues of national concern. But, it is difficult to see how this could generally be regarded as a positive factor in co-operative law reform projects across national boundaries.

Different workloads

At any one time, a law reform agency will usually have several inquiries running at the same time. At the time of the privacy references, the practice of the ALRC was, generally — and, I suggest, sensibly — to have only two (usually major) projects on the go at any one stage. The corollary was, again in my view sensibly, that the ALRC was subject to strict reporting timelines. In contrast, the NSWLRC was involved in seven inquiries in 2006,[33] though, in accordance with normal practice, that Commission was not required to report on any of the projects within any particular timeframe.

The heavy workload of the NSWLRC effectively meant that it could not complete its review of the cause of action report before the ALRC reported within its own timeframe. Effectively, this meant that the final views of the NSWLRC on a statutory cause of action for invasion of privacy were not available to the ALRC.

Different organizational cultures and processes

Like all organizations, law reform agencies tend to develop their own cultures. Sometimes those cultures can diverge substantially from other law reform agencies. For example, it is conceivable that an agency in country A may have a culture of extensive consultation, while that in country B may prefer to rely on the assistance of experts in carrying out its functions. If each agency were to insist on its "own way of doing things", a joint cross-border reference between the agencies in countries A and B may not be viable; and, if it occurred, it would certainly produce a very strange report, one that was subject to consultation only in country A, the results of which may be completely irrelevant in country B.

---

[33] See NSWLRC, *Annual Report 2005–06* (2006) <http://www.lawlink.nsw.gov.au/lawlink/lrc/ll_lrc.nsf/pages/LRC-ar> accessed 23 January 2012.

The ALRC and the NSWLRC had no differences of this nature at the time of their privacy references. Attention has, however, already been drawn to two differences in their practice that may have effected the outcome of the privacy inquiries, namely, the differing practices relating to their workloads and to the timeframes on references.

Moreover there was a difference in approach between the ALRC and the NSWLRC in the production of consultation papers and their relationship to consultation. The ALRC's general approach to its task was to issue three papers in any project: an issues paper, followed by a discussion paper, followed by a report. Each paper built on the last, filling out and, where necessary, modifying the previous paper by reference to further research and to the views of consultees and submitters, which were relevant at all stages of the process.[34] In contrast, the NSWLRC generally issued a consultation paper after significant research and some preliminary consultation, and then moved to a final report after a period of intense consultation. The NSWLRC's report did not generally attempt simply to build on the prior consultation paper, and, indeed, sometimes bore little relation to it. This provided flexibility as far as further research was concerned, as well as flexibility in taking into consideration the results of consultations. In the context of the privacy references, no problems arose out of these varying practices. However, issues could arise in a joint project relating to the timing of relevant consultations and the consequent ability of one agency effectively to analyse, share in and make use of, the results of the consultations of the other agency, in the production of the variety of papers that are generated in the course of the inquiry.

Different expert opinions

Both the ALRC and the NSWLRC generally use expert advisory committees to assist in their work, and each Commission had its own advisory committee to assist in its privacy reference. In the end, this may have made a difference to the understanding of each Commission about what a statutory cause of action for invasion of privacy should look like. The work of the NSWLRC's international expert advisory committee, which relied heavily on teleconferencing,

---

[34] This aspect of the ALRC's approach, in contrast to the production of only one consultation paper, are commented on in Parliament of Australia, The Senate, Legal and Constitutional Affairs References Committee, *Inquiry into the Australian Law Reform Commission* (April 2011) [5.9]–[5.13], and Dissenting Report [1.22].

prompted the Commission to enlist the services of Parliamentary Counsel in New South Wales to draft legislation to reflect its views, with the various and developing iterations of that legislation forming the basis of the teleconferences and subsequent correspondence. This proved extremely influential in developing the Commission's final proposals. Unfortunately, the views of the advisory committee only crystallized at a late stage in the Commission's inquiry, and, at this stage, it was, as already explained, too late for their consideration by the ALRC.

There is, of course, a simple solution to problems that can arise from the receipt of potentially differing advice from expert committees, namely, to set up a joint advisory committee. To be effective, the joint committee must, however, work in a way that suits the timetables of both Commissions — something that was not possible in the privacy inquiries of the ALRC and the NSWLRC.

Resolving disagreements on reform proposals

In any co-operative law reform inquiry, there is always going to be the likelihood of disagreement between the law reform agencies involved about the substance of their recommendations.[35] The major disadvantage of such disagreement is that the inquiry may end up devoting a significant, perhaps disproportionate, amount of time in an attempt to resolve such disagreement. This will generally be misconceived. While a united front is generally (and obviously), a more powerful outcome in promoting the cause of reform, particularly after a long inquiry, disagreements between law reform agencies can helpfully highlight the issues that need to be exposed to further public scrutiny. Dissenting views are, after all, known in law reform commission reports, and such views may prove important in exposing recommendations to further scrutiny.

A failure of co-operation?

Many of the practical difficulties involved in co-operative inquiries between law reform agencies can, as indicated, be resolved. The difficulties that

---

[35] Examples are found in *Uniform Evidence Law*, (ALRC Report 102, NSWLRC Report 112. VLRC Final Report, 2005). The Commissions were not ad idem on Recommendations 5–2 and 18–3.

prevented the ALRC and the NSWLRC from presenting uniform proposals on a statutory cause of action for invasion of privacy could not. The difficulties were institutional and happenstance. This does not mean that the co-operation between the two Commissions was unsuccessful or a failure. On the contrary, there is a great deal in common between the two sets of recommendations, and, importantly, the two Commissions early reached agreement on the fundamental structure of the proposed reforms, namely, in the creation of a statutory cause of action (rather than a statutory tort), which would divorce the development of the protection of privacy in civil law from any proposed strictures that may be imposed by the law of tort or by "tortious thinking".

In its recent issues paper dealing with the enactment of a statutory cause of action for invasion of privacy, the federal government has given more or less full consideration to the differences on the topic between the ALRC, the NSWLRC and the Victorian Law Reform Commission.[36] Importantly, the legislation developed by the NSWLRC in conjunction with NSW Parliamentary Counsel forms one of the appendices to the Paper.[37]

It is, however, a matter of regret that the issues paper overlooks, plays down or simply fails to appreciate, important (often subtle) differences between the proposals of the NSWLRC and the ALRC, and hence fails to expose both to proper scrutiny.[38] There are at least four such differences. First, the NSWLRC's recommendations more clearly locate greater protection of privacy within the emerging context of human rights law, rather than within the law of tort. Secondly, the NSWLRC proposes a test for the cause of action based simply upon "reasonable expectation of privacy", without the qualification, with which some common law authority flirts,[39] that the invasion should be "highly offensive to an objective reasonable person".[40] Thirdly, the

---

[36] See Issues Paper (n 12).

[37] Ibid, Appendix B.

[38] For a comparative analysis and evaluation of the proposals of the two Commissions and of the VLRC, see N Witzleb, "A Statutory Cause of Action for Privacy? A Critical Appraisal of Three Recent Australian Law Reform Proposals" (2011) 19 *Torts Law Journal* 104.

[39] See *Jones v Tsige* [2012] ONCA 32, [70]; *Hosking v Runting* [2005] 1 NZLR 1, [117]; *Australian Broadcasting Corporation v Lenah Game Meats Pty Ltd* (2001) 208 CLR 199, [42] (Gleeson CJ). Compare *Campbell v MGN Ltd* [2004] 2 AC 457, [94] (Lord Hope).

[40] See NSW Law Reform Commission, *Invasion of Privacy* (Report 120, 2009) [5.4]–[5.13].

NSWLRC's report includes draft legislation that gives certainty to the new cause of action by identifying a non-exhaustive list of circumstances relevant to determining whether or not an individual's privacy has been invaded.[41] Fourthly, the NSWLRC's report locates the new cause of action within the existing framework of Australian law by spelling out its relationship to defamation (particularly as far as defences to the action are concerned) and by expressly preventing the development of a common law action for invasion of privacy, whose existence alongside the proposed action could be a source of confusion.[42]

The Government's Response to an Inquiry

The considered (and ongoing) response of the federal government to the ALRC's recommendations for privacy law reform compared to the lack of response by the NSW government to the NSWLRC's review of privacy,[43] illustrates what Justice Kirby (as he then was) identified as the "institutional flaw" in current law reform machinery: "how to secure governmental, legislative and official attention once law reform reports are produced". As Kirby explained: "[u]nless there is interest and a sufficiently long attention span, anything but the simplest law reform proposal will often wait a long time until someone powerful in the Parliament or the bureaucracy lifts a voice and moves the proposal forward".[44] There is a corollary to Kirby's point: governments will pay attention to reports if, for whatever reason, they have an interest in doing so. Two examples are given in this chapter. The first is the response of the NSW government to the NSWLRC's inquiries into the interface between freedom of information and privacy legislation. Those reports, on contained topics that the Commission could review in a short period of time to fit in with the government's legislative program, were commissioned in order to sort out the confusion in proposed legislation concerning the issue of access to personal information in the context of wider access to government information, and in order to identify the policy options that applied to the relationship between the proposed Offices of the Information and Privacy Commissioners. The second

---

[41] See Civil Liability Amendment (Privacy) Bill 2009 cl 74(3) in ibid, Appendix A.
[42] Ibid [6.6]–[6.12], [8.1]–[8.3].
[43] Text to nn 10–16.
[44] M Kirby, "Are We There Yet?" in Opeskin and Weisbrot (n 3) 433, 445.

example is the action of the federal government in responding to the phone hacking scandal in the United Kingdom by bringing forward that government's consideration of the desirability or otherwise of introducing a statutory cause of action for invasion of privacy.

The lack of consistency in responding to law reform agencies' reports is obviously unsatisfactory in so far as it leads to some reports simply being ignored, or being ignored for long periods of time, creating a perception that the role of the law commission in the process of law reform is a marginal one and that the resources spent in commissioning the report have been wasted. One way of dealing with this is to require a government to table a law commission report in Parliament within a specified period of time. One explanation for the differing responses of the federal and NSW governments to the respective reports of their Commissions on privacy reform, may be attributable to the requirement, in the ALRC's constituent Act, to table reports of the Commission in Parliament within the first 15 sitting days after the Attorney General has received the report.[45] At the time of the NSWLRC's delivery of its final report of the privacy reference in 2010, there was no similar requirement in New South Wales. Perhaps in response to the government's failure to release that report in a timely fashion, the legislation was amended in 2011 to require the Attorney General to table any report of the Commission in Parliament within 14 sitting days of its receipt.[46]

Legislation may go further than this and require the government to report to Parliament, from time to time, on how it intends to respond to recommendations of a law reform commission. The Law Commission Act 2009 of the UK Parliament, amending the Law Commissions Act 1965, provides that the Lord Chancellor must report annually to Parliament on the extent to which the government has implemented, or not implemented, proposals of the Law Commission. The report must include the government's plans for dealing with unimplemented proposals and specify any decision not to implement those proposals.[47] This provision is enhanced by a further provision that allows for a "protocol" to be entered into between the Lord Chancellor and the Commission to set out how Ministers of the Crown, government departments and the Law

---

[45] See Australian Law Reform Commission Act 1996 (Cth) s 23.

[46] See Law Reform Commission Act 1967 (NSW) s 13(5), as amended by the Courts and Other Legislation Amendment Act 2011 (NSW) sch 1.5.

[47] Law Commissions Act 1965 (UK) s 3A.

Commission should work together.⁴⁸ The protocol made pursuant to this provision contains sections dealing with the response of the government to reports of the Commission, requiring the government, among other matters, to make an interim response to the Commission, generally within six months of publication of the report, and to make a full response (including, where relevant, a timetable for implementation) as soon as possible after the delivery of the interim response. The Commission is also given the opportunity to discuss and comment on the proposed rejection, or substantial modification, of any of its proposals.⁴⁹

Provisions such as these go a long way to address law reform's "institutional flaw". But they may not be a complete answer. This is because the response that they elicit from the government may, conceivably, be unhelpful because it is evasive or non-committal. This may be particularly so where a government has referred an issue to a law reform agency for reasons other than an interest in the findings of the agency. In a recent article, Laura Barnett has argued that, compared to Parliamentary Committees and Ad Hoc Commissions of Inquiry, Law Reform Commissions are the least likely to have their inquiries triggered by politics.⁵⁰ While this may, no doubt, be true as a comparison, it is also true that one way of dealing with a difficult policy issue that is politically sensitive is to "bury" it by sending it to a law reform agency in such a way — for example, by framing extremely wide terms of reference — that the government can be sure that by the time the commission reports the issue will no longer be live; or, if it is, that it can be dealt with in changed circumstances; or, even, that it may no longer be the government that has to deal with the matter.

The real answer to the "institutional flaw" lies in the recognition of, and commitment to, the value of a law reform agency as a body that is able to provide governments and the general body politic with independent advice on matters of legal policy⁵¹ — "independent" in the sense that the advice is

---

⁴⁸ Law Commissions Act 1965 (UK) s 3B.

⁴⁹ See Law Commission for England and Wales, *Protocol between the Lord Chancellor (on behalf of the Government) and the Commission* (Law Com No 321, 2010) [18]–[22].

⁵⁰ L Barnett, "The Process of Law Reform: Conditions for Success" (2011) 39 *Federal Law Review* 161, 172.

⁵¹ See M Tilbury (n 27) 319–325; P Hennessy, "Independence and Accountability of Law Reform Agencies" in Opeskin and Weisbrot (n 3) 72, 76–83.

formulated without fear or favour and free from any direction or control of the government of the day.[52] It is true that law reform agencies now come in a variety of forms, reflecting their recent historical development from the part-time (sometimes ad hoc) committees of the first half of the twentieth century to the permanent commissions of the second half, and, beginning in the last decade of the twentieth century, to agencies whose members are unlikely to be full-time though supported by some full-time staff.[53] But the *machinery* of any particular law reform agency cannot change the nature of its primary *function* to provide independent advice on legal policy.

It follows that the reforms to law reform processes that ought to be pursued are those that at least promote and strengthen the ability of law reform agencies to perform this function. This is precisely what the recent amendments to the Law Commissions Act in England, and the protocol that has resulted from those amendments, do. Other possible reforms directed to this end could include:

- A statutory statement of the independence of the law reform agency in its constituent document.
- A guarantee of public and other funding for the law reform agency that provides the agency with the necessary resources to achieve its objectives in a proper and timely fashion.
- The abolition of any requirement that only the government could initiate law reform inquiries, enabling the law reform agency to be both self-referencing and able to accept suggestions for law reform from other sources.
- The power of a law reform agency to decline to undertake a particular inquiry requested by the government.
- The ability of the law reform agency to set time limits on any inquiry it undertakes having regard to its resources.
- The ability of the law reform agency to publish its own reports.

While it is always possible to identify reforms to law reform processes that would enable law reform agencies to perform more efficiently their primary

---

[52] See D Weisbrot, "The Future for Institutional Law Reform" in Opeskin and Weisbrot (n 3) 18, 27–29; P Hennessy (n 51) 76; W Hurlburt, *Law Reform Commissions in the United Kingdom, Australia and Canada* (Juriliber, 1986) 455–456.

[53] See esp Chapters 6 (Hughes) and 7 (Warner).

task of giving independent advice on legal policy, it is becoming less obvious that executive governments really want such advice. The abolition of the Canadian Law Commission in 1991 and the de-funding of its successor, the Law Commission of Canada, in 2006 are testimony to this,[54] as is the recent "downsizing" of the ALRC in 2010. Yet the Senate's inquiry into this downsizing had nothing but praise for the ALRC.[55] That the organs of government are not speaking with one voice suggests that factors that particularly affect executive governments have resulted in such governments having lost the will or courage to cope with, or to respond rationally to, genuine independent advice. The reasons are, no doubt, complex, but, as a recently retired federal government minister in Australia has pointed out, at least one has to do with the relationship between politicians and the media, who (like celebrities and the media) feed off each other in a 24-hour news cycle that "has little tolerance for complex social and economic issues . . . to such an extent that the contest of ideas is being supplanted by the contest for laughs".[56]

Conclusion

Troubled by nothing but the obvious, Lady Augusta Bracknell, one of Oscar Wilde's great creations who, like Elvis, did not really die and now continues to enjoy a formidable presence as a netizen,[57] would undoubtedly have considered as careless having not one, but four, reviews of the same subject at the same time in two such closely related countries as Australia and New Zealand — especially in view of the fact that the references have produced a multiplicity of often overlapping consultation papers and reports. However, as this chapter points out, the nature of the law itself and the practices of organizations create difficulties in the area of multi-jurisdictional law reform that go beyond the obvious.

The concern of Lady Bracknell and of all citizens should rather be directed to the absurdity of having an independent expert body to assist in the task,

---

[54] See Chapter 6 (Hughes).
[55] Parliament of Australia, The Senate, Legal and Constitutional Affairs References Committee, *Inquiry into the Australian Law Reform Commission* (April 2011).
[56] See Lindsay Tanner, *Sideshow: Dumbing Down Democracy* (Scribe Publishing, 2011) 1.
[57] For example <http://labraknell.blogspot.com> accessed 23 January 2013.

essential in any society, of the continuous and progressive development of the law, and then to marginalize it, by pretending that it does not exist, ignoring its recommendations or, simply, not funding it properly (without even having the courage to abolish it). Therein lies the real challenge of reforming law reform in the twenty-first century.

Part E

Final Word

Chapter 14
Reforming Law Reform: Concluding Reflections

Michael Kirby

The Decline of Institutional Law Reform

Lord Scarman provided the challenge of full-time institutional law reform in 1965. Before then, such law reform as was proposed had to be done in very small bites; by part-time committees; meeting at the end of busy days; generally in armchairs; followed at the end by a stiff glass of whisky to banish the troublesome cares of reform. We are now faced with the decline and fall (at least temporarily) of the Scarman model: the full-time, professional, well-resourced law reform agency. In Canada, the federal body created to perform the task has been abolished: not once but twice. In Ontario, where a major full-time institution, described by Patricia Hughes, long flourished, it has been replaced by a part-time body with a small budget.[1] In several Australian states, a hybrid institute has replaced the earlier models, reliant on busy academics and robbed of significant public subventions.[2] Even the Australian Law Reform Commission (ALRC), despite the marked success of its implementation track record, has suffered serious blows to its personnel, facilities, programme and funding.[3]

So the question presented at the end of this book is not how institutional law reform can be improved in Hong Kong, and elsewhere. It is whether full-time law reform agencies have any realistic part to play in the legal systems of common law countries. What are the reasons for the apparent rise in hostility to the Scarman idea? If we can analyse them, we may well be able to overcome them and breathe fresh life into the concept of institutional law reform

---

[1] See Chapter 6 (Hughes).
[2] See Chapter 7 (Warner).
[3] See Chapter 2 (Kirby).

that looked so promising just 45 years ago. This obliges us to think deeply about the institutions and processes of law reform, not only in Hong Kong, but also in other countries, with similar legal systems: the United Kingdom, Canada and Australia.

Reasons for Hostility and Standstill

Institutional territorialism

One possible reason for the "standstill", Allan Chiang's descriptive noun that captures the reality of much institutional law reform today,[4] would seem to be the territorialism of power. Those who have and wield power over the development of legal change, legislative and executive, sometimes like to retain complete control over the process.

By definition, law reform bodies are likely to be independent. Their staff, consultants and other participants may see issues and urgencies of reform in ways different from government. In particular, finance ministers, and their officials, in any government, tend to resent lawyers and other interlopers who intrude into areas that they regard as their own. Unfortunately, some law reform projects, as for example on bankruptcy, insolvency and insurance contracts, can have significant economic consequences. In the nature of politics today, finance ministries tend to have and wield enormous power. And that includes the power to frustrate and terminate the reform process.

Government sensitivity

Occasionally, excuses for delay will be offered by reference to the sensitivity of law reform proposals made to elected governments, and especially when they are at or near the times of elections. Whereas a minister can effectively exercise control over the timing of activities performed by officers in the executive government, there may not be the same control over timing of law reform reports. Some delay in tabling such reports, and making them public, may afford a breathing space. But, in the nature of the operation of executive government, public officials will generally be more attentive to political sensitivities than independent law reform bodies which see their duty as being

---

[4] See Chapter 11 (Chiang).

owed to a longer term ideal of law improvement. Officials in government departments and agencies can be extremely risk-averse, as can some politicians. Many projects of law reform may be seen, rightly or wrongly, to be risky and controversial, or certainly time consuming and distracting. This may help to explain the inclination of some officials never to lose control over any topic that could come back to cause annoyance or embarrassment.

I have a feeling that this is why, after an interval of 45 years of the Scarman model, a new generation of officials, with strong instincts of control have reacted with less open-mindedness than their predecessors did to the advantage of external stimuli for the development of the law. Putting it quite bluntly, some officials are what are popularly described today as "control freaks". Timid, elected politicians can come to appreciate such officials and to accept their assertion that their main object in life is to protect the minister from danger. In the surprisingly accurate BBC television programme, *Yes Prime Minister*, the leading *dramatis personae* illustrated the symbiotic relationship that can quickly develop between elected politicians and government officials. The circumstances in Hong Kong may require some adjustments. But the basic integers of the relationship are the same.

Staffing and drafting

An instance of the foregoing problem can be seen in the disinclination to provide proper resources to institutional law reform, which now exists in one form or another in many (perhaps most) jurisdictions of the common law world. Institutional law reform was never well resourced or strongly supported. Still, by comparison to today, the situation in the 1970s looks like a "golden age". Although law reform agencies have emphasized the utility of securing available drafting skills, to convert law reform proposals into statutory form where that is appropriate, this facility has generally been denied to the agencies in recent years. The consequence is that proposals are rarely, if ever, ready in Australia (as once they were) for rapid adoption where the political will existed. There is always now the "pause that refreshes" because of the necessity to secure a legislative draft before anything serious could happen.

In Australia, the large reduction in the staff component of the ALRC in recent years contrasts markedly with the huge contemporary growth of the staff of the federal Attorney General's Department. In the 1970s, when the latter was much more modestly staffed, the excellence and centrality of its legal role in government was universally acknowledged. Its leaders, who were all officers with enduring federal experience and a broad vision, appreciated the institutional value of stimulating proposals for law reform from a source different from the permanent bureaucracy. In this, they had their eyes fixed on a longer-term perspective; not necessarily the short-term political agenda and programme of the government of the day. The result of this change has been a demoralization of those, in several jurisdictions, who work in law reform. The brave hopes of the 1970s have all too often been dashed by the perceived need to control outcomes for political purposes and to avoid risks that are viewed as unnecessary.

Avoiding controversy

One source of risk is controversy. The very process of institutional law reform is designed to address and harness controversy by regular procedures of consultation. Such procedures are likely on occasion to encourage controversy, as regularly happened in the work of the ALRC. Even a project on child welfare law became "hot" because of questions that were raised in a discussion paper about corporal punishment of children; their access to sex education; and their lawful age of consent for medical treatment. Controversy is the stuff of modern societies. However, many politicians and permanent officials feel a keen desire to control, limit and disguise such controversy, although this may simply delay its emergence to circumstances providing less structured influence over outcomes.

Change and fragility of government

Whether in circumstances of universal elections or otherwise, governments can sometimes be, or at least feel, fragile, resulting in a desire to avoid challenges that demonstrate vulnerability. The close general election results in recent years in Australia, the United States of America, Canada and the United Kingdom, suggest an interval of weakness in electoral democracy responding to current policy divisions.

This, in turn, may make governments and officials nervous about the controversies they cannot fully control. This may help to explain the diminished enthusiasm today for the structured controversies of institutional law reform, compared to what existed in the 1970s and 1980s. It may help to explain the disinclination to spend resources on institutional law reform and a preference for resources to be expended on government officials whose thinking and outcomes can more easily be controlled and influenced. Thus, the independence of law reform agencies may be seen as a challenge to many proponents of "strong" and "decisive" government, according to party political programmes.

Political opposition

Some analysts suggest that social democratic governments may be more supportive of institutional law reform than conservative governments. The idea of creating the United Kingdom Law Commissions was first advanced by Lord Gardiner LC before and during the Wilson Labour Government. Similarly, the ALRC was created by the Whitlam Labor Government, under a progressive Attorney General, Lionel Murphy. On the other hand, some politicians, nominally in conservative governments, prove strong advocates of law reform. In a sense, true conservatives will seek to make the institutions of law and law making more effective and responsive to community needs.

This was the approach of Prime Minister Malcolm Fraser and his Attorney General, Robert Ellicott QC, in Australia. By comparison to the present severe cutbacks of the ALRC, the past President (Professor David Weisbrot) has described the years of the conservative Howard Government as a "golden age" for the ALRC. Conservative governments can find utility in institutional law reform for carrying forward dialogue, consultation and engagement that find ways to secure reform. Occasionally, governments with narrow, particular-interest agendas of reform, may not be much interested in the broader issues of technical or non-political law reform, that typically engage law reform agencies.

Jealousy and hostility

An effective law reform agency, by its processes of consultation, may prove more capable of engaging with the public over issues of law reform that matter to many community groups. This engagement (and the attendant publicity) can sometimes irritate politicians and officials. They may contrast the lack of public and media attention to their own agendas and, in fairness, to their own large and perhaps greater contributions to effective law reform because they have the direct support of government. These considerations have, from time to time, affected governmental and official attitudes to institutional law reform in Australia.

Disappearing political champions

Anyone who has much to do with the process of law reform will affirm the high importance of having political champions who support both the process and most outcomes. This was certainly so in Australia in securing the major reforms of administrative law under successive Coalition (conservative) and Labor governments. Strong support from the political top can even help to overcome doubts and cautious hesitations on the part of officials (frequently a voice for leaving things well alone). Those who try to get significant reforms of social legislation often recount the key roles played by particular individuals, convinced of the importance of reform or perhaps aware from family circumstances of the injustice of present laws. At a recent symposium that I attended in the Caribbean, Dame Billie Miller, a leading woman politician, told of the key part played by a male prime minister who was converted to the need to change the laws on women's reproductive health. Likewise, particular champions of gay law reform have played a role in securing the repeal of anachronistic sodomy laws, including in Britain, Australia and Hong Kong. In the United Kingdom, the chance fact that Sir John Wolfenden (Chair of the Committee of Homosexual Law Reform) had a gay son may have opened his eyes to the need for reform. But in the absence of champions and chance events of this kind, hostility and political official caution may impede law reform.

Finding champions for law reform agencies and specifically for particular projects is a time-consuming search. In Australia, Mr Ralph Jacobi MP, a Labor backbencher, was a prime mover in securing the enquiry into insurance contracts law reform and in demanding legislative follow up. How do we secure such champions? To what extent can law reform agencies themselves promote and encourage their emergence?

Confusing consensus and unanimity

The present volume reveals a frequent logjam in action on law reform reports in Hong Kong.[5] A repeated phenomenon is the need for a report upon the

---

[5] See Chapter 8 (insolvency law) (Ng); Chapters 11 (privacy) (Chiang) and 12 (Bacon-Shone).

report. Although, in Australia, the ALRC has provided at least two major reports on reform of the law for the protection of privacy, a cautious government has now produced a still further discussion paper to explore options on the subject.[6] In earlier times, government would simply make up its mind on the basis of the law reform report.

Likewise, in Hong Kong, on subjects such as insolvency law and also privacy protection, much caution is exhibited.[7] There appears to be a confusion in contemporary politics between requiring a broad consensus in favour of a reform proposal (perhaps with necessary variations) and waiting for complete unanimity to emerge in society. On most topics of law reform, particularly those related to controversial questions of social policy, unanimity will never emerge. That is the nature of a community that permits free discussion, a vigorous media and active civil society organizations. The logjam in building agreement to law reform is a major obstacle today to securing legislative action. Endless committees and enquiries seem to have become a hallmark of contemporary elected governments.

Faults in law reform

It must be conceded that some of the faults that have arisen in the process of law reform derive from law reform agencies themselves. All too often, they have been over-ambitious in exploring projects on which they embark. And slow in executing their reports. Where the project is assigned by, or with the input of, government, delay will risk the possibility that those who were behind the reform project in the first place may have moved on and out of politics. In such circumstances, the law reform agency may have lost its relevant champion and supporters.

Law reform itself needs to be efficient in producing reports, whilst allowing fully for social survey examinations of aspects of reform that may be neglected in the standard preparation of legislation. In the ALRC, early delivery of law reform reports was initially seriously delayed. This problem has been substantially overcome by the Attorney General (whose reference is required for a project) fixing a deadline for reports, which has ordinarily been adhered to.

---

[6] See Commonwealth of Australia, Department of the Prime Minister and Cabinet, *A Statutory Cause of Action for Serious Invasion of Privacy* (AGPS, Canberra, 2011).

[7] See n 5.

Fear of economic costs

Most law reform proposals have an economic cost attached to them, as do many court decisions, where the common law is re-expressed. Thus, the United States Supreme Court decision in *Gideon v Wainright*[8] and the High Court of Australia's decision in *Dietrich v The Queen*[9] had most significant economic implications. As a result of those decisions, effectively, the state was required to provide legal counsel to indigent accused facing serious criminal trials.

Virtually every law reform report involves cost consequences. Yet, until recently, these costs were rarely spelt out. Necessarily, finance officials and ministers have to weigh up such cost consequences against other competing priorities, including other possible law reforms. Because few, if any, law reform bodies have members or consultants who are skilled in economics, they may not always have taken into account all of the cost implications of their proposals. Occasionally, this could have been a reason why reform proposals were put on the backburner or rejected altogether.

Where proposals have important cost consequences for business, it is to be expected that well-organized lobbyists will oppose the suggested changes in the law and urge revision, delay or rejection. To overcome such hurdles, law reform agencies need to obtain, and record, cost advice so as to counter the opposition. As Professor Martin Partington points out, the Law Commission of England and Wales has recruited experienced economists to help with at least those projects having potential cost significance to government.[10] Sometimes such voices are needed as counterweights to the usually conservative attitudes in the Treasury to any proposal that might involve the need to raise more revenue or to find funds from other sources. At the very least, access to the Treasury, for advice on costs implications, may be essential in cases involving business and administrative law, with their high cost potentials.

Timing is all

Timing can be crucial to the success of law reform proposals. Especially in the instance of long serving governments, weak governments, unstable

---

[8] 372 US 335 (1963).
[9] (1992) 177 CLR 292.
[10] See Chapter 5 (Partington).

governments or governments lacking in self-confidence, gaining the ear of crucial politicians and officials becomes critical.

A common problem has been that officials, who may have been tutored in the theoretical and practical necessities of a particular reform, tend to move on and upwards. They are then lost to the law reform agency and replaced by new officials (or perhaps new ministers) with different personalities, attitudes and levels of knowledge and empathy for the reform proposal. A change in government can also be vital. Sometimes it can be positive, as was the election of the Hawke Labor Government in Australia in 1983. This led to virtually immediate steps being taken to implement the ALRC proposals on insurance contracts and privacy law reform. However, it can also be very damaging to the reform process, not only where the new government is hostile to the reform proposals but also in the time delays that inevitably accompany educating the new government about those proposals.

Full-time staff and volunteers

Law reform agencies have always invoked the assistance of volunteers, most especially part-time commissioners, consultants, academics, experts and community groups. Yet the big change that was introduced in the 1970s was a shift in the appreciation that the core functions of the agency needed dedicated, full-time personnel, both commissioners and staff. A worrying feature of the current trend has been the noticeable shift back to volunteers.

The demands that can be placed upon volunteers are necessarily more modest, as explained by Professor Kate Warner[11] and Ms Hughes.[12] Anyone wanting to maintain a facade of law reform activity, whilst spending virtually nothing on it and ensuring that the output would never seriously burden the decision-making capacity of government, will return to the safe haven of part-time volunteers. Those who see the challenges of law reform as larger and more urgent will regard such a shift as deleterious and retrograde.

Social justice and lawyers' law

The reality of small part-time bodies is that normally they will, effectively, be restrained from entering upon large-scale projects that would involve social

---

[11] See Chapter 7 (Warner).
[12] See Chapter 6 (Hughes).

science research and questioning of fundamental values in the law. Of course, a more modest conception of the role of law reform will tend, at least for a time, to present fewer challenges to governments and officialdom. However, the difficulty of this approach is that the larger and more controversial challenges of law reform may then be neglected or ignored altogether. Or powerful interests in society (such as the print media in relatively few hands) will mobilize a bullying campaign to prevent politicians and officials tackling the truly urgent challenges that confront society: such as media invasion of individual privacy, telephone hacking, highly partisan reporting and excessive political manipulation.

To examine issues of this kind, unless ad hoc enquiries outside the bureaucracy are to be established, it is essential to have a regular system of law reform which, like the judiciary, will be independent of powerful interests, courageous and thorough, and thereby of greater support and assistance to the law making institutions of society.

Internationalization

One of the features that flourished after the first wave of Scarman-model law reform agencies was the exchange of information and materials between professional law reform bodies throughout the English-speaking world. Whilst this no doubt continues to some extent and is enhanced by the Internet, the cutbacks in resources made available to law reform agencies, have reduced the personal and other exchanges.[13] The common language, similar legal systems and institutions and shared professionalism were a distinctive advantage of the growth of institutional law reform that is now under threat.

It is not sufficient that a report should be implemented in other jurisdictions (as the ALRC report on *Human Tissue Transplants* was copied throughout South America), the sharing of reform proposals reflected the identical problems faced by differing countries at roughly the same time and often because of much the same technological and social stimuli. Contacts between professional law reform agencies, across national borders, helped many with the efficient discharge of the law reform task. The same level of co-operation may not exist between officials working solely for the executive government of their own jurisdiction.

---

[13] Consider Chapter 13 (Tilbury).

Enhanced and diminished consultation

In the context of the Ontario law reform agency, Patricia Hughes has explained the steps that are taken to consult vulnerable groups or categories of the population who may need special help to be able to express their experience and explain their concerns about the current law.[14] In Canada, this includes, for example, a true dialogue between anglophone and francophone citizens and lawyers. It also includes, in particular projects, the need to consult children, migrants, deaf and otherwise physically impaired citizens and groups. Although government will increasingly be obliged to take such measures seriously, law reform agencies pioneered the diverse processes of public consultation. By thorough procedures to test the waters and to secure widespread feedback, the chances of achieving long-term reforms were greater than the situation where, traditionally, the changes were worked up internally by hard-pressed officials, often working to a severe deadline, or externally by overworked judges and legal professionals.

The need for crises

Allan Chiang, describing the acceptance of privacy law reform in Hong Kong, in the context of data protection, has pointed out the beneficial impact of the European Union *Directive* on privacy that presented a danger that Hong Kong might lose access to processing personal data because it was unable to guarantee effective legal protections for data privacy.[15] Certainly, where a law reform report dovetails successfully into a solution for a current matter of high controversy, there is a greater chance of action to implement the report. Perhaps, it should not be so. But these are the realities of the ways in which law is conceived, evolves and is developed in common law countries.

The law commission idea was aimed at providing institutional mechanisms that would make the process of law reform more logical, systematic and effective. Yet is the flame that was lit by Lord Scarman only flickering now? What can be done to restore it to full force?

---

[14] See Chapter 6 (Hughes).
[15] See Chapter 11 (Chiang).

Marginal Utility and Marginal Costs

If, as this book urges us to do, we reflect upon the impediments to institutional law reform that the book discusses, we will come to a number of conclusions.

First, law reform is not the most important challenge for society. Large social and economic reforms are often stimulated by international movements and by events that have little to do with the law at all. Even in the world of law reform itself, at least some enquiries will conclude that no change to the law is required. This was the conclusion to which the ALRC came when it investigated the possibility of and need for introducing systems of inquisitorial procedure in the place of the adversarial tradition of the common law. The ALRC concluded in favour of the status quo.

Likewise, some changes that are required in society are purely administrative or economic. It is a mistake to consider that a law reform project has failed if it does not result in legislation. All of this being said, the fact remains that some changes in legislation are required from time to time and the current procedures are simply inadequate, and too slow, to adjust and update the legal system in a way that will effectively renew it, modernize and simplify it, and adapt it to a rapidly changing global environment. This is where the shoe currently pinches. An efficient law-making system would deliver more effective machinery for regular change and improvement in the law.

Secondly, once law reform is achieved, it is a mistake to believe that it is accomplished forever. A failing even of the Scarman model was the inadequacy of the institutional attention to follow up and audit law reform legislation to make sure that it continues to be relevant and effective. This too constitutes a continuing institutional failing of the operation of law-making in contemporary societies. It is a particularly acute failing in common law countries because the underlying legal system is built on the model of judge-made law. This responds in a pragmatic way to individual problems brought to the courts. At least the civil law system proclaims a search for underlying broad concepts. In the common law world, the legal system is a kind of chaos that tends to disdain codification. It is highly detailed, particular and technical. It therefore presents greater challenges for institutional renewal. Unfortunately, the current institutions of renewal frequently fail to deliver.

Thirdly, the most serious defect in the model of institutional law reform developed by Lord Scarman was its failure to provide an effective process to translate the proposals in law reform reports into parts of the living law.

This omission was not the fault of Scarman, as such. It was just assumed that, when thorough processes of investigation and consultation were concluded, the well-reasoned suggestions of such accomplished commissioners would be quickly translated into action by a grateful legislature. The dangers in that assumption were drawn to notice in the first annual report of the ALRC in 1975.[16] Even then, at the very outset of well-funded institutional law reform, priority attention was urged on the question of implementation. Various efforts were made in that direction in Australia. They were sometimes supported and encouraged by the Parliamentary Committees on Constitutional and Legal Reform. At one stage, they procured an undertaking from the Hawke government to provide responses to law reform reports, one way or the other, within a short period. However, these became somewhat formal. And then they faded away.

In New Zealand, a similar process evolved in relation to the reports of the Law Commission of that country. But its implementation showed, once again, that a great deal depended on the personalities, commitment and interest of the relevant ministers. These were to prove variable.

Appropriately, perhaps, the greatest progress in this area has been achieved, and that quite recently, by the Law Commissions in the United Kingdom. In March 2010, a protocol was agreed between the Law Commission of England and Wales and the government, with a view to improving the rate at which Law Commission reports were implemented. The protocol was not withdrawn when the Brown government was defeated and replaced at the general election by the Coalition government led by Mr David Cameron.

In devising its eleventh programme of law reform, published on 20 July 2011, the Law Commission of England and Wales worked in accordance with the protocol. As yet, it is still uncertain whether the protocol will operate successfully. This will only be known when the projects started under the protocol have been reported and the government of the day responds, as was contemplated. The idea is that the heightened government support for the Commission's projects and the requirements for liaison during the lifetime of those projects would ensure that the reports were implemented more often and more quickly. According to the information received, the government

---

[16] ALRC, *Annual Report 1975* (ALRC 3) Foreword vii, [44]; ALRC, *Annual Report 1976* (ALRC 5) Foreword xiii, [16]–[22] ("Implementation of Law Reform"). See also A F Mason, "Where Now?" (1975) 49 *Australian Law Journal* 570, 572–73.

departments in the United Kingdom have so far been following what they needed to do under the protocol. In its terms, the protocol stated that it would be applied "as far as possible" to projects then already in the pipeline. The response to this promise has apparently been disappointing because the British government has not, so far, been able to meet the requirements for responding to reports, either on an interim basis (as soon as possible or within six months) or finally (as soon as possible or within 12 months). However, hope springs eternal. None of the reports published since the signing of the protocol, and for which a response is due in the stated time scales, has yet been treated in such a way.

The first of the reports by the Lord Chancellor to Parliament on how matters stand on the unimplemented reports of the Law Commission, was presented by him in January 2011. There was some degree of disappointment in the lack of information then provided. However, it is still hoped that the time will come when this annual procedure will become a useful additional way of ensuring that the Commission's reports are not forgotten. Moreover, the fact that a report is made to Parliament will hopefully provide an opportunity to government and opposition members to call the government to account.

The introduction of these changes in the United Kingdom is definitely a step in the right direction. Still the problem remains of securing governmental attention and focus upon an agenda that has essentially been fixed elsewhere and may not accord with the priorities of the government's own agenda. In the United Kingdom, at the moment, the government's agenda involves its declared determination to restore the country's financial position. The Law Commission has played its part in this process by reducing its budget by 5% in 2010–11, and by accepting a reduction in the grant from the Ministry of Justice of 25% over the ensuing four years. It is hoped that this reduction (comparable to that faced by the ALRC in Australia) will be mitigated in Britain by the Commission's ability to attract income from other government departments.

Good news has followed with the approval by the House of Lords of the procedure for considering Law Commission bills. These followed a pilot run in which two bills, drafted by the Law Commission, were placed on the statute book in accordance with the semi-automatic procedure adopted for such consideration. These were the Perpetuities and Accumulations Act 2009 (UK) and the Third Parties (Rights Against Insurers) Act 2010 (UK). Since then, the Consumer Insurance (Disclosure and Representations) Act 2012 and the

Trusts (Capital and Income) Act 2013 have been enacted in accordance with the procedure. The object of this procedure is to allow uncontroversial and technical Law Commission bills to proceed by way of second reading debate in a committee room rather than on the floor of the House of Parliament. Time on the floor of the House is always at a premium. In the United Kingdom, as elsewhere, the new procedure is hoped to allow more such bills to be taken forward. It all depends on the selection of uncontroversial and technical programme items and acceptance of the procedures by those who have the power to stop it.

From the foregoing, it is clear that some progress is being made in Britain, inch by painful inch, in improving the parliamentary machinery of law-making to cope with the modern necessities of institutional law reform. It has not yet reached a post-modern era in the United Kingdom. However, if the protocol agreed between the government and the Law Commission operates to produce a speedier ministerial acceptance of reports, with prompt moves towards legislation, bills drafted in the Commission will be able to go through the Law Commission procedure in Parliament or to be picked up immediately by the relevant departments of state. If all of this can come together, it will be a distinct step forward. It will be one that gives encouragement and inspiration, providing a model for institutional law reform agencies elsewhere in the world.[17]

Throughout the English-speaking world, the growth of the functions of government, and of its complexity, has imposed enormous burdens on legislators. Those burdens meet an absolute barrier when they effectively make demands upon legislators that exceed those that can reasonably be imposed upon them as human beings. Moreover, as elected officials, they must constantly be engaged with the society they represent. This is why the search is now on for machinery of law-making that can expedite effective responses

---

[17] See Law Commission Act 2009 (UK); Law Commission for England and Wales, *Protocol between the Lord Chancellor (on behalf of the Government) and the Commission* (Law Com No 321, 2010); Lord Chancellor's Report to Parliament <http://webarchive.nationalarchives.gov.uk/+/http://www.justice.gov.uk/publications/report-law-commission-proposals-jan-2011.htm> accessed 4 July 2012; Law Commission, *Annual Report 2010–11* (Law Com 328) Pt 3; Law Commission, *Eleventh Programme of Law Reform* (Law Com 330); Law Commission, *The Work of the Law Commission 2011–2015: Incorporating the Eleventh Programme* <http://www.justice.gov.uk/lawcommission/publications/programmes-law-reform.htm> accessed 4 July 2012.

to law reform reports and provide fast-track mechanisms to translate those reports into law, particularly where the proposals are of a technical and non-controversial kind.

Even where there is some risk of controversy in a report from a law reform agency, the position is now surely approaching in our law-making mechanisms that the slow, highly particular and individual examination of reform proposals has become, in itself, part of the obstacle to translating those proposals into action. Eventually, an economic equation has to be considered in the social context to which law responds. Is the marginal utility of such individualized consideration of detailed proposals, that have already been examined most closely by a law reform agency, equal to or greater than the marginal cost of the delay in justice involved in such examination; and the risk of inertia and complete failure of the law-making process?

When the answer to this last question is in the affirmative, attention begins to shift to two procedural reforms in law reform that will facilitate improvement of the process of law-making. The first is a restoration of the procedure still followed in the Law Commissions in the United Kingdom, and originally followed in the ARLC, of providing draft bills with all reports where legislative reform is recommended, so as to expedite implementation and to ensure consideration of the relevant governmental choices. Secondly, there is a need for two further procedures for implementation of law reform proposals. The first is the traditional, full debate procedure. The second, for non-controversial and technical matters, is a fast-track process of the kind now being implemented experimentally in the United Kingdom.

Those who are concerned with the effectiveness of law-making and the continued relevance of electoral democracy in a complex world of enormous ongoing change will turn their attention to this institutional need for adjustment. Without such adjustment, our legislators will be of increasing irrelevance to a large portion of law-making in society. They will increasingly fail to deliver on the urgent needs of law reform presented to society by technology and social change. They will render even more fictitious the assumptions that electoral democracy can serve a modern, complex, dynamic and changing community effectively. They will put great pressures on other law-makers (such as courts and officials) to remake the law whilst pretending otherwise.

It is because these are large questions, about the effective operation of elected institutions and maintenance of the rule of law in contemporary society, that they deserve close attention. And action. This is needed not only by those who are engaged in, and committed to, institutional law reform. It is required by all those who truly respect elected legislatures; favour the rule of law; and seek to promote their continued relevance to today's world of complex and rapid change.

The issues facing legal reform in Hong Kong arise in a somewhat unusual and peculiar constitutional setting. They are therefore distinct, special, even unique.[18] However, because the issues are shared by every modern community as it seeks to reconcile democratic institutions with contemporary realities, their subject matters are as important in Australia, Canada and the United Kingdom as they are in Hong Kong and in many places beyond. Progress is being made. But it is very slow, uneven and in some places non-existent.

When the challenges seem overwhelming, daunting and discouraging, we can look about us in Hong Kong to the mighty changes that have been achieved both here and in China in a mere hundred years. Then we can take encouragement from the astonishing capacity of the human species to adapt to changing times and to be a force for change and hopefully for human and environmental betterment.

---

[18] See, especially, Chapter 3 (Wong).

Index

advocacy, *see* civil society advocacy
Alberta Law Reform Institute, 6, 90, 117
anti-discrimination law, *see* equal opportunity law
Australian Capital Territory Law Reform Advisory Council, 119–20
Australian Law Reform Commission, 23, 31–32, 36–39, 239–40, 259, 261–62, 263, 265, 267, 268, 271

Basic Law, *see* law reform in Hong Kong
Bill of Rights Ordinance, *see* law reform in Hong Kong
British Columbia Law Institute, 91–92

Canadian law reform commissions, 88–89
civil society advocacy
  effect of government policy on strategy of, 199
  equal opportunity law and, 181, 188–89, 192–93, 198–99
  labour law reform and, 152–53
  role in law reform, 152–53, 170–71, 173–74, 179, 188
consultation, *see* law reform commissions, public consultation on government policy
Court of Final Appeal
  law reform and, 11–12

Department of Justice (Hong Kong), 44, 57, 59, 158, 212, 215, 217

equal opportunity law reform in Hong Kong
  business community and, 179, 185
  discrimination on more than one ground, 192–94, 199–203
  future of, 203–4
  history of anti-discrimination law, 174–90
  indirect discrimination, 201–3
  public opinion and, 181–82
  women's movement and, 179–81
  see also civil society advocacy, international influences on law reform in Hong Kong, law reform in Hong Kong, public consultation on government policy, Race Discrimination Ordinance (Hong Kong)

Federation of Law Reform Agencies of Canada, 92

government bureaux, *see* law reform in Hong Kong
government responses to law reform proposals, 18–19, 47–50, 63–65, 81–82, 181–85, 186–99, 241–43, 251–53, 262–65, 271–73

Hong Kong Court of Final Appeal, *see*
    Court of Final Appeal
Hong Kong law
    need for reform of, 15–16
Hong Kong Law Reform Commission
    composition of, 45, 55–57, 60, 61
    consultation and, 9, 46
    criticisms of, 61–62
    draft legislation and, 54, 56, 57
    establishment of, 13, 23–24, 45, 54–56
    full-time commissioners and, 14,
        16–18, 63
    general characteristics of, 56–57
    government response to reports of,
        18–19, 47–48, 61–62
    Guidelines on response to reports of,
        49–50
    implementation of reports of, 15,
        18–20, 47–50, 63–65, 208–11,
        236, 238
    implementation rates, 14–15
    independence of, 9, 46, 59
    law revision and, 13–14, 55, 62
    mission of, 13
    need for, 9–10
    non-statutory body, 59
    privacy law reform and, 207–8
    processes of, 25, 59–61
    reputation of, 14–15
    resources, 143
    secretariat, 46
    sources of references, 57, 61
    sub-committees and, 14, 45–46, 60–61
    timeliness of reports of, 16, 18, 62–63
    see also law reform commissions, law
        reform in Hong Kong

ILO conventions and standards in
    Hong Kong, 153–56
implementation of law reform proposals,
    see law reform commissions
insolvency law reform in Hong Kong
    background to, 135–37

evaluation of, 141–43
reform in other jurisdictions, 141–42
reform of bankruptcy law, 136–38
reform of winding up provisions,
    138–41
international influences on law reform
    in Hong Kong, 8, 152–56, 158,
    173–75, 183–86, 192, 194–99

Labour Advisory Board (Hong Kong)
    composition of, 158–59
    role in law reform, 160
    support for, 159–60
Labour Department (Hong Kong)
    role in law reform, 157–58
labour law
    suitability as law reform project, 158,
        169
labour law reform in Hong Kong
    context of, 148–51
    course of reform, 146–48
    discrimination in the workplace,
        152–53
    future of, 169–71
    nature of, 145–48
    need for, 145–46, 147–48, 169
    obstacles to, 145–46
    role of courts in, 164–69
    role of government bureaux in,
        157–60
    role of Hong Kong Law Reform
        Commission in, 169–70
    role of trade union lobby in, 161–63
    see also international influences
        on law reform in Hong Kong,
        Labour Advisory Board
        (Hong Kong), Labour
        Department (Hong Kong), law
        reform in Hong Kong, private
        members' bills and law reform
Law Commission of Canada, 92–93
Law Commission of England and Wales
    Commissioners of, 70–72

Index

consultants to, 74
consultation, 80, 84
economists at, 73
establishment of, 4, 53–54, 67–69
government response to reports of, 81–82
impact analysis of recommendations, 73–74, 81
implementation process, 83
implementation rates, 82–83
law revision and, 72–73, 83
lawyers working at, 72–73
legislative drafters at, 73, 80–81
output of, 82
processes of law reform (protocol with government), 77–82
programmes of work, 74–78
project selection, 75–78
research, 79
research assistants at, 73
Law Commission of Ontario
consultation, 99–101, 103–6, 107–8
establishment of, 90–91, 116
funding of, 91
membership of, 91
projects, 96–99, 102–3
relationship to government, 107
see also law reform commissions
law commissions, *see* law reform commissions
law reform
actors and agencies involved in, 7, 44–45, 113
courts and, 3–4, 10–12, 29–30, 40, 164–69, 232
crises as trigger for, 151, 170, 177, 212–13, 221–26, 241–42, 269
crowded field of, 7, 113
executive and, 4, 8, 84–85, 260–61, 262–63
government agencies and, 5, 8–9, 44, 78, 81–82
legislatures and, 4, 8, 40, 273–75

need for, 3–5, 26, 28–32, 43–44, 67–69, 84, 274–75
specialist agencies, 7, 12–13, 44–45, 113, 114, 142, 158–60
see also consultation, government response to law reform proposals, law reform commissions, law reform in Hong Kong, social science research
Law Reform Commission of Canada, 92
see also Law Commission of Canada
Law Reform Commission of Hong Kong, *see* Hong Kong Law Reform Commission
law reform commissions
chairing of, 60, 70–71, 91, 93
characteristics of, 5, 30–31, 87–88
communication strategies of, 85
consultation processes, 33–36, 39–40, 84, 94–95, 99–101, 105–6, 121, 123, 126–27, 263–64, 269
controversial subjects and, 31–32, 208–11, 262
co-operation between law reform agencies, 108, 240, 244–49, 268
cost benefit analysis of reports, 73–74, 81, 266
cost of, 5, 17, 40, 111, 143
decline of full-time professional commissions, 5–6, 259–60
drafting legislation and, 19, 20, 31, 57, 261, 274
empirical research and, 79, 122–23
establishment of permanent full-time commissions, 4–5, 67–69
future of, 40–41, 270–75
government response to recommendations of, 241–43, 251–52, 264–65, 270–72
establishment of permanent full-time commissions, 4–5, 67–69
implementation procedures, 19–20, 83, 252–54, 272–74

incidence of, 5, 27
independence of, 9, 38–39, 84–85
institute/part-time agencies, 6–7, 27–28, 90–92, 116–20, 259, 267–68, 269, 272–73, 274
international context of, 43–44, 244–45, 268
judging the success of, 82–83, 110–11, 124–25
models of, 45, 58–59, 127–28
need for, 3–4, 28–32, 34, 84, 273–75
non-lawyers and, 61, 84, 266
outreach activities, 95
philosophy of, 92–93, 99
political champions and, 264
possible reforms of, 20–21, 254–55, 265, 270–75
post-report activity, 81–82, 109–110
practical focus of work of, 39, 87–88, 93
project examples and types, 31–32, 35, 59, 74–75, 94–99, 123–24, 267–68
project selection and, 85, 94, 102–3, 265
purpose, 4
relationship with communities, 107–8
relationship with government, 103, 107, 142, 260–64, 266–67
staffing issues, 103, 142, 261–62, 267
volunteers and, 14, 46, 60–61, 267
see also Australian Law Reform Commission, consultation, Hong Kong Law Reform Commission, social science research, timeliness of law reform proposals, university-based law reform agencies
Law Reform Committee (England), 68
Law Reform Committee (Hong Kong), 13, 23, 54
law reform in Hong Kong

Basic Law and, 4, 152–53, 177, 207
Bill of Rights Ordinance, 177–79, 207
bureaux, role in, 8–10, 19, 44, 47, 49–50, 157–60, 181–86, 212, 213–21, 232–34
controversial subjects and, 208–11
general factors affecting, 7–13, 43–44, 148–51, 171
interaction with Mainland China, effect of, 8, 17, 26, 44
interest groups and, 8, 18, 179, 185, 236–37
LegCo, legislation and, 4, 8, 18, 19–20, 43–44, 150, 192–93
need for reform of, 15–20
NGOs and, 152–53, 170, 184–85
possible reforms of, 20–21, 26
public demonstrations and, 9, 150–51, 177, 184
resumption of Chinese sovereignty and, 17, 44
see also Department of Justice (Hong Kong), equal opportunity law reform in Hong Kong, Hong Kong Law Reform Commission, international influences on law reform in Hong Kong, labour law reform in Hong Kong, Office of the Privacy Commissioner for Personal Data, private members' bills and law reform, public consultation on government policy
law revision, 13–14, 55, 83
Law Revision Committee (England), 68
LegCo, see law reform in Hong Kong

Manitoba Law Commission, 89–90

New South Wales Law Reform Commission, 239–40
New Zealand Law Commission, 243

Index

Northern Ireland Law Commission, 69
Nova Scotia Law Reform Commission, 89–90

Octopus incident, 221–26
Office of Privacy Commissioner for Personal Data, 212
   role in law reform, 212, 213–15
Ontario Law Reform Commission, 88
   see also Law Commission of Ontario

Personal Data Privacy Ordinance
   background to, 208–10
   nature of, 211–12
   perceived inadequacies of, 214–15
   reform of, 212–14
   review of, 215–21
privacy law
   constitutional protection of in Hong Kong, 207
   reach of, 207, 243
privacy law reform in Australia, 240–43, 249–55
privacy law reform in Hong Kong
   evaluation of, 235
   factors driving, 208–9, 221–26, 229–30, 233–35, 236–37
   reports of the Law Reform Commission, 207–8, 231–32
   see also law reform in Hong Kong, Octopus incident, Personal Data Privacy Ordinance, public consultation on government policy, social sciences
private members' bills and law reform, 163–64, 179–80
public consultation on government policy, 163–64, 181–86, 193–94, 215–21, 226, 234–35
   government response to public consultation, 188, 193–94, 227–29, 237–38

Race Discrimination Ordinance (Hong Kong), 186–91
racial discrimination, *see* equal opportunity law reform in Hong Kong

Saskatchewan Law Reform Commission, 89–90
Scottish Law Commission, 4, 69
sentencing advisory councils
   incidence of in Australia, 114
   independence of sentencing law reform and, 115–16
   relationship to law reform commissions, 114–15
social sciences
   use of in law reform, 32–36, 39, 123–24, 237–38, 267–68
South Australian Law Reform Institute, 27, 120
Standing Committee on Company Law Reform (Hong Kong), 12, 44–45, 136
Statute Law Committee (England), 67–68

Tasmania Law Reform Institute
   consultation and, 126–27
   establishment of, 27, 117
   evaluation of, 127–31
   functions of, 118
   funding of, 118, 129
   implementation record, 124–25
   projects, 118, 120–23
   source of projects, 118–19
   structure of, 117
timeliness of law reform proposals and reports, 16, 39, 62–63, 126, 265, 266–67
trade unions and law reform, *see* labour law reform in Hong Kong

Uniform Law Conference of Canada, 92, 93

universities
- co-operation with law reform agencies, 7
- relationship with in-house and other law reform bodies, 108–9

university-based law reform agencies
- advantages and disadvantages of, 127–31
- Australia, 116–20
- Canada, 90–92
- role in legal education, 98, 120, 128–29
- *see also* Alberta Law Reform Institute, Australian Capital Territory Law Advisory Council, Law Commission of Ontario, Tasmanian Law Reform Institute

Victorian Law Reform Commission, 243

volunteers, *see* law reform commissions